Breakthrough Language Series

ITALIAN

Giovanni Carsaniga
Professor of Italian Studies,
La Trobe University (Melbourne)

General editor Brian Hill
Head of the Language Centre, Brighton Polytechnic

Series advisers
Janet Jenkins International Extension College, Cambridge
Duncan Sidwell Principal Modern Languages Adviser, Leicestershire LEA
Al Wolff Producer, BBC School Radio

Pan Books London and Sydney

Acknowledgements

The task of collecting recordings in Italy was made easy by the cooperation of many casual acquaintances, whom I must necessarily thank collectively. Several shops gave me permission to eavesdrop on the conversations between their staff and customers, both of whom managed to carry on with their business as if I had not been there.

My particular thanks go to Dr Giuseppe Deluca, Aldo Visco-Gilardi, Dr Dino Bressan, Dr Attilio Cernuschi, Osvaldo Grassi, Professor and Mrs T. Bolelli, the directors and staff of the Ente Provinciale del Turismo in Milano and Pisa, the station managers and staff of Domodossola and Pisa railway stations, the comptroller and staff of the passenger terminal, Galilei Airport, the manager and staff of the Ristorante Il Balanzone, Milano, and the Royal Victoria Hotel, Pisa.

The author and publisher would also like to thank the Polytechnic of Central London for the studio recordings, Mr Kym Horsell of the Computer Centre, La Trobe University, and the author's wife for help in preparing the vocabulary list, and the following for permission to use copyright material:

Marco and Paride Bruzzone for the photographs on pages 8, 18, 33, 47, 51, 62, 66, 67, 75, 76, 80, 89, 96, 102, 103, 104, 107, 118, 121, 129, 145, 146, 163, 173, 174, 178, 189, 191, 194, 195, 201, 213, 214 and 215.
J. Allan Cash Ltd for the photographs on pages 47, 70 and 187.
The Italian Trade Centre for the photographs on pages 139 and 157.
The Italian State Tourist Office for the photographs on pages 185 and 207.

Tape production: Gerald Ramshaw
Acting: Marisa Dillon-Weston, Gigi Gatti, Giancarlo Ciccone
Book design: Gillian Riley
Illustrations: Rowan Barnes-Murphy

First published 1982 by Pan Books Ltd,
Cavaye Place, London SW10 9PG
9 8 7 6 5 4 3

ISBN 0 330 26792 2
Phototypeset by Input Typesetting Ltd, London SW19 8DR
Printed in Great Britain by
Richard Clay (The Chaucer Press) Ltd, Bungay, Suffolk

Breakthrough Language Packs

Other titles in the series
Breakthrough French
Breakthrough German
Breakthrough Spanish
Breakthrough Greek

Contents

How to use this course

Following this course will help you understand, speak and read most of the Italian you are likely to need on holiday or on business trips. The course is based on recordings made in Italy of ordinary Italian people in everyday situations. Step by step you will learn first to understand what they are saying and then to speak in similar situations yourself.

Before producing the course we talked to hundreds of people about why and how they learn languages. We know how important it is for learning to be enjoyable – and for it to be usable as soon as possible. Again and again people told us that there was not much point in knowing all the grammar if you were unable to ask simple questions. In this course you will learn to ask simple questions very early on – and the only explanations of grammar will be those that actually help you understand and use the language.

General hints to help you use the course

- Have confidence in us! Real language is complex and you will find certain things in every unit which are not explained in detail. Don't worry about this. We'll build up your knowledge slowly, selecting only what is most important to know at each stage.
- Try to study regularly, but in short periods. 20–30 minutes each day is usually better than 3½ hours once a week.
- To help you learn to speak, say the words and phrases out loud whenever possible.
- If you don't understand something, leave it for a while. Learning a language is a bit like doing a jigsaw or a crossword: there are many ways to tackle it and it all falls into place eventually.
- Don't be afraid to write in the book and add your own notes.
- Do revise frequently. (There are revision sections after every three units.) It helps to get somebody to test you – and they don't need to know Italian.
- If you can possibly learn with somebody else you will be able to help each other and practise the language together.
- Learning Italian may take more time than you thought. Just be patient and above all don't get angry with yourself.

Suggested study pattern

Each unit of the course consists of approximately fourteen pages in the book and ten minutes of tape. The first page of each unit will tell you what you are going to learn and suggest what we think is the best method for going about it. As you progress with the course you may find that you evolve a method of study which suits you better – that's fine, but we suggest you keep to our pattern at least for the first two or three units or you may find you are not taking full advantage of all the possibilities offered by the material.

The book contains step-by step instructions for working through the course: when to use the book on its own, when to use the tape on its own, when to use them both together, and how to use them. On the tape the presenter Marisa will guide you through the various sections. Here is an outline of the study pattern proposed.

Dialogues

Listen to the dialogues, first without stopping the tape, and get a feel for the task ahead. Then go over each one bit by bit in conjunction with the vocabulary and the notes. You should get into the habit of using the PAUSE/STOP and REWIND buttons on your cassette recorder to give yourself time to think, and to go over the dialogues a number of times. Don't leave a dialogue until you are confident that you have at least understood it. (Symbols used in the notes are explained on p. 6).

Key words and phrases Study this list of the most important words and phrases from the dialogues. If possible, try to learn them by heart. They will be practised in the rest of the unit.

Practise what you have learnt This section contains a selection of exercises which focus your attention on the most important language in the unit. To do them you will need to work closely with the book and often use your tape recorder – sometimes you are asked to write an exercise and then check the answers on tape: other times to listen first and then fill in answers in the book. Again, use your PAUSE/STOP and REWIND buttons to give yourself time to think and to answer questions. Pauses have been left to help you to do this.

Grammar At this stage in a unit things should begin to fall into place and you are ready for the grammar section. If you really don't like grammar, you will still learn a lot without studying this part, but most people quite enjoy finding out how the language they are using actually works and how it is put together.

Read and understand and *Did you know?* In these sections you will be encouraged to read the kind of signs, menus, brochures, and so on you may come across in Italy and you will be given some practical background information on Italian customs and culture.

Your turn to speak Finally, back to the tape for some practice in speaking the main words and phrases which you have already heard and had explained. The book only gives you an outline of the exercises, so you are just listening to the tape and responding. Usually you will be asked to take part in a conversation where you hear a question or statement in Italian followed by a suggestion in English as to how you might reply. You then give your reply in Italian and listen to see if you were right. You will probably have to go over these spoken exercises a few times before you get them absolutely correct.

Answers The answers to all the exercises (except those given on tape) can be found on the last page of each unit.

If you haven't learned languages using a tape before, just spend five minutes on Unit 1 getting used to the mechanics; practise pausing the tape, and see how long the rewind button needs to be pressed to recap on different length phrases and sections.

Don't be shy – take every opportunity you can to speak Italian to Italian people and to listen to real Italian. Try listening to Italian broadcasts on the radio or tuning in to the excellent BBC radio and television broadcasts for learners.

Buona fortuna e buon lavoro!

At the back of the book

At the back of the book is a reference section which contains:

p. 217 the written part of the revision sections which occur after every third unit on the tape
p. 227 a short grammar summary with definitions of grammatical terms (noun, adjective, etc.). The section also covers the main rules of Italian grammar
p. 231 an Italian-English vocabulary list containing all the words in the course
p. 239 a brief index to enable you to look things up in the book.

The Italian language

Each language has its own peculiarities and character. Here are a few points to remember when learning Italian.

- The spelling of Italian is much simpler than the spelling of English. By and large an Italian letter will always correspond to one sound only. Similarly an Italian sound will always be spelled in the same way. Of course correct pronunciation (of single sounds or words) and intonation (of whole sentences) cannot be taught through a book: that's why it is so important that you should listen to, and imitate, the speakers recorded on your cassette tape.
- Italian is an inflected language: one, that is, where the endings of certain classes of words, and changes in their endings, indicate the role those words play in the sentence, and consequently help to understand the meaning of that sentence. In English that is mostly indicated by word order. In Italian, on the other hand, word order is relatively flexible: **mi piace il caffè nero, il caffè nero mi piace, il caffè mi piace nero** all mean (admittedly with slightly different emphasis) 'I like black coffee'.

  There are easy rules to predict word endings and their change, and we shall be giving the most important ones. Do not worry too much however if you get some endings wrong: your Italian listeners will be able to understand you all the same in most cases, and that's surely more important at this stage than one hundred per cent accuracy.
- In English if you put different personal pronouns (such as 'I, you, we, they' etc.) before a verb you get different verb forms. In Italian verb forms change their endings according to the person: **parlo** I speak, **parli** you speak, **parliamo** we speak, **parlate** you (pl.) speak, **parlano** they speak. That's why in Italian personal pronouns are rarely used, mostly for emphasis. Verb endings change according to fixed and mostly predictable patterns: you'll see they are quite easy to memorize.
- Italian has only recently become a viable national *spoken* language. Even today about one third of the Italian population are native speakers of a dialect (which may be as different from the standard language as English is from French) and learn Italian at school. Bear that in mind if you hear, while in Italy, something totally different from what you have been taught to expect in this course. Many Italians are just as likely as you are to speak 'substandard' Italian, but that does not stop them from speaking and communicating effectively, nor should it hinder you!

Symbols and abbreviations

☐ If your cassette recorder has a counter, set it to zero at the start of each unit and then fill in these boxes with the number showing at the beginning of each unit dialogue. This will help you to find the right place on the tape quickly when you want to wind back.

➧ This indicates a key word or phrase in the dialogues.

m.	masculine	pl.	plural
f.	feminine	lit.	literally
sing.	singular	adj.	adjective

1 Ciao! Tutto bene?

What you will learn

- how to greet people
- how to say where you're from
- how to say where you live
- how to introduce someone
- how to answer a customs officer

Before you begin

The dialogues on tape are divided into three groups. First listen carefully to each group, without looking at the book. Marisa, on tape, will tell you what the dialogues are about, and that should enable you to get the gist of what is being said. After listening to each group rewind your tape. Listen again to the dialogue(s) in the group one by one, at the same time reading the text. Then study the vocabulary and notes. To do that, you must use the *stop* or *pause* buttons on your cassette recorder. Do not move on to the next dialogue unless you have understood what you are studying.

Finally rewind your tape and listen to all the dialogues once more, trying to remember as much as possible of their meaning without referring to the notes. If necessary, repeat the procedure until you know what they are about. These instructions apply to all lessons in this course.

After studying the dialogues move on to the next two sections, while the language of the dialogues is still fresh in your mind. Check your progress through the various sections by ticking off the items in the following checklist:

Study guide

	Dialogues 1, 2: listen straight through without the book
	Dialogues 1, 2: listen, read and study one by one
	Dialogues 3–5: listen straight through without the book
	Dialogues 3–5: listen, read and study one by one
	Dialogue 6: listen straight through without the book
	Dialogue 6: listen, read and study notes
	Learn the *Key words and phrases*
	Do the exercises in *Practise what you have learnt*
	Study *Grammar* and do the exercises
	Do *Read and understand*
	Read *Did you know?*
	Do the tape exercises in *Your turn to speak*
	Finally, listen to all the dialogues again without the book

Dialogues

If you have a cassette recorder with a counter put it to zero as you begin playing the tape, and note the counter reading for each dialogue in the box. This way you'll be able to find the dialogue more quickly when you want to listen to it again.

1 *Gianni and Emma exchange greetings on the telephone*

Emma Pronto.
Gianni Pronto.
Emma Ciao, sono Emma.
Gianni Ciao Emma.
Emma Ciao Gianni.
Gianni Tutto bene?
Emma Tutto bene.

tutto bene everything's OK (lit. all well)
Gianni a shortened form of **Giovanni**, John

2 *Giovanni meets Marcella and her mother*

Giovanni Ciao. Chi sei?
Marcella Sono Marcella.
Giovanni Di dove sei?
Marcella Sono di Milano.
Giovanni E dove abiti?
Marcella Abito a Lurago Marinone. Questa è la mia mamma.
Sisa Io sono la mamma di Marcella.
Giovanni Buon giorno, signora.

di Milano from Milan
e dove abiti? and where do you live?
abito a . . . I live in . . .
Lurago Marinone a village some 20 miles north of Milan
la mamma di Marcella Marcella's mum

The most important expressions are marked with a ➧; these are the ones you should try to remember. They will be listed again on p. 13.

1 ➧ **pronto** This is what you say when you begin a telephone conversation. It normally means 'ready' but in English you would say 'hallo'. Note that the same Italian word may have different English translations in different contexts.

➧ **ciao** hi! hallo! bye bye; used both on meeting and on parting by people who are on first-name terms (including adults talking to children), or by people who know each other very well. For a more formal greeting see dialogue 2.

➧ **sono Emma** I'm Emma. **Sono** is a form of the verb **essere** (to be). For the whole verb, see p. 17.

2 **chi sei**? who are you? Note that **ch-** is always pronounced 'k-'.

➧ **di dove sei**? where are you from? If you are talking to a person you don't know well you should ask **di dove è**? using the polite form for 'are you?' which is the same as the 'he/she' form. (See *Grammar* p. 17.)

➧ **questa è la mia mamma** this is my mum. **Questa è Marcella** this is Marcella; but, when introducing or pointing to a boy or a man you say **questo è Gianni** this is Gianni.

Note the use of io (I) for emphasis when Marcella's mother introduces herself. It would not normally be necessary.

➧ **buon giorno** good day, but used for good morning and good afternoon. From late afternoon on say **buona sera** good evening. Before retiring at night say **buona notte** good night. All three may be written as one word: **buongiorno, buonasera, buonanotte.** Note that, when addressing a 13-year-old girl like Marcella you use the informal **ciao**: but use the more formal greeting when talking to adults you don't know well, or with whom you are not on first name terms, like Marcella's mother.

signora is the word used to address a married or an elderly woman (even if unmarried). Unlike 'Mrs' in English, **signora** does not have to be followed by the woman's name. The same applies to **signorina** (Miss). **Signore** is used for men. If you know the man's surname you must add it and shorten **signore** to **signor**: **buon giorno signor Gilardi**.

The following three dialogues are all about going through customs.

3 *A customs officer asks a train passenger a few questions*

Guardia di finanza Buon giorno signora. Passaporto, passaporto prego. Grazie.
Viaggiatrice Prego.
Guardia di finanza Qualcosa da dichiarare?
Viaggiatrice No.
Guardia di finanza Valuta? Titoli di credito? Oro?
Viaggiatrice No.
Guardia di finanza Sigarette? Tabacco? Superalcoolici?
Viaggiatrice No.
Guardia di finanza Valigia?
Viaggiatrice È qui.
Guardia di finanza. Va bene. Tutto bene. Grazie.
Viaggiatrice Prego.
Guardia di finanza Buon giorno.
Viaggiatrice Buon giorno.

guardia di finanza customs officer
viaggiatrice female passenger, traveller
passaporto passport
valuta currency
titoli di credito bonds, securities
oro gold
sigarette cigarettes
tabacco tobacco
superalcoolici spirits
valigia suitcase
qui here
va bene it's OK

4 *More questions from a customs officer at the airport*

Guardia di finanza Buon giorno. Che ha da dichiarare?
Turista Non ho niente da dichiarare.

turista tourist (man or woman)

5 *This time the tourist has something to declare: he has more cigarettes than he is allowed to take duty-free*

Guardia di finanza Che ha da dichiarare?
Turista Delle sigarette.
Guardia di finanza Quanti pacchetti?
Turista Venti pacchetti. Quanti pacchetti si possono portare? . . .
Guardia di finanza Si possono portare due pacchetti. Uno aperto.
Turista Due pacchetti soltanto?
Guardia di finanza Due pacchetti.

delle sigarette some cigarettes
venti twenty
si possono portare one can bring
due two
uno aperto one open
soltanto only

3 ➧ **prego** please. This is also used as the standard reply to **grazie** (thanks) when it would be translated as 'it's alright' or 'don't mention it'.

➧ **qualcosa da dichiarare?** anything to declare?

➧ **no** no. The opposite is **sì** yes.

4 **che ha da dichiarare?** what have you got to declare?

➧ **non ho niente da dichiarare** I have nothing to declare. A useful phrase, also in conjunction with other verbs:
non ho niente da studiare I have nothing to study
non ho niente da fare I have nothing to do.

non . . . niente is 'nothing' or 'not . . . anything': **non dichiaro niente** I'm not declaring anything, **non è niente** it's nothing.

ho and **ha** come from the verb **avere** (to have). The whole verb is on p. 17.

Note that *h* is never pronounced in Italian. When it is found between *c* and *e* or *i*, as in **che, dichiarare, pacchetti** (packets), it indicates that the *c* has a 'hard' sound (like *ch-* in *ch*emistry or *k-* in *k*it, as opposed to a 'soft' sound as in *ch*eese).

The customs officer addresses the tourist in the polite form:
che <u>ha</u> da dichiarare? what have you got to declare? (See p. 17.)

5 ➧ **quanti pacchetti?** how many packets? but
quante sigarette? how many cigarettes?
quanto tabacco? how much tobacco?
quanta valuta? how much currency?
(See *Grammar* p. 16.)

6 *Five Italian students, taking summer courses in English, introduce themselves to Giovanni.*

Lorena Io mi chiamo Lorena. Sono una studentessa dell'università di Bologna.

Enrico Io mi chiamo Enrico. Studio anch'io a Bologna.
Giovanni E da dove vieni Enrico? Sei di Bologna?
Enrico No, non sono di Bologna. Vengo dall'Abruzzo.

Giovanni Come ti chiami?
Cesarina Mi chiamo Cesarina. Vengo dalla provincia di Mantova. Abito in un paese chiamato Suzzara.

Annamaria Io mi chiamo Annamaria. Sono studentessa all'università di Bologna.

Enza Sono Enza. Vengo da Lecce. Studio a Bologna. Sono qui per imparar l'inglese.

studentessa female student
Abruzzo a region in central Italy
Mantova Mantua
Lecce a town in South-East Italy

6

dell'università di Bologna of Bologna university (lit. of the university of Bologna). In this dialogue you will also find the phrases **all'università** at the university, **dall'Abruzzo** from the Abruzzi, **dalla provincia** from the province. **Dell', all', dall'** and **dalla** will be explained further on p. 30.

io mi chiamo Lorena my name is Lorraine (lit. I call myself Lorraine). **Io** can be omitted: **mi chiamo Cesarina** my name is Cesarina.

studio anch'io a Bologna I too study at Bologna.

➧ **da dove vieni?** where do you come from? **Da** is the normal translation of 'from', see also **vengo da Lecce** I come from Lecce. If you ask a person you don't know well where he/she is from, you must say **da dove viene?**

➧ **non sono di Bologna** I'm not from Bologna. Note the following:
- to deny something, place **non** before the verb: **non mi chiamo Enrico** my name is not Henry, **non vengo da Lecce** I don't come from Lecce.
- **di** normally means 'of' as in **l'università di Bologna** the university of Bologna. In phrases like **sono di Milano, non sono di Bologna,** the Italians use **di** because they mean being a citizen *of* a particular place.

➧ **come ti chiami?** what's your name? If you are talking to a person you don't know well you should ask **come si chiama?**

➧ **abito in un paese chiamato Suzzara** I live in a small town called Suzzara. **In** is used in most cases to indicate location: **è in Italia** he is in Italy, **studio in Inghilterra** I'm studying in England, **abito in un paese** I live in a small town. The exception is with names of towns: **abito a Suzzara** I live in Suzzara, **abito a Londra** I live in London. **Paese** can mean both 'town' and 'country' i.e. Italy, England etc.

sono qui per imparar l'inglese I'm here to learn English. **Imparar** is short for **imparare,** to learn. **Inglese** means 'English' – the language and the nationality:

➧ **sono inglese** I'm English. Italians usually refer to everyone from Great Britain as **inglese,** even if they come from Scotland, Wales or Ireland.

Key words and phrases

Here are the most important words and phrases that you have met in this unit. First are those you may need to know how to say: try to learn them by heart.

To learn

buon giorno	good morning, good afternoon
buona sera	good evening
ciao!	hi! hallo! 'bye
sono	I am
sono Emma/Enrico	I'm Emma/Henry
sono inglese	I'm English
sono di Londra	I'm from London
abito	I live
abito in Inghilterra	I live in England
abito a Londra	I live in London
vengo	I come
vengo da Manchester	I come from Manchester
non	not
non sono inglese	I'm not English
non vengo da Londra	I don't come from London
non ho niente da dichiarare	I've nothing to declare
questo è . . .	this is . . .
questo è Enrico	this is Henry
questa è Cesarina	this is Cesarina
sì	yes
no	no
grazie	thank you
prego	don't mention it

Now practise saying these aloud – they're on tape after the dialogues. You will need to pause the tape after each phrase to give yourself time to speak.

To understand

tutto bene?	everything OK?
chi è?	who are you?
di dove è?	where are you from?
da dove viene?	where do you come from?
qualcosa da dichiarare?	anything to declare?

You will find a summary of the key words and phrases in every unit, immediately after the dialogues. They will not be recorded on tape from now on.

Practise what you have learnt

This part of the unit is designed to help you cope more confidently with the language you have met in the dialogues. You will need both the book and the cassette to do most of the exercises but all the necessary instructions are *in the book*. You will have an opportunity to speak at the end of the unit.

1 Who comes from where and who lives or studies where? Listen to the questions and answers on tape, and write the appropriate name, chosen from the people on the right after each location. (Answers p. 20.)

a. Abruzzo ....

b. Bologna ....

c. Lecce ....

d. Milano ....

e. Suzzara ....

f. Lurago ....

Marcella
Enza
Cesarina
Enrico
Lorena

2 Listen to our actress introducing herself, then answer the following questions by ticking the correct box. (Answers p. 20.)

1. Come si chiama?
- **a.** ☐ Marina
- **b.** ☐ Gina
- **c.** ☐ Laura

2. È italiana?
- **a.** ☐ sì
- **b.** ☐ no

3. Di dove è?
- **a.** ☐ Rapallo
- **b.** ☐ Ravenna
- **c.** ☐ Ragusa

4. Dove abita?
- **a.** ☐ in Italia
- **b.** ☐ in Inghilterra

3 Listen to the dialogue on tape. When you are sure you have understood it answer the following questions by ticking the correct box. (Answers on p. 20.)

1. What time of day is it? **a.** ☐ morning
   b. ☐ evening
2. Why is the girl here? **a.** ☐ as a tourist
   b. ☐ to learn English
3. Where does she come from? **a.** ☐ Venice
   b. ☐ the Abruzzi
   c. ☐ Rome
4. Does she want to smoke? **a.** ☐ yes
   b. ☐ no

4 Write in the appropriate greeting, **ciao** or **buon giorno** before the names of the people below. When you have finished, check your answers by listening to the recorded greetings on tape. At a later stage, when you are quite sure of your answers, you may use this exercise as a speaking exercise, and say the greetings aloud *before* each recorded phrase. You will need to stop the tape to give yourself time to speak.

a. .... signora Giraldi.

b. .... Marcella.

c. .... signor Giraldi.

d. .... signorina.

e. .... Enrico.

f. .... Enza.

Grammar

Gender and number

In the notes to dialogues 2 and 6 you have learned that words like **questo** this, and **quanto** how much, change their ending according to the noun they refer to. Here is the complete pattern for **questo**:

questo è Enrico this is Henry
questa è Cesarina this is Cesarina
questi sono Enrico e Giovanni these are Henry and John
queste sono Cesarina e Lorena these are Cesarina and Lorena

questo refers to one male individual (masculine singular)
questa to one female individual (feminine singular)
questi to more than one individual, either both males or of both sexes (masculine plural)
queste to more than one female (feminine plural).
Masculine and *feminine* are distinctions that apply to *all* Italian nouns, for instance:

questo è oro this is gold
queste sono sigarette italiane these are Italian cigarettes

Exercise 1 Write the appropriate forms of **questo** in the dotted spaces below. (Answers p. 20.)

a. .... è Gianni

b. .... è Enza

c. .... sono Marcella e la mamma di Marcella

d. .... sono Enrico e Annamaria

e. .... sono studenti italiani

f. .... sono studentesse italiane

The explanation about **questo** (above) also applies to **quanto**:

sing.
m. **quanto oro?** how much gold?
f. **quanta valuta?** how much currency?
pl.
m. **quanti passaporti?** how many passports?
f. **quante valigie?** how many suitcases?

Note that some nouns have the same endings as **questo** and **quanto**, that is, they belong to the same pattern.

	sing.	*pl.*
m.	**pacchetto**	**pacchetti**
f.	**sigaretta**	**sigarette**

Italian nouns which end in **-o** are nearly always masculine, and those which end in **-a** are nearly always feminine. Their plurals are formed as shown above.

Verbs

Italian verbs fall into three main classes according to the ending of their *infinitive* (the dictionary entry word). Verbs ending in **-are**, like **abitare** to live in, **chiamare** to call, **dichiarare** to declare, **imparare** to learn, **studiare** to study, belong to the first class (or first *conjugation*). Normally the endings of verbs belonging to the same class are the same.

imparo	I learn	**impariamo**	we learn
impari	you (informal) learn	**imparate**	you (pl.) learn
impara	he/she learns *or* you (polite) learn	**imparano**	they learn

There is no difference in Italian between 'I learn' and 'I am learning'.

Exercise 2 Taking **imparare** as a model, fill in the missing forms of **abitare** in the following dialogue. (Answers p. 20.)

Clelia Filippo, dove .... ?

Filippo .... a Bologna. E tu, Clelia, dove .... ?

Clelia .... a Milano.

Filippo Marcella e la mamma dove .... ?

Clelia .... a Lurago.

Filippo E Cesarina dove .... ?

Clelia .... a Suzzara.

Here are two very important verbs which don't fit the same pattern as **imparare** – they are *irregular*. Try to learn them by heart.

Essere to be

sono	I am	**siamo**	we are
sei	you (informal) are	**siete**	you (pl.) are
è	he/she is *or* you (polite) are	**sono**	they are

Avere to have

ho	I have	**abbiamo**	we have
hai	you (informal) have	**avete**	you (pl.) have
ha	he/she has *or* you (polite) have	**hanno**	they have

Read and understand

Here are a few simple Italian notices. See how they relate to the points you have learned so far.

This is just one of the various ways of signposting toilets. The words are the plurals of **SIGNORA** and **SIGNORE** respectively.

This is one of the signs that light up in aircrafts before take-off and landing. **Vietato** (forbidden) comes from the verb **vietare** to forbid, in the same way as **chiamato** (dialogue 3) comes from **chiamare**. You may also find this sign in theatres, cinemas, public offices and public transport.

This comes from **entrare** to enter.

This comes from **uscire** to go out.

Did you know?

Regions

Italy is divided into nineteen **regioni** which have a certain degree of administrative autonomy from central government (see map on p. 20). Some 120 years ago many of these **regioni** (Piemonte, Lombardia, Veneto, Toscana, Lazio, Campania) were either independent states or the seats of government of larger independent states. Earlier on in Italian history political fragmentation was even greater: at some stage nearly all important Italian towns were capital towns in their own right, which explains their individual variety and unparalleled artistic richness. Regional dialects, much different from the standard language and from each other, are still in widespread use, and often impart a characteristic flavour (**accento**) to the standard language.

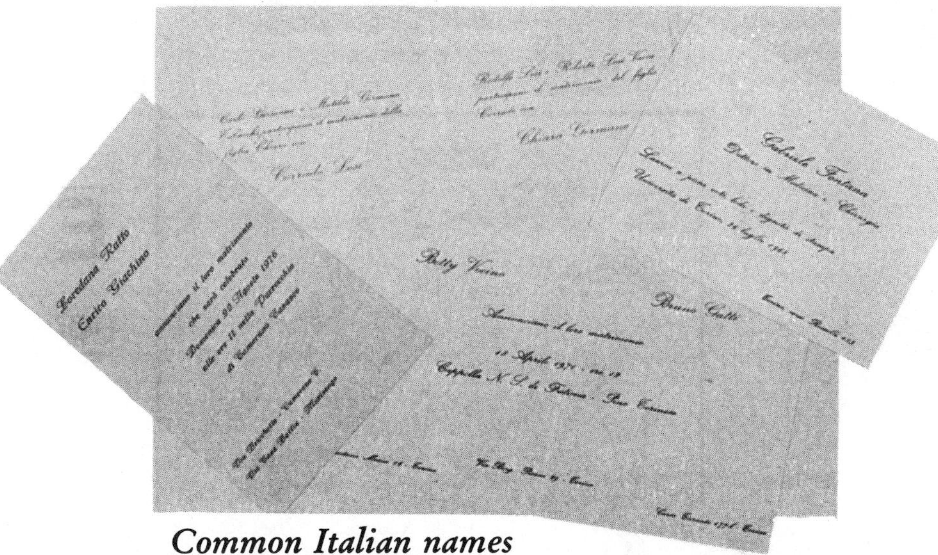

Common Italian names

The vast majority of Italians still bear a 'Christian' name hallowed in the Catholic tradition as the name of a saint. The giving of non-traditional names was discouraged in the past, or even forbidden. Many common names have English equivalents: no need to translate Adriano, Alberto, Alessandro, Anna, Bernardo, Carlo, Caterina, Cristina, Elisabetta, Elena, Emilia, Franco, Laura, Lorenzo, Marco, Maria, Michele, Paolo, Riccardo, Susanna, Teresa, Vincenzo, etc. Some names are reminiscent of Italy's Roman past, like Attilio, Mario, Fabio, Tullio (often with a feminine counterpart in **-a**). Many others have no English counterpart, e.g. Mauro. Note that a few names ending in **-a** are masculine: Andr*e*a and Nic*o*la in Italy are always given to boys, never to girls. (The letters in *italics* show where you should stress these words.) In stating their identity, Italians often place their surname before their name, e.g. Rossi Carlo.

Titles

Titles are used more frequently in Italian than in English. All university graduates, not only medical ones, are entitled to call themselves **dottore** – men, and **dottoressa** – women (though the actual use of titles is generally less common in addressing women). Engineering graduates are called **ingegnere** (no feminine form). All secondary and tertiary teachers are called **professore** – men or **professoressa** – women. **Cavaliere** and **commendatore**, corresponding to two grades in the Italian honours system, are common courtesy titles often given to males (whether they have actually received an honour or not).

Your turn to speak

This section contains exercises for which you will have to work only with your cassette recorder. You will be practising the most important language in the unit. Try not to refer to the book. Instructions and checks will be given on tape. Read the paragraph on *Your turn to speak*, p. 5, before you start.

1 In the first exercise you will practise giving negative answers – saying no to a customs officer.
New word: French, **francese**

2 In the second exercise you will say who you are and introduce yourself. You will also learn the Italian for:
Scottish **scozzese**
Welsh **gallese**
Irish **irlandese**

Answers

Practise what you have learnt p. 14 Exercise **1** (**a**) Enrico (**b**) Lorena (**c**) Enza (**d**) Marcella (**e**) Cesarina (**f**) Marcella.

p. 14 Exercise **2** (**1**) b (**2**) a (**3**) c (**4**) b.

p. 15 Exercise **3** (**1**) b (**2**) b (**3**) b (**4**) b.

Grammar p. 16 Exercise **1** (**a**) questo (**b**) questa (**c**) queste (**d**) questi (**e**) questi (**f**) queste.

p. 17 Exercise **2** abiti/abito/abiti/abito/abitano/abitano/abita/abita.

2 *Arrivi e partenze*

What you will learn

- how to understand simple train and flight announcements
- how to ask where someone is going and understand the reply
- numbers 1–20
- how to ask the way to places in the station
- how to ask about trains leaving and arriving
- about the Italian railways, Italian officials and the Italian language today

Before you begin

Points to remember from Unit 1:

1 Pointing words
questo è . . ., questa è. . . ., questi sono. . ., queste sono. . .

2 **-are** verbs e.g. **abitare** to live
abito, abiti, abita, abitiamo, abitate, abitano

3 Two genders: masculine and feminine, with different endings for the singular and plural
pacchetto pacchetti
valigia valigie

Study guide

You will be following the same study pattern as in Unit 1 and if you want to remind yourself of the best way to work, why not read the introduction to the course again on p. 4?

Remember to check your progress through the various sections by ticking off the items in the study guide below as you complete them. It will also give you a guide to the order to follow.

	Announcements 1, 2: listen straight through without the book
	Announcements 1, 2: listen, read and study one by one
	Dialogue 3: listen straight through without the book
	Dialogue 3: listen, read and study notes
	Dialogues 4, 5: listen straight through without the book
	Dialogues 4, 5: listen, read and study one by one
	Dialogue 6: listen straight through without the book
	Dialogue 6: listen, read and study notes
	Learn the *Key words and phrases*
	Do the exercises in *Practise what you have learnt*
	Study *Grammar* and do the exercises
	Do *Read and understand*
	Read *Did you know?*
	Do the tape exercises in *Your turn to speak*
	Finally, listen to all the dialogues again without the book

Dialogues

1 *First, two announcements recorded in an Italian railway station*

Treno locale per Treglia, Varzo, Iselle, Briga, è in partenza dal binario numero cinque.

Treno espresso per Milano centrale, Venezia, delle ore nove, è pronto sul binario numero tre.

treno locale	local train (i.e. one that stops at every station)
per	for
Treglia, Varzo etc.	places where the train stops
treno espresso	fast train
Milano Centrale	Milan Central (Station)
pronto	ready, waiting

2 *More station announcements*

Locale per Livorno è in partenza dal binario sei. Locale per Livorno è in partenza dal binario sei. Ferma a Tombolo.

Diretto da Roma Termini per Genova, Torino, è in arrivo al binario sei.

Rapido da Roma Termini per Genova, Torino, è in arrivo al binario sette.

sei six
da from
Roma Termini main station in Rome
sette seven

3 *Giovanni is talking to two travellers on a train*

Viaggiatore Va a Pisa, no?
Giovanni Sì, vado a Pisa.
Viaggiatore Dopo Pisa dove va?
Giovanni Vado forse a Siena, a . . . a Firenze, e poi torno a Milano. E Lei va soltanto a Roma? . . .
Viaggiatore . . . soltanto a Roma, e domani sera rientriamo di nuovo in Alessandria.
Giovanni *(to another passenger)* E Lei dove va?
2° Viaggiatore Vado a Roma.

viaggiatore male passenger, traveller
dopo after
forse perhaps
Firenze Florence
poi then
Lei you (polite)
domani sera tomorrow evening
di nuovo again

1 ➧ **è in partenza** is departing. On train timetables look for **partenze** (departures). Note the verb **partire** (to leave).

➧ **dal binario numero cinque** from platform number 5. The numbers 1–20 are very important and can be found listed on p. 27.

delle ore nove 9 a.m. (lit. of the hours nine).

sul binario numero tre at platform number 3.

2 **locale** the stopping train; **diretto** the semi-fast train; **rapido** the non-stop (intercity) train. Note that these words can all *either* be adjectives describing **treno** (as in dialogue 1) *or* can be used by themselves, as in this dialogue, as nouns.

ferma a Tombolo it stops at Tombolo.

➧ **è in arrivo al binario sei** is arriving at platform 6. Look for **arrivi** (arrivals) on train timetables. Note the verb **arrivare** (to arrive).

3 **va a Pisa, no?** you're going to Pisa, aren't you?

➧ **vado** I go, I'm going, and **va** you're going, are both parts of the verb **andare** (to go). This is one of the important verbs you will need to learn and it can be found in *Grammar* on p. 31.

➧ **dove va?** where are you going? You should also learn the phrase **dov'è?** where is? which is a combination of **dove** and **è**.

➧ **torno a Milano** I'm going back to Milan. **Torno** is from the verb **tornare** (to go back, to return).

rientriamo . . . in Alessandria we're going back to Alessandria.

4 *Airport announcements*

ATI arrivo volo tre sette quattro da Alghero.

ATI partenza per Milano volo tre quattro zero, imbarco all'uscita sei.

British Airways partenza per Londra volo BA cinque due nove, imbarco dall'uscita numero sei. Volo BA cinque due nove per Londra, uscita numero sei.
Chiamata finale per il volo BA cinque due nove per Londra. Imbarco immediato uscita numero sei.

ATI initials of **Aero Trasporti Italiani,** Italian national airline
volo flight
quattro four
uscita exit, channel
chiamata finale final call
immediato immediate

5 *And now Giovanni is checking in at the airport. He is worried in case he has to pay excess weight for his suitcase*

Impiegata Buon giorno.
Giovanni Vado a Londra e . . . ho questa valigia.
Impiegata Benissimo. Quanti chili pesa?
Giovanni Non lo so.
Impiegata Pesa venti chili. Allora, il peso consentito è di venti chili. Benissimo.
Giovanni Non c'è eccedenza.
Impiegata Non c'è eccedenza.
Giovanni Molte grazie.
Impiegata A Lei.

impiegata female employee
benissimo very good, OK
peso consentito weight allowance

4

tre sette quattro as in English, numbers of three figures and above are often spelled out figure by figure: 'three seven four' instead of 'three hundred and seventy-four'.

imbarco boarding (lit. embarkation). Announcements are often given in Italian in telegraphic style, omitting verbs which would be used in corresponding British announcements.

5

ho questa valigia I have this suitcase. The word for 'this' is **questa** because **valigia** is feminine. The plural is **queste valigie** these suitcases. With **treno** it would be **questo treno** this train, plural, **questi treni** these trains.

- **quanti chili pesa?** how many kilos does it weigh? She could also have said **quanto pesa?** how much does it weigh? Remember that you can ask a lot of useful questions using **quanto**, e.g. **quanti voli per Londra?** how many flights to London?, **quanto costa?** how much does that cost?

- **non lo so** I don't know (lit. I don't know it).

- **non c'è eccedenza** there's no excess. **Non c'è** is a very useful expression, e.g. **non c'è treno** there's no train, **non c'è uscita** there's no way out. The plural is **non ci sono**, e.g. **non ci sono treni** there are no trains, **non ci sono voli per Londra** there are no flights to London. **C'è** and **ci sono** will be practised in Unit 3.

a Lei thank[ing] you (lit. to you). This is short for **grazie a Lei**.

6 *Information on hotels from the tourist office*

Impiegato Pronto, mi dica signora. L'Ente del Turismo parla. Buona sera.
Sì, dunque: qualche numero telefonico.
Allora, l'Ariston, due quattro due cinque cinque.
California: otto nove zero sette due sei.
L'albergo Capitol: quattro nove cinque nove sette. Cinque nove sette.
La Pace: cinque zero due due sei sei.
L'albergo Roma: due due sei nove otto.
Pronto. Segnato? Va bene. Prego, le pare. Buona sera.

impiegato male employee
dunque right
allora right, so
Ariston, California etc. names of hotels
otto eight
nove nine

6 **mi dica** (or simply **dica**) tell me, is the standard expression used by shop assistants, waiters, public employees etc., and corresponds to 'can I help you?'.

l'Ente del Turismo parla the Tourist Office speaking. **Parla** may be translated both as 'he/she speaks' and 'he/she's speaking'.

qualche numero telefonico a few telephone numbers.

l'albergo Capitol, la Pace the Capitol Hotel, the Peace (Hotel). **L'** and **la** both mean 'the' (see *Grammar* p. 30).

segnato? have you taken it down? (lit. marked?).

le pare has no precise equivalent in English. The whole expression **prego, le pare** (which is in reply to thanks from the inquirer) may be loosely translated as 'no trouble at all'.

Key words and phrases

To learn

dov'è . . . ?	where is . . . ?
vado a (Roma)	I'm going to (Rome)
torno a (Londra)	I'm going back to (London)
non lo so	I don't know
non c'è . . .	there's no . . .
treno	train
uscita	way out
non ci sono . . .	there are no . . .
voli per (Londra)	flights to (London)
treni per (Roma)	trains to (Rome)
quanti (treni)?	how many (trains)?
quante (valigie)?	how many (suitcases)?
quanto costa?	how much does that cost?

To understand

dove va?	where are you going?
(il treno) è in partenza	(the train) is departing
dal binario numero (sei)	from platform (6)
(il volo) è in arrivo	(the flight) is arriving
mi dica	can I help you?

Numbers from 1 to 20

0	**zero**	11	**undici**
1	**uno**	12	**dodici**
2	**due**	13	**tredici**
3	**tre**	14	**quattordici**
4	**quattro**	15	**quindici**
5	**cinque**	16	**sedici**
6	**sei**	17	**diciassette**
7	**sette**	18	**diciotto**
8	**otto**	19	**diciannove**
9	**nove**	20	**venti**
10	**dieci**		

You can also hear these pronounced on tape straight after dialogue 6.

Practise what you have learnt

The answers for all these exercises are on p. 34.

1 Listen to the train announcements on tape. Write the platform numbers from the boxes below next to the origin or destination announced for the trains arriving at or leaving from each of them.

a. ROMA ....

b. EMPOLI, PONTEDERA, PISA ....

c. MILANO, BOLOGNA ....

d. BOLOGNA, VERONA, BRENNERO ....

e. SIENA, EMPOLI ....

f. PRATO, PISTOIA ....

1	2	4	7	11	18

2 Listen once more to the same train announcements. This time for every platform number specify the type of train (**locale, rapido, diretto, espresso**), and tick whether it's arriving or leaving.

Tipo di treno	Binario	In arrivo	In partenza
	1		
	2		
	4		
	7		
	11		
	18		

3

Look at the following pieces of luggage being checked in at the airport. Listen to the baggage handler's voice on tape giving their weight, and write the weight on the appropriate label.

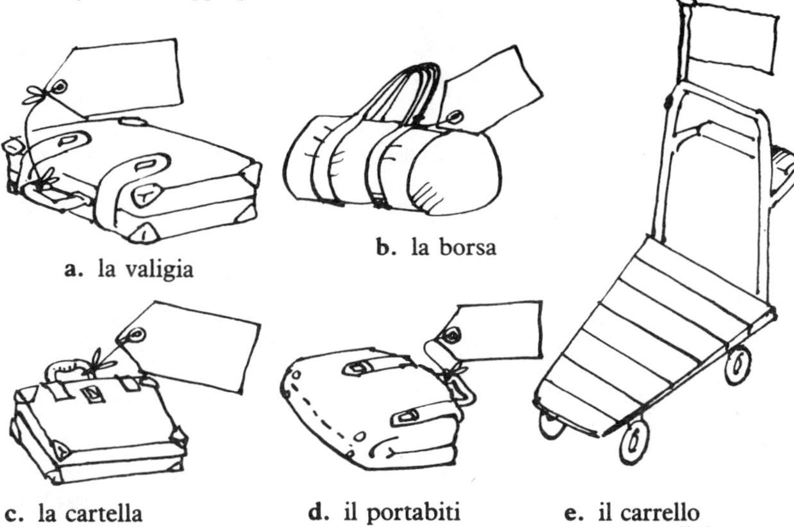

a. la valigia

b. la borsa

c. la cartella

d. il portabiti

e. il carrello portavaligie

4

Listen to the airport announcements on tape. For every one of the destinations on the board below write down the three-figure flight number.

	Destinazione	Volo numero		
a.	Roma			
b.	Palermo			
c.	Napoli			
d.	Londra Gatwick			
e.	New York			

5

On your cassette the Tourist Office employee is giving another caller the telephone numbers of a few local hotels. Take down the numbers, writing them after each hotel's name.

a. Albergo Aurora ....

b. Hotel Continentale ....

c. Albergo Lido ....

d. Albergo Internazionale ....

e. Albergo dei Viaggiatori ....

f. Albergo del Sole ....

Grammar

Translation of 'the' in the singular

In Italian there are different words for 'the' with masculine and feminine nouns, in the singular and in the plural.

- **il** is used before all singular masculine nouns beginning with a consonant, e.g. **il treno** the train, **il rapido** the fast train; but
- **lo** is used before masculine nouns beginning with **z-** and **s-** + another consonant, e.g. **lo studente** the student, **lo zucchero** sugar. (**Lo** is also used before words beginning with **ps-** and **gn-**, but you will come across very few examples.)
- **la** is used before feminine singular nouns beginning in a consonant, e.g. **la valigia** the suitcase, **la bilancia** the weighing scales.
- **l'** is used before any singular noun, masculine or feminine, beginning with a vowel, e.g. **l'albergo** (m.) the hotel, **l'uscita** (f.) the way out.

It is important to try to remember the gender of Italian nouns, but don't worry too much if you make mistakes with 'the'. You will still be understood, and the most important thing is to speak confidently, even at the cost of a few mistakes. (You will learn the plural forms of 'the' in Unit 4.)

Exercise 1 Write the correct translation of 'the' before the following singular nouns. Treat all nouns ending in **-o** as masculine, in **-a** as feminine. (Answers p. 34.)

a. ....espresso

b. ....uscita

c. ....pacchetto

d. ....numero

e. ....imbarco

f. ....partenza

g. ....arrivo

h. ....telefono

Dal, al, sul etc.

Certain prepositions, **a** (to, at), **da** (from), **di** (of), **su** (on), **in** (in) combine with **il, lo, la** and **l'** producing the following forms:

a		al		allo		all'		alla	**to the**
da		dal		dallo		dall'		dalla	**from the**
di	+ il	del	+ lo	dello	+ l'	dell'	+ la	della	**of the**
su		sul		sullo		sull'		sulla	**on the**
in		nel		nello		nell'		nella	**in the**

e.g. **dal binario** from the platform
allo studente to the student
della casa of the house
nell'albergo in the hotel
sul treno on the train
sullo sgabello on the stool
dall'uscita from the exit
nella birra in the beer

If you find this list daunting, there's no need to learn it by heart. Just note it so that you can recognize the forms later.

You will often find these combinations in Italian where 'the' would not be used in English, e.g. **in arrivo al binario sette** arriving at platform seven, **imbarco dall'uscita numero sei** boarding from gate six, etc.

Here are two important irregular verbs in the present tense:

Venire to come		*Andare* to go	
vengo	I come	**vado**	I go
vieni	you come	**vai**	you (pl.) go
viene	he/she/it comes you (polite) come	**va**	he/she/it goes you (polite) go
veniamo	we come	**andiamo**	we go
venite	you (pl.) come	**andate**	you go
vengono	they come	**vanno**	they go

Look at the following questions:

dove vai? dove va? dove andate?

They all translate 'where are *you* going?' but they mean three different kinds of 'you'. You use **dove vai?** when talking to a child, a friend or a relation. You use **dove va?** (the polite form) when talking to a person you don't know very well, whom you would address by his/her family name and/or title. You use **dove andate?** in the plural, with more than one person, whether friends or strangers.

Exercise 2 Here we'll concentrate on the polite form. Fill in the verbs in the following dialogue about where people come from (**venire**) and where they are going (**andare**). Remember that **da** means 'from'. (Answers p. 34.)

a. E Lei da dove ....?

b. .... da Alessandria.

c. E dove ....?

d. .... a Roma.

e. .... soltanto a Roma?

f. No, ... anche a Firenze, forse a Siena.

g. (*addressing another traveller*) Anche Lei .... da Alessandria?

h. No, ... da Torino.

i. Dove .... ? A Roma?

j. No, ... a Napoli.

Read and understand

Look at the noticeboard below. See whether you can answer the following questions. (Answers on p. 34.)

1 At what time does the flight from Alghero arrive in Pisa?

....

2 Where does it go on to?

....

3 How many flights do not use Pisa airport as a stopover, but originate and terminate there?

....

4 If you arrived at Pisa airport at about eight p.m. (or 20.00), would you be able to catch a flight to Rome?

....

Did you know?

Italian railways

The Italian railway system **Ferrovie dello Stato** (or **FS**), is largely nationalized, with only a few surviving privately owned narrow-gauge lines mostly over short distances. It is generally acknowledged to be one of the most efficiently run public services in the country, and good value for money. If you travel to Italy by railway (and, even if you don't, you may consider using railways once you're there), you can usually get discounts for return trips, for students, and for family groups. Reduced fares also apply to 'rover' tickets, allowing you unlimited travel over short periods, also to special occasions (such as International Trade Fairs), package tours and rail-drive combinations.

It is worth using express trains, paying the **supplemento rapido** (express train surcharge) where applicable, and booking seats in advance if possible. Avoid international express trains between Northern Europe and Southern Italy at peak holiday times: they *will* be overcrowded and late. Remember that porters are a fast disappearing race and station trolleys hard to come by: luggage with wheels or a collapsible trolley can be extremely useful. Information about your journey is usually available from prominently displayed noticeboards and electronic panels, often including the sequence of carriages in the trains. Through coaches are clearly labelled: look out for them.

People in uniform

You may be surprised at the variety of uniformed officers you will see while in Italy. Apart from railway officials (if you travel by train), your papers will be checked at the frontier by a plain-clothes police inspector, usually accompanied by a **Carabiniere** in navy-blue uniform with red collar badges. **Carabinieri** are a special corps of the Italian Army performing police duties. You may also see grey-uniformed State Police (**Pubblica Sicurezza**) or Railway Police officers (**Polfer** or **Polizia Ferroviaria**), and Customs and Excise officers (**Guardia di Finanza**) in battle green with bright yellow collar badges. In towns you will see **Vigili Urbani** members of the local traffic police force, and an increasing number of armed security guards mostly stationed outside banks.

Italian 'as she is spoken'

Even today about one third of the Italian population (some 20 million people) are *not* native speakers of Italian, but were brought up in one of the various local 'dialects' (languages as different from each other and from Standard Italian as Italian differs from French or Portuguese) and learned Italian at school. A few old people in remote areas may speak only their dialect. The majority speak Standard Italian with a more or less marked regional accent, often with a few minor departures from the accepted grammatical standard.

Your turn to speak

This is the section where you get a chance to speak and you'll be working alone with your cassette recorder.

Here are a few of the things you should now be able to say by using and re-combining together words and expressions you have just learned:

Questions **dov'è . . . ?** where is . . . ?
da dove . . . ? where from . . . ?

Statements **non c'è . . .** there is no . . .
non lo so I don't know (it)
non so . . . I don't know . . .
vengo da . . . I come from . . .
vado a . . . I'm going to . . .
By the way, **vado a . . .** can mean 'I'*ll* go' as well as 'I go' and 'I'm going'.

1 The first exercise on tape practises the expressions above, so read them several times before you start. You should then try to do the exercise without looking at your book. Marisa will tell you what to do.

2 In this second exercise you'll be using the same expressions but this time you'll be taking part in a conversation. Imagine you're on holiday and want to go somewhere by train. You see a railwayman at the local railway station and ask him some questions. You'll need a new and important phrase **per piacere**, please.

Answers

Practise what you have learnt p. 28 Exercise **1** (**a**) 2 (**b**) 4 (**c**) 18 (**d**) 1 (**e**) 7 (**f**) 11.

p. 28 Exercise **2** **binario 1:** diretto, in partenza; **binario 2:** rapido, in partenza; **binario 4:** locale, in partenza; **binario 7:** locale, in arrivo; **binario 11:** locale, in partenza; **binario 18:** espresso, in arrivo.

p. 29 Exercise **3** (**a**) 12k (**b**) 6k (**c**) 2k (**d**) 4k (**e**) 1k.

p. 29 Exercise **4** (**a**) 459 (**b**) 275 (**c**) 310 (**d**) 528 (**e**) 764.

p. 29 Exercise **5** (**a**) 32–78–61 (**b**) 36–54–24 (**c**) 45–20–17 (**d**) 43–00–72 (**e**) 76–33–41 (**f**) 53–25–48.

Grammar p. 30 Exercise **1** (**a**) l' (**b**) l' (**c**) il (**d**) il (**e**) l' (**f**) la (**g**) l' (**h**) il.

p. 31 Exercise **2** (**a**) viene (**b**) vengo (**c**) va (**d**) vado (**e**) va (**f**) vado (**g**) viene (**h**) vengo (**i**) va (**j**) vado.

Read and understand p. 32 (**1**) 7.55 (**2**) Milan (**3**) 2 (**4**) no.

3 *Ci sono camere libere?*

What you will learn

- how to tell other people about your profession or occupation
- how to book a room in a hotel
- how to ask for information about what is, or is not, available
- numbers 20–1000
- about tourist accommodation in Italy

Before you begin

Points to remember from Unit 2:

1 verbs **venire** and **andare**

vengo	**vieni**	**viene**	**veniamo**	**venite**	**vengono**
vado	**vai**	**va**	**andiamo**	**andate**	**vanno**

2 negative statements

non c'è . . .	**non c'è eccedenza,**	**non c'è uscita**
non ci sono . . .	**non ci sono treni,**	**non ci sono voli per Londra**

3 saying one doesn't know
non so, non lo so, non so da dove viene questo treno

Study guide

	Dialogues 1, 2: listen straight through without the book
	Dialogues 1, 2: listen, read and study one by one
	Dialogues 3, 4: listen straight through without the book
	Dialogues 3, 4: listen, read and study one by one
	Dialogues 5–7: listen straight through without the book
	Dialogues 5–7: listen, read and study one by one
	Learn the *Key words and phrases*
	Do the exercises in *Practise what you have learnt*
	Study *Grammar*
	Do *Read and understand*
	Read *Did you know?*
	Do the tape exercise in *Your turn to speak*
	Listen to all the dialogues again without the book
	Do the *Revision* section for Units 1–3 on p. 217.

Dialogues

1 *Giovanni meets a lady on a train. They discuss the work they do*

Giovanni Io sono un insegnante. Sono professore di italiano. Insegno l'italiano in Inghilterra. E Lei?
Signora Io sono una segretaria. Lavoro in una ditta di Milano.
Giovanni E suo marito?
Signora Mio marito è commerciante.

insegno I teach (from **insegnare**, to teach)
lavoro I work (from **lavorare**, to work)
ditta firm
mio my
commerciante (m.) businessman, dealer

2 *A member of a group of bee-keepers tells Giovanni where they are going.*

Giovanni Io sono un turista inglese che va a Pisa.
Signore Noi andiamo a Roma a un congresso, un congresso di apicultura.
Giovanni E Lei è un apicultore?
Signore Sì, eh, sono un vecchio apicultore, ecco . . .
Giovanni Da quanti anni fa l'apicultore?
Signore Eh, trentacinque anni adesso.

il turista (m.), la turista (f.) tourist
che who
congresso conference, congress
apicultura bee-keeping; **apicultore (m.)** bee-keeper; **ape (f.)** bee
vecchio old
ecco there you are
adesso now

1 ➧ **io sono un insegnante** I'm a teacher. There are two simple ways of stating your profession or occupation. You either say: **sono un insegnante, sono una segretaria** (I'm a secretary) (see *Grammar* p. 45), or you say **sono insegnante, sono segretaria**. You will find the Italian for some other occupations in *Key words and phrases* on p. 42.

insegnante is the general word for 'teacher' of all categories, both male and female; **professore** is the title appropriate to secondary and tertiary male teachers (female teachers are called **professoressa**).

➧ **e Lei?** what about you? **e suo marito?** what about your husband? When addressing people in the polite form, the feminine pronoun **Lei** is used whenever necessary. To make it clear that it means 'you' and not 'she' the capital **L** is often used. Here **suo** means 'your' (in other contexts it means 'his', 'her(s)': see *Grammar* p. 45).

2 ➧ **da quanti anni fa l'apicultore?** how many years have you been a bee-keeper? Another way of stating one's occupation or trade, particularly if it involves some form of manual work, is to use the verb **fare**, to do, to make (which has an irregular present: see *Grammar* p. 45):
che cosa fa? what do you do?
che lavoro fa? what work do you do? what's your work?
faccio l'apicultore I'm a bee-keeper
faccio la segretaria I'm a secretary
Note that in this case the name of the profession or trade must be preceded by the word for 'the'.

➧ **trentacinque** thirty-five. You should learn the numbers 20–1000 which are explained in *Key words and phrases* on p. 42.

3 *Giovanni is booking in at a hotel. The receptionist tells him that the hotel is rather full, but he may be able to accommodate him*

Portiere Buona sera.
Giovanni Buona sera.
Portiere Buona sera. Mi dica, signore. Desidera qualcosa?
Giovanni Ha delle camere libere?
Portiere Sì. Quante persone sono?
Giovanni Siamo in quattro.
Portiere Che camera desidera? A un letto, due letti . . .
Giovanni Una camera con due letti, e due camere a un letto. Una camera a due letti con bagno, e le due camere a un letto anche senza bagno.
Portiere Anche senza bagno? Va bene. Per quanti giorni si trattiene?
Giovanni Cinque giorni.
Portiere Cinque notti, eh. Ma vediamo . . . Ci ho l'albergo un po' completo. Ci ho poco posto . . . Va bene, posso . . . posso sistemarli. Una a due letti con bagno . . .
Giovanni Sì.
Portiere . . . e due a un letto senza bagno. Sì, sì, posso sistemarlo.
Giovanni Va bene.

portiere (m.) receptionist
che camera desidera? what (sort of) room do you want?
letto bed
anche even, (in other contexts: also)
vediamo let's see, let's have a look
posso sistemarli/lo I can accommodate you

4 *A shop assistant is unable to supply a very shy customer with the black jumper she requires*

Commessa Una maglia nera? No, signora, mi dispiace. L'abbiamo finite in nero. Ce l'ho colorate.
Signora Mmm . . . allora . . .
Commessa Mi dispiace proprio, ma non ho altro di nero . . . Grazie, buona sera.

maglia a word used to describe anything knitted: a jersey, a jumper, a pullover, a vest
nero, nera black
l'abbiamo finite in nero we're out of black ones
ce l'ho colorate I've got them in other colours

3 ◆ **desidera qualcosa?** do you want anything? You could answer using **desidero** . . . *I want*, or simply by stating what you want and adding *please*, **per piacere**

◆ **ha delle camere libere?** have you (got) any rooms free? **Delle** and **dei** are the plurals of **della** and **del** (see also Units 2 and 4) used with the meaning 'some' or 'any': **ha delle valigie**? have you got any luggage? **ci sono dei treni per Roma**? are there any trains for Rome?

◆ **siamo in quattro** there are four of us: **siamo in sei** there are six of us.

◆ **con** with; **senza** without: **con bagno o senza**? with or without bath? **con doccia** with shower; **con colazione e cena, ma senza pranzo** with breakfast and evening meals, but without midday meals; **con un letto matrimoniale** with a double bed.

◆ **per quanti giorni si trattiene?** how many days are you staying? Two things to note here:
- the forms of **trattenere** are similar to those of **venire**: **vengo/trattengo, vieni/trattiene** etc. For a full list, see p. 31.
- **trattenere** actually means 'to retain', 'to detain' or 'to entertain', according to the context. To mean 'I'm staying' the Italians actually say 'I'm detaining myself' – **mi trattengo**. For **mi, si**, etc., see *Grammar* p. 45.

The receptionist might have simply asked **per quanti giorni?**, and the short reply would be **cinque giorni**.

ci ho l'albergo un po' completo the hotel is rather full. **Un po'** is short for **un poco**, a little. **Poco** on its own means 'very little', 'hardly any', e.g. in the phrase **ci ho poco posto** I have hardly any space.

4 ◆ **no, signora, mi dispiace** no, Madam, I'm sorry; **mi dispiace proprio** I'm really sorry. This is a very useful phrase which you should learn both to recognize and to use (but *not* as a translation of 'sorry!' when you have just trodden on someone's toes, when you should say **scusi**, excuse me).

non ho altro di nero I've nothing else in black. This phrase could also be used by a hotel receptionist: **non ho altro** I've nothing else, **non ho altre camere** I've no other rooms, I've no more rooms.

5 *Giovanni asks a lady in the tourist office whether there are any department stores nearby*

Giovanni Signora, ci sono dei grandi magazzini qui vicino?
Signora Vicino a Piazza Duomo c'è l' . . . la Rinascente, e in via Torino c'è sia la STANDA che la UPIM.

Piazza Duomo (or: **Piazza del Duomo**) Cathedral Square
La Rinascente, STANDA, UPIM names of three well-known chains of department stores (the last is an abbreviation)
sia . . . che . . . both . . . and . . .

6 *Giovanni is asking another tourist office employee where public telephones can be found*

Giovanni Ci sono dei telefoni pubblici qui vicino?
Signorina C'è l'ufficio dei telefoni in mezzo alla Galleria, Galleria Vittorio Emanuele.
Giovanni E si può telefonare anche all'estero?
Signorina Sì, può telefonare anche all'estero.

in mezzo a in the middle of, in the centre of
si può . . .? can one . . .?
all'estero abroad
può you can

7 *Giovanni asks another hotel receptionist where the telephone office is*

Giovanni Dov'è l'ufficio dei telefoni?
Portiere In piazza Facchini, piazza Facchini. Sulla sinistra c'è questa piazza, e sotto la torre dove c'è l'orologio trova l'ufficio.
Giovanni Molte grazie.
Portiere Prego.

piazza square
sotto underneath, below
torre (f.) tower
trova you'll find (from **trovare**, to find)

5 ➧ **c'è** there is; **ci sono** there are. This dialogue, and the next, concentrate on these expressions, which are very commonly used in Italian:
ci sono dei grandi magazzini qui vicino? are there any department stores nearby?
c'è la Rinascente there is Rinascente
ci sono la STANDA e l'UPIM there are STANDA and UPIM
ci sono dei telefoni pubblici? are there any public telephones?
c'è l'ufficio del telefono in piazza Facchini there's the telephone office in Facchini square.

ci there, can be used only in conjunction with a verb; with **essere**, as in the above examples, or with other verbs:
ci andiamo we are going there
ci lavoro I work there
It is often used when there is no equivalent in English, especially with **avere**, as in the examples in dialogue 3:
ci ho l'albergo un po' completo
ci ho poco posto.

6 **l'ufficio dei telefoni** is a special office where one can make trunk and international telephone calls. It is often more convenient than using payphones which require large quantities of coins or **gettoni** (telephone tokens).

Galleria is the name given to two huge glass-covered arcades in the centre of Milan and Naples, which enclose elegant marble-paved pedestrian precincts with luxury shops, restaurants, bars, public offices etc.

7 ➧ **sulla sinistra** on the left; **sulla destra** on the right. You can also say: **a sinistra, a destra.**

orologio clock or watch: the same word is used in Italian for any sort of timepiece irrespective of size.

Key words and phrases

Your profession or occupation

sono . . .	I am . . .
(un) dottore/(una) dottoressa/ (un) medico	a doctor (man/woman)
(un/una) negoziante	a shopkeeper
(uno) studente/(una) studentessa	a student
in pensione	retired
faccio . . .	I am . . .
l'operaio (m.)/l'operaia (f.)	a factory worker
il dattilografo/la dattilografa	a typist
il/la telefonista	a switchboard operator
e Lei che cosa fa?	and what about you? and what's your work?
che lavoro fa?	what work do you do?

At the hotel

ha delle camere libere?	have you got any rooms free?
desidero una camera . . .	I want a room . . .
a due letti	with twin beds
a un letto	with one bed (i.e. a single)
con un letto matrimoniale	with a double bed
con bagno	with bath
senza bagno	without bath
con doccia	with shower
siamo in (quattro)	there are (four) of us
mi trattengo (sette) giorni	I'm staying (seven) days
c'è un bagno?	is there a bathroom?
c'è una doccia?	is there a shower?
ci sono (dei) telefoni pubblici qui vicino?	are there (any) public telephones nearby?
ci sono (dei) grandi magazzini qui vicino?	are there (any) department stores nearby?

Now the phrases you need mainly to understand.

desidera qualcosa?	do you want anything?
mi dispiace	I'm sorry
quanti giorni si trattiene?	how many days are you staying?
sulla sinistra/a sinistra	on the left
sulla destra/a destra	on the right
non ho altro	I've nothing else

Numbers from 20 to 1000

(See also *Grammar summary* p. 227.)

20 **venti**	60 **sessanta**	100 **cento**
30 **trenta**	70 **settanta**	200 **duecento**
40 **quaranta**	80 **ottanta**	300 **trecento etc.**
50 **cinquanta**	90 **novanta**	1000 **mille**

All other numbers in between are formed, as in English, by combining hundreds, tens and units in that order:

34 **trentaquattro** thirty-four   276 **duecento settantasei** two hundred (and) seventy-six

The final vowel of the tens is omitted before **uno** and **otto**:

21 **ventuno**   358 **trecento cinquantotto**

(but not the final vowel of **cento**: 101 **centouno**, 308 **trecento otto**).

Practise what you have learnt

1 For each of the various people illustrated below choose the appropriate profession or occupation from those in the box. Then listen to the tape to check your answers.

a. .... **b.** .... **c.** ....

d. .... **e.** .... **f.** ....

g. .... **h.** ....

insegnante
negoziante
telefonista
operaia
dottore
segretaria
studentessa
portiere

2 All the following questions may be asked both as they are printed below, and by placing the appropriate form of **del, della** etc. before the noun. Check back to the list on p. 30, then write the required form in the dotted space. You won't need your cassette recorder, the answers are on p. 48.

a. Ha .... camere, per favore?

b. Ci sono .... telefoni pubblici qui vicino?

c. Avete .... docce in questo albergo?

d. Ci sono .... grandi magazzini qui vicino?

e. Ha .... maglie nere, per favore?

3 Listen to the hotel receptionist sending various visitors to their rooms, and write the number allotted to each visitor, choosing it from the box below, after each name. (Answers on p. 48.)

a. Signor Jones ....

b. Signor e signora Smith ....

c. Signor Gilardi ....

d. Signora e signorina Rossi ......

e. Dottor White ....

f. Professor Bianchi ....

320	79	102	227	35	412

4 In the three short dialogues on tape, Signor A, Signorina B and Signora C regret that they haven't got what they are being asked for, or say that it is not available. Identify what it is they do not have or cannot direct their questioner to, and put a cross in the appropriate box below. (Answers p. 48.)

Signor A
a. ☐ two bedrooms
b. ☐ a twin-bedded room

Signorina B
a. ☐ a telephone
b. ☐ the public telephone office

Signora C
a. ☐ luggage trolleys
b. ☐ railway porters

5 In the following dialogue the traveller's part has been omitted. Her replies are jumbled, together with other incorrect replies, after the dialogue. Choose the correct ones, and write them in the appropriate place.

Portiere Buongiorno, signora. Dica.

Signora ....

Portiere Vediamo . . . Sì, signora. Una camera a un letto?

Signora ....

Portiere Sì, l'abbiamo. Come la desidera, con bagno o senza?

Signora ....

Portiere Sì, l'abbiamo anche con doccia. Per quante notti?

Signora ....

Portiere Allora: una camera a due letti con doccia per tre notti. Va bene. Posso sistemarla.

Signora ....

Portiere La trecentocinque.

Per tre notti.
Dov'è la camera?
Che numero?
Mi trattengo solo un giorno.
Due camere a un letto.
Ha una camera libera?
Con doccia non c'è?
Senza bagno.
No, una camera a due letti per me e per mio marito.

And now check your answers by listening to the dialogue on tape. Then listen to it a second time, this time stopping the tape after the receptionist's questions, so that you can take the part of the traveller.

Grammar

Nouns ending in -e, -i

sing.	*pl.*
negoziante	**negozianti**
insegnante	**insegnanti**

Unlike the nouns studied in Unit 1, where one can guess the gender from their endings (e.g. **letto, letti** m.; **camera, camere** f.), these nouns have no separate masculine and feminine endings. Some, like **lo studente**, are masculine; some, like **l'ape** (bee), are feminine; and others, like those in the example above, can be both (**il negoziante** m., **la negoziante** f.). The gender of all these nouns will be given in the vocabulary lists.

A number of adjectives, e.g. **inglese** English, **scozzese** Scottish, **locale** local, **internazionale** international etc., follow the same pattern and end in **-e** in the singular and **-i** in the plural, whether masculine or feminine. Note that in phrases like **treno locale, studente italiano, signore scozzesi** noun and adjective 'agree', even though they don't have the same ending.

Translation of 'a', 'an'

un	**turista** **insegnante** **segretario**	before all masculine nouns
uno	**studente**	before masculine nouns beginning with **s** followed by another consonant (**st, sp, sch,** etc) **gn-, ps-, z-**
una	**turista** **segretaria**	before feminine nouns beginning with a consonant
un'	**università**	before feminine nouns beginning with a vowel

Fare to do

faccio	I do
fai	you do
fa	he/she/it does
facciamo	we do
fate	you do
fanno	they do

Sapere to know

so	I know
sai	you know
sa	he/she/it knows you (polite) know
sappiamo	we know
sapete	you know
sanno	they know

Like many verbs in common everyday use, **fare** and **sapere** have irregular present tenses. Remember also the verb **trattenere** (to detain, to stay), which follows the same pattern as **venire** (see Unit 2).

Mi, ti, si, ci, vi

mi trattengo cinque giorni	I('ll) stay five days
dove si trova?	where is it?
come si chiama?	what's his/her name?

Some Italian verbs like **chiamare** to call, **trovare** to find, and **trattenere** to detain, may be preceded by the words **mi** (me), **ti** (you), **si** (him-/her-/itself, themselves), **ci** (us), **vi** (you, pl.). These have a 'reflexive' meaning, that is, they refer back to the subject of the verb (as if **mi trattengo** meant 'I detain myself'). In English, however, it is mostly unnecessary to translate them literally: in other words, you don't translate **si chiama** as 'he calls himself', but simply as 'he's called'.

Read and understand

Here is a registration form, such as you may be asked to complete when you book in at an Italian hotel.

Cognome ....
Nome ....
Luogo e data di nascita ....
Nazionalità ....
Passaporto N° ....
Abitante a ....
in ....
Data d'ingresso in Italia ....

Answer the following questions. (Answers p. 48.)

1 Which should you fill in first?
a. ☐ your first name
b. ☐ your family name
2 Which should you fill in first?
a. ☐ your place of birth
b. ☐ your date of birth
3 Supposing you are British, which would the correct word be, after **nazionalità**?
a. ☐ **britannico**
b. ☐ **britannica**
4 What would you write after **abitante a**?
a. ☐ the town where you live
b. ☐ the street where you live.

Learn to recognize these notices.

RICEVIMENTO reception (**ricevere** to receive)

CASSA cashier, cash desk

TELESELEZIONE payphone with STD

Did you know?

Tourist accommodation

The terms **albergo** and **hotel** (which the Italians pronounce without the **h-**) are interchangeable. Less luxurious types of establishment are called **pensione**, guest house, and **locanda** or **alloggio** roughly corresponding to simple bed-and-breakfast type accommodation. The term **ostello** is reserved for youth hostels (also called **albergo della gioventù**).

A particularly useful type of establishment, without a counterpart in Britain, is the **albergo diurno**, or simply **diurno**, 'day-time hotel'. As its name suggests it does not have overnight accommodation, but it does offer most services available in hotels, such as toilets, baths, showers, hairdresser, manicure, laundry and valet service, etc., but not a restaurant service nor a room for the night.

In many Italian towns you can find **alberghi** and **pensioni**, often of a quite respectable standard, occupying only a part of a block of flats, with the reception on the third or fourth floor of the building.

Hoteliers are required by law to display in every room, usually behind the door, the cost of the accommodation, inclusive of **IVA** (VAT) and **tassa di soggiorno** (local tourist tax). Unless the cost is specified as being **per persona** it refers to the charge for the room, which may be occupied by more than one person. Breakfast is seldom included in the price, though the habit of making an inclusive charge is spreading. Anyway it is often better and cheaper to have breakfast in a nearby café. Full board is called **pensione completa**, and half board **mezza pensione**. Not all hotels have a restaurant, and in those which do, the standard of accommodation is no reliable guide to the standard of catering.

Tourists travelling with caravans, motor-homes or tents will find a bewildering variety of campsites of all sizes and standards. It's difficult to generalize but on the whole those recommended by well-known tourist organizations are usually reliable and it is possible to find quite satisfactory campsites that have not been included in any list or noted on any map. The Italian word **campeggio** tends to be superseded by the international word 'camping'.

Your turn to speak

In this exercise you'll be asked to book a room in a hotel, using the phrases you've learned in this unit. Follow the instructions on tape.

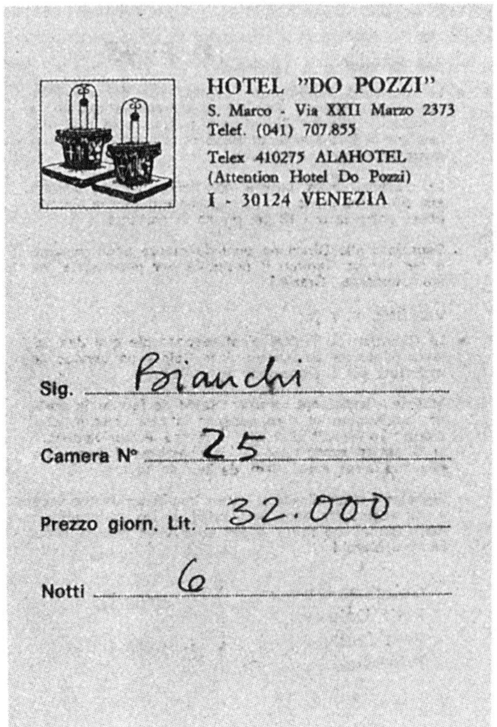
HOTEL "DO POZZI"
S. Marco - Via XXII Marzo 2373
Telef. (041) 707.855
Telex 410275 ALAHOTEL
(Attention Hotel Do Pozzi)
I - 30124 VENEZIA

Sig. Bianchi

Camera N° 25

Prezzo giorn. Lit. 32.000

Notti 6

Revision

Next you should do a short revision section which goes over the language you have studied in Units 1–3. Turn to p. 217 for the written part of the exercises. The tape exercises follow straight after this unit on your cassette.

Answers

Practise what you have learnt p. 43 Exercise **2** (**a**) delle (**b**) dei (**c**) delle (**d**) dei (**e**) delle.

p. 43 Exercise **3** (**a**) 320 (**b**) 227 (**c**) 102 (**d**) 412 (**e**) 79 (**f**) 35.

p. 44 Exercise **4** Signor A (b)
Signorina B (a)
Signora C (a)

Read and understand p. 46 (**1**) b: **cognome** = family name (2) a: **luogo** = place (**3**) b: **britannica** (**4**) a: you would put the street where you live after the word **in** . . .

4 *Che cosa prende?*

What you will learn

- how to ask how much something costs
- how to order breakfast
- how to order drinks and snacks
- how to understand what is available
- numbers from 1001 onwards

Before you begin

Points to remember from Unit 3:

1 verbs
chiamare

mi chiamo	**ti chiami**	**si chiama**
ci chiamiamo	**vi chiamate**	**si chiamano**

fare		**sapere**	
faccio	**facciamo**	**so**	**sappiamo**
fai	**fate**	**sai**	**sapete**
fa	**fanno**	**sa**	**sanno**

2 nouns and adjectives in **-e**

negoziante	**scozzese**
negozianti	**scozzesi**

3 how to ask 'is there?' 'are there?'
c'è un telefono? ci sono camere libere?

Study guide

	Dialogues 1–3: listen straight through without the book
	Dialogues 1–3: listen, read and study one by one
	Dialogues 4–6: listen straight through without the book
	Dialogues 4–6: listen read and study one by one
	Learn the *Key words and phrases*
	Do the exercises in *Practise what you have learnt*
	Study *Grammar* and do the exercise
	Do *Read and understand*
	Read *Did you know?*
	Do the tape exercises in *Your turn to speak*
	Finally, listen to all the dialogues again without the book

Dialogues

1 *Giovanni asks the hotel receptionist how much the rooms cost*

Giovanni Quanto costano queste camere? Mi dica solo la camera e mezza pensione.

Portiere Mezza pensione? Io le posso dire tutti i prezzi . . . (va bene) . . . poi Lei può vedere. . .

Giovanni Mm, mi dica . . . mi dica allora tutti i prezzi.

Portiere Dunque, la doppia, cioè quella a due letti con bagno, con la colazione del mattino, con pane, burro, marmellata, o cioccolata, o té, quello che Lei desidera, ventinovemila quattrocento lire per due persone, tasse, servizio, tutto incluso. Ventinovemila quattrocento. Mentre invece le singole, cioè le singole senza bagno, con la colazione del mattino, tredicimila e quattrocento cinquanta per camera.

Giovanni Va bene, va benissimo, allora le prendo.

solo only
mezza pensione half board
le posso dire . . . I can tell you . . .
poi Lei può vedere . . . then you can see . . .
dunque well, then
doppia double (room)
cioè that is
quello che Lei desidera what you want
ventinove twenty-nine
tasse taxes
servizio service
tutto incluso all included
mentre invece while on the other hand
singole single (rooms)
tredicimila quattrocento cinquanta 13,450

2 *Giovanni asks the hotel receptionist about methods of payment*

Giovanni E per il pagamento Lei accetta travellers' cheques e anche carte di credito?

Portiere Sì, sì, qualsiasi tipo di pagamento.

Giovanni Io ho una carta di credito VISA.

Portiere VISA va benissimo.

Giovanni VISA va benissimo.

Portiere Sì, sì, va bene, sì, sì.

Giovanni Allora . . .

Portiere VISA, o anche American Express, o Eurocard. Qualsiasi carta.

Giovanni Va bene.

Portiere Grazie.

carte di credito credit cards

1 **quanto costano queste camere?** how much do these rooms cost? And, for only one room: **questa camera quanto costa? Quanto costa/quanto costano** can go either at the beginning or at the end.

mi dica here has its literal meaning of 'tell me'.

tutti i prezzi all the prices. **I** is the plural of **il** (see *Grammar* p. 59).

la colazione (del mattino) (morning) breakfast. The standard Italian **colazione** consists of a hot drink: **caffè** (black coffee), **caffè e latte** or **caffellatte** (white coffee, lit. coffee and milk) – called **cappuccino** when made using an espresso coffee machine – **té** (tea), **cioccolata** or **cioccolato** (chocolate), with **pane** (bread), **burro** (butter) and **marmellata** (jam). If you want marmalade ask for **marmellata d'arance**, lit. orange jam. The word **colazione** can also mean 'lunch'.

ventinovemila quattrocento lire twenty-nine thousand four hundred lire. To understand prices in Italian it is important to know the numbers over 1000 (see p. 56).

va bene it's OK; **va benissimo** it's excellent. This extremely frequent expression may also be used in conjunction with a noun, e.g. **questa camera va bene** this room is OK; **queste camere vanno bene** these rooms are OK; **la cioccolata va benissimo** the chocolate will do fine.

allora le prendo I'll take them, then.

2 **accetta travellers' cheques?** do you accept travellers' cheques? **Accetta** is from **accettare**, to accept.

qualsiasi tipo di pagamento any type of payment. **Qualsiasi**, meaning 'any whatever', always stays the same and can only be followed by a singular noun: **qualsiasi carta** any (credit) card; **qualsiasi documento va bene** any document will do.

allora . . . You will find transcribed in these dialogues many words like **be'** (**bene**), **dunque, ecco, allora, senta** etc., which carry no real meaning. They are used merely as sentence openers or stopgaps and are consequently difficult or impossible to translate. They are the equivalent of 'really', 'right', 'OK', etc. used in English conversation.

3 *The receptionist gives Giovanni the hotel's address and telephone number, and asks him for his identity papers*

Portiere L'indirizzo è: Albergo Vittoria, Lungarno Pacinotti numero dodici. Il telefono . . . eh . . . se chiama di fuori Pisa, zero cinquanta, due trentatré otto due. E poi con comodo quando scendono, mi fa un favore se mi portano i loro passaporti, o carte d'identità. Qualsiasi documento va bene.
Giovanni Abbiamo carte d'identità. Va bene lo stesso?
Portiere Va bene lo stesso, sì, sì.
Giovanni Molte grazie.
Portiere Prego.

con comodo at your convenience
quando scendono when you (pl.) come down (from **scendere**)
carte d'identità identity cards

4 *Giovanni asks a waiter what he can have for breakfast*

Giovanni Mi dica che cosa c'è per colazione?
Cameriere Eh, caffè col latte, oppure del té o del cioccolato con pane, burro, e marmellata. Se poi vuole anche qualche cos'altro si può fare delle uova à la coque, o omelette, o qualche cos'altro del genere.
Giovanni Va bene, molte grazie.
Cameriere Prego, niente.

cameriere (m.) waiter
col latte with milk (**col** = **con il**)
oppure or
se poi vuole if you then want
▶ **qualche cos'altro** something else
si può fare one can make
uova à la coque soft boiled eggs
del genere like that (lit. of the kind)

5 *Signor Gabrielli, Signor Ranieri and Giovanni order drinks at the bar*

Giovanni Io prendo un Campari soda. E Lei che cosa prende, signor Gabrielli?
Gabrielli Un Bitter Campari.
Giovanni Signor Ranieri, che cosa prende Lei?
Ranieri A me un analcoolico.
Giovanni Senza alcool . . .
Ranieri Benissimo.
Giovanni E io prendo un Campari soda.
Ranieri (*to the barman*) A me un analcoolico.
Gabrielli Un Bitter Campari. Col limone.
Ranieri Dico analcoolico, eh?
Giovanni E un Campari soda.

analcoolico alcohol-free (aperitif)
a me for me (lit. to me)
col limone with lemon
dico I say

3 **l'indirizzo è . . .** the address is . . . In Italian addresses the number always comes *after* the street name. **Lungarno** in Pisa and Florence are river walks (lit. 'along the Arno').

se chiama di fuori Pisa if you call from outside Pisa.

♦ **mi fa un favore se . . .** you('ll) do me a favour if . . . This useful phrase may be completed in any number of ways: **. . . se mi portano i loro passaporti** . . . if you bring me your passports; **. . . se mi porta un caffè** . . . if you bring me a coffee; **. . . se mi cambia venti sterline** . . . if you change me £20. The simpler expression **per favore** or **per piacere** is much more common: **mi porta un caffè per favore, per piacere mi cambia venti sterline** etc.

♦ **lo stesso** all the same; **va bene lo stesso** it's fine all the same; **passaporto o carta d'identità è lo stesso** passport or ID card it makes no difference.

4 ♦ **che cosa c'è per colazione?** what is there for breakfast? (**. . . per pranzo?** for lunch? **. . . per cena?** for dinner?). **Che cosa?** (lit. what thing?) is a very useful and common way of starting a question.

♦ **prego, niente** don't mention it: it's nothing. **Niente** (nothing) is often used as a negative before a noun, e.g. **niente uova!** no eggs; **niente latte nel té** no milk in the (my) tea, etc.

5 ♦ **io prendo . . .** I'm having (lit. I take); **che cosa prende?** what will you have? (lit. what do you take?). Other examples of **che cosa** questions: **che cosa desidera?** what do you want? can I help you? (in shops); **che cosa fa?** what do you do? what are you doing? In all these questions **che** can be omitted.

un Bitter Campari etc. Some aperitifs are alcohol-free (**analcoolici**) but all of them are bitter. Aperitifs known by their brand name followed by the word **soda** are sold in small one-glass bottles, already mixed with soda water. Digestive liqueurs, normally drunk after meals, are even more fiercely bitter, and are collectively know as **amari**, plural of **amaro** bitter. There are more names for drinks in dialogue 6 and in *Key words and phrases*.

6 *Giovanni asks the buffet trolley attendant in a train about the drinks and snacks he sells*

Giovanni Allora, Lei che cosa ha sul suo carrello?
Venditore Spuntini, panini, biscotti, dolci. Poi da bere c'è . . . c'è succo di frutta, limonata, Campari soda, Bitter, chinotto . . .
Giovanni Ci ha anche il caffè caldo?
Venditore Sì.
Giovanni In queste bottigliette qui che cosa c'è?
Venditore Whisky.
Giovanni Ah, queste sono bottigliette di liquori.
Venditore Sì.
Giovanni Quanto costa una di queste bottigliette?
Venditore Millecinquecento.
Giovanni Millecinquecento. E il caffè a quanto lo vende?
Venditore Trecentocinquanta lire.
Giovanni Quanto costa un panino?
Venditore Un panino . . . di che gusto? . . . Col salame, oppure col tonno e pomodoro, o frittatina?
Giovanni Frittatina?
Venditore Costa ottocento.
Giovanni Ottocento.

venditore (m.) vendor, salesman
sul suo carrello on your trolley
spuntini snacks
biscotti biscuits
dolci cakes
succo di frutta fruit juice
limonata lemonade
chinotto a sort of bitter orange
caldo, -a hot
bottigliette small bottles
liquori liqueurs
millecinquecento 1500

6

panini filled bread rolls, the Italian equivalent of sandwiches. They come in all shapes and sizes and with a variety of fillings.

da bere to drink. Used in phrases like: **che cosa c'è da bere?** what is there to drink? **da bere c'è . . .** to drink there is . . . Similarly: **che cosa c'è da mangiare?** what is there to eat? **non c'è niente da mangiare** there's nothing to eat. This is basically the same use of **da** as in **non ho niente da dichiarare** I've nothing to declare (Unit 1).

ci ha . . . Ci means 'there' and need not be translated into English in this case.

in queste bottigliette qui in these little bottles. Italian speakers, especially when pointing to objects, often reinforce **questo, -a** by adding **qui** (here).

a quanto lo vende? for how much do you sell it?

di che gusto? how do you want your roll? (lit. what taste?). The vendor then offers a choice between **salame** (no need to translate this!) **tonno e pomodoro** tuna fish and tomato, or **frittatina** omelette. Other possibilities are: **formaggio** cheese, **prosciutto** ham.

Key words and phrases

Those you may wish to say.

Paying for things

quanto?	how much?
quanto è?/quant'è?	how much is it?
quanto costa?	how much does it cost?
quanto costano?	how much do they cost?
accetta (travellers' cheques)?	do you accept (travellers' cheques?)

Breakfast

che cosa c'è per colazione?	what is there for breakfast?
per me . . . caffè	for me . . . black coffee
caffellatte	white coffee
cappuccino	white espresso coffee
té – col latte	tea – with milk
col limone	with lemon
cioccolato/cioccolata	chocolate (drinking and eating)
pane	bread
burro	butter
marmellata	jam

Drinks and snacks

che cosa prende?	what will you have?
che cosa c'è da bere?	what is there to drink?
che cosa c'è da mangiare?	what is there to eat?
prendo . . . una birra	I'll have . . . a beer
un'aranciata	an orangeade
un aperitivo	an aperitif
dell'acqua	some water
un succo di frutta	a fruit juice
un panino	a roll
al salame	a salami roll
al prosciutto	a ham roll
al formaggio	a cheese roll
niente, grazie	nothing, thanks

Other expressions

va bene	it's OK, OK
va benissimo	it's excellent, excellent
va bene lo stesso	it's fine all the same

Those you may need to understand.

vuole qualcos'altro?	do you want something else?
di che gusto?	what filling? what flavour?

And learn the numbers on the next page, p. 56.

Numbers

After **mille** one thousand, the word for -thousand is **-mila**:

duemila two thousand
seimila six thousand
ventimila twenty thousand
centotrentasettemila one hundred and thirty-seven thousand etc.

Numbers are formed as in English, e.g.
348.932 **trecentoquarantottomila novecento trentadue**
three hundred (and) forty-eight thousand nine hundred and thirty-two

- Note that no number above one thousand is ever counted in hundreds, therefore eighteen hundred and forty-eight is: **milleottocentoquarantotto** (one thousand eight hundred and forty-eight).
- Groups of more than three figures are separated by a *point*: 1.486.
- The decimal point is indicated by a comma: 6,81.
- One million is **un milione**, two million **due milioni** etc. With present-day inflation, prices using these high figures are within the scope of ordinary tourists, since, at the time of writing (early 1982) **un milione di lire** is worth about £450.

For summary list of numbers, see p. 230.

To practise numbers ask someone to give you a number in English and you try and say it in Italian. You should aim to get faster and faster at working it out.

Practise what you have learnt

1 Listen to an employee of the Ente del Turismo giving some hotel prices over the 'phone, and pair the name of the hotel with the price given. (Answers p. 62.)

Albergo dei Cavalieri ....

Albergo Duomo ....

Albergo Ariston ....

Albergo Arno ....

Lire 25.000

Lire 83.000

Lire 46.000

Lire 24.000

What do these prices relate to?

☐ a single room without bathroom
☐ a double bedroom with bathroom and breakfast
☐ a double bedroom with bathroom, no breakfast

2 A married couple is ordering breakfast. Listen to the dialogue on tape and write in the space provided the items each of them has ordered. Be careful – the words in the bubble contain a few items neither of them has ordered. (Answers p. 62.)

Husband ....

....

Wife ....

....

uova à la coque
omelette
cappuccino
pane
cioccolata
succo di frutta
caffellatte
marmellata
tè
burro

3 Draw lines to link the following questions and answers so that they make sense together. You don't need your cassette, the answers are on p. 62.

Questions		Answers
Sigarette, liquori, valuta estera?		Mi dispiace: non c'è niente da mangiare.
Ha panini, o biscotti?		È un aperitivo senza alcool.
Che cos'è un analcoolico?		Non ho niente da dichiarare.
Che cosa c'è da bere?		Cinquantamila lire, camera e colazione.
Per favore, quant'è?		Aranciata, birra, chinotto, quello che vuole.

4 For each of the following items choose the appropriate form:
quanto costa . . . ? or **quanto costano . . . ?**
You don't need your cassette, the answers are on p. 62.

a. .... la colazione?

b. Questi biscotti .... ?

c. .... il caffè caldo?

d. Questi dolci .... ?

e. .... un chinotto?

f. .... queste bottigliette di liquore?

g. I panini .... ?

h. .... un succo di frutta?

Grammar

Translation of 'the' in the plural

(For singular see Unit 2, p. 30.)
The plural of **il** is **i: il treno** **i treni**
The plural of **l'** (m.) and **lo** is **gli: l'albergo** **gli alberghi**
lo studente **gli studenti**
The plural of **l'** (f.) and **la** is **le: la camera** **le camere**
l'aranciata **le aranciate**

Dal, al, sul etc.

The combination of certain prepositions with the plural of 'the' gives the following forms (for singular see Unit 2, p. 30.)

a		**ai**		**agli**		**alle**
da		**dai**		**dagli**		**dalle**
di	+ **i**	**dei**	+ **gli**	**degli**	+ **le**	**delle**
su		**sui**		**sugli**		**sulle**
in		**nei**		**negli**		**nelle**

e.g. **agli studenti** to the students **dagli alberghi** from the hotels
nelle camere in the rooms **sui treni** on the trains

Exercise 'Not just one . . . but all . . . !' Complete the following sentences – the first one has been done for you as an example. (Answers p. 62.)

a. Non solo una bottiglietta, ma tutte le bottigliette.

b. Non solo una sigaretta, ma ....

c. Non solo uno studente, ma ....

d. Non solo un treno, ma ....

Potere to be able to, can

posso	I can
puoi	you can
può	he/she/it can you (polite) can
possiamo	we can
potete	you can
possono	they can

Volere to want

voglio	I want
vuoi	you want
vuole	he/she/it wants you (polite) want
vogliamo	we want
volete	you want
vogliono	they want

Mi, ti, ci, vi, si

Apart from the translations 'myself', 'yourself' etc. mentioned in Unit 3 p. 45 these words can also have the following meanings:

mi me — **mi dica** tell me
ti you (informal) — **ti telefono questa sera** I'll call you tonight
ci us — **ci può sistemare?** can you accommodate us?
vi you (pl.) — **vi porto la colazione** I'll bring you breakfast
si corresponds to 'one' in phrases like:
si può fare one can do (it) **si prende il treno** one takes the train

Read and understand

DITTA, RESIDENZA O DOMICILIO UBICAZIONE ESERCIZIO, CODICE FISCALE ALBERGO DIANA via CAVOUR 128. VILLA S. MARTINO	RICEVUTA FISCALE n. 304
Sig. M. Rossi - 381	li 17.9.81
QUANTITA, NATURA E QUALITA DEI SERVIZI	CORRISPETTIVO I.V.A. INCLUSA
Pernottamento / camera con bagno + colazione 35,350 x 3	106.050
Bar	5.200
Ristorante	38.950
Lavanderia	12.630
Telefono	2.400
TOTALE L.	165.230

This is the sort of bill you will receive from an Italian hotel. It's called **ricevuta fiscale** (statutory receipt) and you are obliged by law to keep it, since it is evidence that both you and the **esercizio**, a general word for any business or concern, have complied with **IVA** (VAT) legislation. Look carefully at the bill and see whether you can answer the following questions.

1 What is the date of the receipt? **a.** ☐ 3rd April
b. ☐ 17th September

2 How many rooms were booked? **a.** ☐ one
b. ☐ three

3 Was breakfast included? **a.** ☐ yes
b. ☐ no

4 Was any meal taken at the hotel restaurant? **a.** ☐ yes
b. ☐ no

5 How were drinks paid for? **a.** ☐ by charging them to the account
b. ☐ cash

6 What was the laundry charge? **a.** ☐ 5.200 lire
b. ☐ 12.630 lire

7 Was VAT included in the total? **a.** ☐ yes
b. ☐ no

Did you know?

Paying your bills

Nearly all Italian hotels will accept one or more of the international credit cards. They will also accept **assegni di viaggio**, which most Italians call by their English name of 'travellers' cheques', and foreign currency, but often at a less favourable rate of exchange than can be had through a bank. Don't be surprised if the rates of exchange vary slightly from bank to bank.

One way of ensuring that you are supplied with the money you need, and can draw as much as you need at short notice, is to use a Eurocheque cash card, which you can obtain from your bank. This allows you to use your cheque book to obtain foreign currency.

In Italian hotels, banks and nearly all bars, restaurants and shops, money matters are dealt with by a **cassiere** (m.) or **cassiera** (f.), and not by the receptionist, waiter or employee who has been attending you. In bars you often have to pay the cashier first, get a receipt and then go to the counter. In banks, bars, etc. listen for the phrase **prego, si accomodi alla cassa** please go to the cash till.

Drinks and snacks

The place to go to for drinks and snacks is the ubiquitous **bar**, which you will find at almost every street corner. Bars come in all sizes, shapes and degrees of luxury. As there are no licensing laws in Italy, you are free to enjoy any drink you fancy, from milk to strong alcoholic concoctions, at any time of day and often of night.

Italian beer is a palatable but mostly undistinguished lager, with low alcoholic content. A glass of **acqua minerale** (mineral water, sometimes not much more than good quality tap water in fancy bottles), may cost as much, and occasionally even more than, a glass of wine. If you like your **acqua minerale** fizzy, say you like it **gasata**, otherwise ask for **liscia** or **naturale**. If you like bitter lemon drinks you may wish to try **aranciata amara** bitter orange, or **chinotto**, made from citrus fruit peel: both drunk straight and never used as mixers. There is a bewildering variety of **aperitivi**, of various degrees of bitterness, some made up by the barman (**aperitivo della casa**), others pre-mixed with soda water bearing familiar brand names.

Caffè made with the espresso machine consists of a few drops of scalding black coffee. If you want more than a few drops ask for **caffè lungo** (lit. long coffee). White coffee is called **cappuccino**, if made on the espresso machine, or **caffè e latte**. You will never be served instant coffee except on trains, or if you specifically ask for it (**caffè solubile**). Most bars have a mouthwatering selection of fresh cakes, buns, biscuits and confectionery. Fresh cakes are called **paste**. Note that the **crema** with which some of them are filled is not cream but a sort of rich custard: the Italian for cream is **panna**.

If your taste is for savoury snacks you may choose between **panini**, soft rolls with a variety of fillings; **tosti**, toasted sandwiches; and **pizzette**, small pizzas to be re-heated in a microwave oven.

Your turn to speak

1 You'll practise ordering breakfast for yourself at your hotel. You'll need to understand **pane tostato** – toast.

2 You'll be ordering drinks at a bar for yourself and a friend. You'll need to say **aranciata amara** – bitter orange.

Answers

Practise what you have learnt p. 57 Exercise **1**

Albergo dei Cavalieri 83.000
Albergo Duomo 46.000
Albergo Ariston 24.000
Albergo Arno 25.000

The prices relate to a double bedroom with bathroom and no breakfast.

p. 57 Exercise **2** Husband caffellalte, pane, burro, omelette
Wife succo di frutta, té, pane, burro, marmellata.

p. 58 Exercise **3**

Sigarette, liquori, valuta estera?	Non ho niente da dichiarare.
Ha panini, o biscotti?	Mi dispiace: non c'è niente da mangiare.
Che cos'è un analcoolico?	È un aperitivo senza alcool.
Che cosa c'è da bere?	Aranciata, birra, chinotto, quello che vuole.
Per favore, quant'è?	Cinquantamila lire, camera e colazione.

p. 59 Exercise **4** (**a**) quanto costa? (**b**) quanto costano? (**c**) quanto costa? (**d**) quanto costano? (**e**) quanto costa? (**f**) quanto costano? (**g**) quanto costano? (**h**) quanto costa?

Grammar p. 59 (**b**) tutte le sigarette (**c**) tutti gli studenti (**d**) tutti i treni.

Read and understand p. 60 (**1**) b (**2**) a (**3**) a (**4**) a (**5**) a (**6**) b (**7**) a.

5 Come faccio per andare in centro?

What you will learn

- how to ask where various places are: a bank, a department store etc.
- how to ask the best way to get to these places
- how to ask where you can change money, telephone etc.
- how to understand simple street directions
- how to understand information about public transport
- how to apologize for not knowing a direction, if asked

Before you begin

Points to remember from Unit 4:

1 verbs

potere **posso, puoi, può, possiamo, potete, possono**
volere **voglio, vuoi, vuole, vogliamo, volete, vogliono**

2 questions
che cosa c'è per colazione?
che cosa prende? **che cosa vuole?**
quanto? **quanto è?** **quanto costa?**

3 'the'

il bagno	**i bagni**	**la colazione**	**le colazioni**
l'aperitivo	**gli aperitivi**	**l'acqua minerale**	**le acque minerali**
lo spuntino	**gli spuntini**		

Study guide

	Dialogues 1, 2: listen straight through without the book
	Dialogues 1, 2: listen, read and study one by one
	Dialogues 3, 4: listen straight through without the book
	Dialogues 3, 4: listen, read and study one by one
	Dialogues 5, 6: listen straight through without the book
	Dialogues 5, 6: listen read and study one by one
	Dialogues 7–10: listen straight through without the book
	Dialogues 7–10: listen, read and study one by one
	Learn the *Key words and phrases*
	Do the exercises in *Practise what you have learnt*
	Study the *Grammar* section
	Do the exercise in *Read and understand*
	Read *Did you know?*
	Do the tape exercises in *Your turn to speak*
	Finally, listen to all the dialogues again straight through

Dialogues

1 *Where is the department store?*

Signorina 1 Scusa, sai dov'è la Rinascente?
Signorina 2 Sì, guarda, è là.

2 *It's very close*

Giovanni Scusi, dov'è la Rinascente?
Signore È proprio di fronte a Lei. Attraversa la strada.
Giovanni Grazie.

proprio just
attraversa cross (from **attraversare**)
strada street

3 *Where is this bank?*

Giovanni Scusi, dov'è la Banca Commerciale?
Signore È a sinistra: venti metri avanti.

4 *Turn left for the nearest bank*

Giovanni Buon giorno, signora.
Signora Buon giorno.
Giovanni Mi sa dire dov'è la banca più vicina?
Signora Guardi, quando esce qui dal negozio va a sinistra e quando arriva al semaforo attraversa la strada e sul marciapiede di fronte c'è il Banco di Napoli.
Giovanni Molte grazie, signora.
Signora Prego.

più vicina nearest
guardi look (**Lei** form)
negozio shop
semaforo traffic lights
marciapiede (m.) pavement

1 **scusa** excuse me (informal **tu** form); otherwise **scusi** (**Lei** form), as in the next dialogue.

guarda look (**tu** form).

è là there it is. Also: **è lì**. Similarly there are two words for 'here': **qua** and **qui**. There is no difference at all in their use.

2 **di fronte** opposite; **di fronte a Lei** opposite you; **di fronte alla stazione** opposite the station; **di fronte all'albergo** opposite the hotel.

3 **venti metri (più) avanti** 20 metres further on. Also **avanti!** come in! forward! move on! Do not confuse this with **davanti** opposite: **davanti alla banca** opposite the bank.

4 **mi sa dire . . .** can you tell me . . .

quando esce when you go out. **Uscire** to go out, to come out, has an irregular present, see *Grammar* p. 73.

va a sinistra you go left. You will also hear expressions like: **alla sua sinistra** on your left; **sulla sinistra** on the left.

la banca is the modern Italian word for 'bank', but in older times it used to be **il banco**, the counter. Some old-established banks use the masculine form in their name: **il Banco di Napoli** the Bank of Naples, **il Banco di Roma** the Bank of Rome.

5 *Where can I change foreign money?*

Giovanni Signorina, vorrei cambiare della valuta straniera. Dove posso cambiare?

Signorina Be', qui fuori del nostro ufficio ci sono differenti banche e uffici cambio. Dunque, c'è la Banca Ponti in Piazza Duomo, ci sono altre banche visibili subito fuori qui del nostro ufficio. Anche alla fine di via Dogana e via Mazzini trova delle banche.

vorrei cambiare I'd like to change
be' well (short for **bene**)
ufficio office
ufficio (pl. **uffici**) **cambio** bureau de change
altro, -a other
visibile (pl. **visibili**) visible
alla fine at the end

6 *Where is the bureau de change?*

Giovanni Scusi, dov'è l'ufficio cambio?
Signore È lì a destra.

7 *Taking the underground*

Giovanni Buon giorno. Come faccio per andare da qui a Piazzale Lima?
Signore Dunque, prende una metropolitana in direzione Marelli e scende alla quarta fermata.
Giovanni Molte grazie.

Piazzale Lima name of an underground station; **piazzale** = type of square
Marelli name of an underground terminus
scende get off (a bus, a train etc.), from **scendere**

5 ➧ **dove posso cambiare?** where can I change (money)? Here are some examples of this phrase with other verbs: **dove posso telefonare?** where can I telephone? **dove posso trovare un albergo?** where can I find a hotel? **dove posso fare colazione?** where can I get breakfast?

➧ **fuori** outside, out; **vado fuori** I'm going out; **qui fuori** out(side) here; **fuori del nostro ufficio** outside our office.

la banca pl. **le banche** bank; the plural form of feminine words ending in **-ca** is **-che**: see *Grammar* p. 73.

dunque like **be'** this is one of those words often used at the beginning of a sentence, with no real translation.

6 ➧ **a destra** right, on the right, on your right. Also: **sulla destra, sulla sua destra.**

7 ➧ **come faccio per andare . . .** how do I get (lit. go) . . . This is another phrase that can be used with a variety of verbs: **come faccio per telefonare?** how do I (use the) telephone? **come faccio per uscire?** how do I get out? (i.e. where's the exit?).

➧ **prende una metropolitana** you take an underground train (**prendere** = to take). The word **metropolitana** is often shortened to **metrò**, changing its gender to masculine: **il metrò**. In Italy Milan, Rome and Naples have embryo underground networks.

➧ **la quarta fermata** the fourth stop. **Fermare** to stop; **ferma a Piazzale Lima?** does it stop at Piazzale Lima? **ferma a tutte le stazioni** it stops at all stations. Note the following numerals: **primo** first, **secondo** second, **terzo** third, **quinto** fifth, **sesto** sixth. They are all adjectives which have the usual pattern of endings, e.g. **primo, prima, primi, prime.** See list on p. 230.

8 *How much is the ticket and how long is it valid?*

Giovanni Buon giorno. Per andare in via Francesco Sforza da qui come devo fare?

Signore Sì, si va sulla . . . sulla piazza, si prende il tram tredici, Via Cappellari, tredici, si scende alla seconda fermata, Corso di Porta Romana, angolo via Francesco Sforza.

Giovanni Quanto costano i biglietti del tram?

Signore Il biglietto del tram costa duecento lire. Si timbra la prima volta su un mezzo di superficie o in metrò, e vale settanta minuti da quel momento.

Giovanni Settanta minuti? Quindi posso prendere più di un tram sempre con lo stesso biglietto.

Signore Sì, il tram più di uno. Il metrò una volta soltanto. Una volta uscito dal metrò non è più possibile riprendere il metrò. I mezzi di superficie invece son liberi. Si può prendere più di una volta lo stesso mezzo.

Giovanni Grazie.

sulla piazza into the square
corso wide, main street
♦ **angolo** (at the) corner (of)
biglietto ticket
mezzo di superficie surface transport
vale it's valid for
minuto minute
da quel momento from that moment
quindi so
lo stesso the same
riprendere to re-take, to take again

9 *Going by public transport to the park*

Giovanni C'è un giardino pubblico a Pisa?

Signore Sì, c'è il Giardino Scotto. Si trova dall'altra parte dell'Arno, nei pressi del Ponte della Fortezza, circa a due chilometri da Piazza del Duomo.

Giovanni Ci si può andare con un mezzo di trasporto? . . .

Signore Sì, c'è un pullman diretto, che parte ogni dieci minuti circa da Piazza del Duomo, il numero tre.

Giovanni Il numero tre. Grazie.

giardino pubblico public park (lit. garden)
Scotto name of a park in Pisa
Arno name of the river flowing through Pisa and Florence
Ponte della Fortezza Fortress Bridge
chilometro kilometre
ci si può andare? can one go there?
pullman diretto non-stop coach

10 *Here is a young lady who cannot give directions*

Giovanni Come si fa per andare in Piazza della Scala?

Signorina Mi dispiace, non lo so perché non sono di Milano.

8 ➧ **come devo fare?** what (lit. how) must I do? Also: **come devo fare per timbrare il biglietto?** how do I stamp the ticket? **Devo** (I must or I have to) comes from **dovere** which has an irregular present tense: see *Grammar* p. 73.

si prende il tram tredici you take (lit. one takes) the number 13 tram; **si scende alla seconda fermata** you get off (lit. one gets off) at the second stop; **si può prendere . . .** you can take (lit. one can take) . . . Note that **si timbra il biglietto la prima volta** may be translated both 'you stamp the ticket the first time' and 'the ticket is stamped the first time'. Where Italians use **si** (one) very frequently, in English you would say 'you', 'we' and, less commonly, 'one'.

➧ **la prima volta** the first time. Other useful expressions: **una volta soltanto** once only; **una volta uscito dal metrò** once out of the tube; **due volte** twice, **tre volte** three times etc.; **questa volta** this time. Note that **volta** means 'time' only in the sense of 'occasion' and has nothing to do with clocks.

➧ **più di un tram** more than one tram; **più di una volta** more than once; **non è più possibile** it's no longer possible. Note that the ending **-bile** in Italian often corresponds to -ble in English: **visibile** visible, **mangiabile** edible, **scusabile** excusable etc.

son liberi are free, i.e. unrestricted. **Son** is short for **sono** and is often used in speech.

9 ➧ **dall'altra parte di . . .** on the other side of . . .; **nei pressi di . . .** or: **nelle vicinanza di . . .** in the vicinity of . . .; **circa** about, approximately.

ogni dieci minuti every ten minutes. **Ogni** is invariable (keeps the same form) and corresponds to 'every', 'each': **da qui ogni tram va alla stazione** from here every tram goes to the station.

➧ **mezzo di trasporto** public transport (lit. means of transport). Only a few Italian towns have managed to keep trams (**il tram** pl. **i tram**). The bulk of public transport is by bus (**l'autobus, gli autobus**), and taxi (**il tassì, i tassì**). Private coaches and long-distance coaches are called **il pullman, i pullman**. Note that all nouns ending in a consonant (mostly borrowed from foreign languages) are invariable. For more information on public transport see *Did you know?* p. 75.

10 **Piazza della Scala** (or **Piazza Scala**) the square in Milan where the Scala Theatre is.

➧ **mi dispiace, non lo so perché non sono di Milano** I'm sorry, I don't know because I'm not from Milan. Also **. . . perché non sono di qui** . . . because I'm not from here, I don't live here.

Key words and phrases

To learn

scusi	excuse me
mi sa dire . . .	can you tell me . . .
dove posso cambiare?	where I can change money?
dov'è la banca più vicina?	where is the nearest bank?
come faccio per . . .	how I can . . .
andare alla stazione?	get to the station?
andare in centro?	get to the town centre?
mi dispiace, non sono di qui	I'm sorry, I'm not from here

Public transport

l'autobus	bus
il tram	tram
il tassì	taxi
la metropolitana / **il metrò**	underground railway

To understand

prende/deve prendere . . .	you take/you must (have to) take . . .
attraversa/deve attraversare . . .	you cross/you must cross . . .
la prima strada a destra	the first street on the right
la seconda via a sinistra	the second street on the left
la piazza di fronte	the square opposite
scende/deve scendere . . .	you get off/you must get off . . .
alla terza fermata	at the third stop
davanti alla stazione	in front of the station
dall'altra parte del fiume	on the other side of the river
è lì/là . . .	it's there . . .
all'angolo di via Roma	on the corner of Rome Street
fuori (dell'ufficio/della banca)	outside (the office/the bank)
questa volta	this time
la quarta volta	the fourth time
più di . . .	more than . . .

Practise what you have learnt

1 On tape you will hear Giovanni asking for directions to a particular place. Listen to the conversation and then tick the correct box. (Answers p. 76.)

1. Giovanni wants to go to **a.** ☐ the Galleria
b. ☐ Piazza del Duomo

2. The bus stop is **a.** ☐ across the street
b. ☐ at the end of the street

3. Which buses go there? **a.** ☐ No. 60 **b.** ☐ No. 65
c. ☐ No. 606 **d.** ☐ No. 705

4. After how many stops should Giovanni get off the bus?
a. ☐ 1
b. ☐ 2
c. ☐ 3

2 There is an alternative to going by bus: **andare a piedi** going on foot. Listen to the next dialogue on tape and tick the correct directions below. (Answers p. 76.)

1. On foot you should walk **a.** ☐ in the same direction
b. ☐ in a different direction

2. At the traffic lights you should turn **a.** ☐ left
b. ☐ right

3. How many squares do you have to cross? **a.** ☐ one
b. ☐ two

4. How long does it take to get there on foot? **a.** ☐ 5 to 6 minutes
b. ☐ 8 to 9 minutes

3 Now Giancarlo wants to get to the centre of the town. Listen to the tape and answer as before. (Answers p. 76.)

1. Where should he look for the tram? **a.** ☐ on his left going out of the station
b. ☐ on his right

2. Which tram should he take? **a.** ☐ No. 1
b. ☐ No. 3

3. Where should he get off? **a.** ☐ Via Redi
b. ☐ Piazza Scala

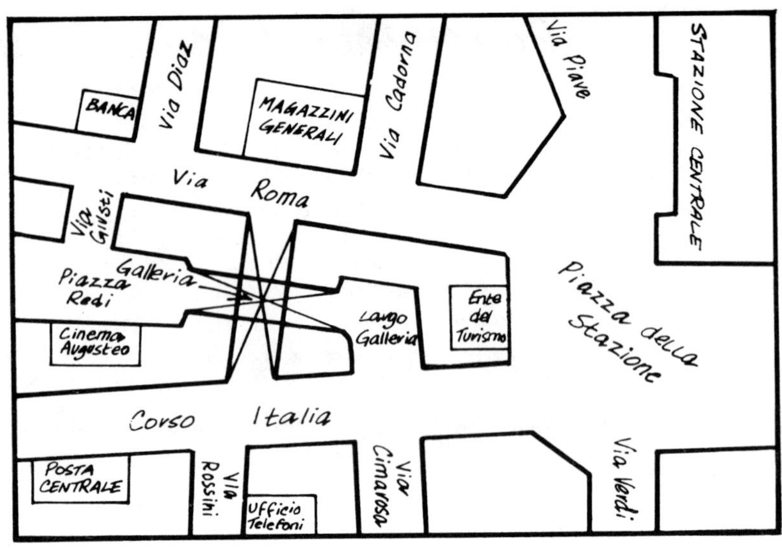

4 Look at this section from an imaginary town map. Complete the following sentences which describe what is shown in the map, inserting expressions from the box below. (Answers p. 76.)

a. La banca è .... di via Diaz e di via Roma.

b. I Magazzini Generali sono .... alla Galleria.

c. Quando .... dalla Posta Centrale, via Rossini è ....

d. Per andare da piazza Redi a largo Galleria .... la Galleria.

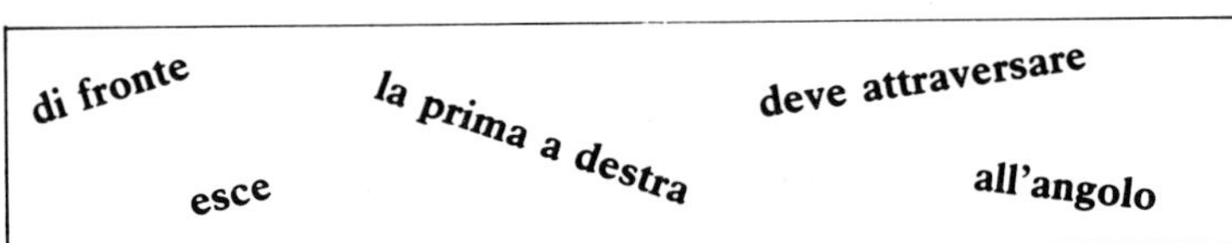

5 Look again at the map, and tick those among the following statements that appear to you to be true. (Answers p. 76.) **Magazzini Generali** = name of department store.

a. ☐ L'Ente del Turismo è in piazza Stazione.
b. ☐ La Galleria ha soltanto due uscite.
c. ☐ La Posta Centrale è di fronte alla Galleria, in Corso Italia.
d. ☐ Il cinema Augusteo è in via Giusti.
e. ☐ Per andare dalla Stazione Centrale all'ufficio dei telefoni, si attraversa la piazza della Stazione, e, quando si è in corso Italia, si prende la seconda strada a sinistra, via Rossini.
f. ☐ La banca è in via Rossini.
g. ☐ I Magazzini Generali sono all'angolo di via Roma e di via Diaz.
h. ☐ Per andare dai Magazzini Generali all'ufficio dei telefoni si attraversa la Galleria.

Grammar

Dovere to have to

devo	I must/have to
devi	you must/have to etc.
deve	he/she/it must you (polite) must
dobbiamo	we must
dovete	you (pl.) must
devono	they must

Uscire to go out

esco	I go out
esci	you go out
esce	he/she/it goes out you (polite) go out
usciamo	we go out
uscite	you (pl.) go out
escono	they go out

More plurals

There are various exceptions to the general rules that follow, but you are unlikely to need to know them at this stage.

Most masculine words ending in **-ico** form their plural in **-ici**:

giardino pubblico park	**giardini pubblici**
amico friend	**amici**

Note that **-c-** followed by **-i-** or **-e-** is pronounced 'soft', as in 'chit' and 'cheese', and therefore the sound changes from singular to plural.

In all other cases words with a **-c-** or a **-g-** in their ending keep in the plural the 'soft' or 'hard' sound they have in the singular. If there is an **-i-** in the singular ending, it *tends* to disappear in the plural (but not *always*).

l'ufficio office	**gli uffici**
l'orologio watch, clock	**gli orologi**
la valigia suitcase	**le valigie** or **valige**
la faccia face	**le facce**

Words ending in **-co**, **-ca**, **-go** and **-ga** add an **-h-** in the plural to keep the **-c-** and **-g-** sounds 'hard' (as in English 'cot' and 'got').

il banco counter	**i banchi**
la banca bank	**le banche**
lo spago string	**gli spaghi**
la paga pay	**le paghe**

Exercise Choose from the box the appropriate words to insert in each uncompleted sentence below. You should use the plural form of the word you choose. (Answers p. 76.)

a. Il Gorgonzola e il Parmigiano sono due .... italiani.

b. In italiano i giardini .... si chiamano anche ....

c. Queste due .... pesano venti chili. Non c'è eccedenza.

d. "Signori, che cosa prendono?" "Due .... "

e. Il Ponte della Fortezza ha quattro ....

analcoolico	**arco (arch)**	**formaggio**	**pubblico**	**valigia** **parco**

Read and understand

Here are various public transport tickets. They display all or most of the following indications:

a. name and/or logo of transport company
b. name of town where service operates
c. serial number
d. type of journey for which ticket is valid
e. period during which ticket is valid
f. price
g. basic instructions and/or regulations
h. edge to be inserted in stamping machine

1 Which of these indications can you see on:
a. the ATM Milan ticket? ....
b. the ATAF Florence ticket? ....

2 How much does the ATAF ticket cost? ....

Did you know?

Urban transport

Public transport in Italian towns is no more, and probably no less efficient and convenient than in Britain, but it is certainly cheaper. Urban transport operates on the flat rate principle: you can go from one end of Milan or Rome to the other for less than one half of what it costs to travel across central London (at 1982 rates). Taxis are often less easy to find. Stick to official taxi-cabs, with taximetres, and steer clear of taxi touts at railway stations and air terminals.

Almost all Italian urban transport companies have gone over to one-man operation, and conductors have been replaced by machines. In most cases all these machines do is to stamp your ticket with the date and time of issue: that is called **convalida** validation, or **obliterazione** cancellation, two words you may see on notices displayed in the vehicle or printed on the ticket itself. You must therefore buy the ticket before you board your bus or tram.

Tickets, often in blocks of ten, can be bought in tobacconists' shops, espresso bars or newspaper kiosks during shop opening times, after which it may be practically impossible to obtain them. On some routes you may find coin-operated ticket vending machines, for which you are supposed to have the appropriate coins ready.

In some towns surface transport tickets are valid for one hour and ten minutes from cancellation: within that time you may use as many trams and buses as you like. In Milan surface tickets are interchangeable with **metrò** tickets, but on the underground they are valid only for one journey, however short.

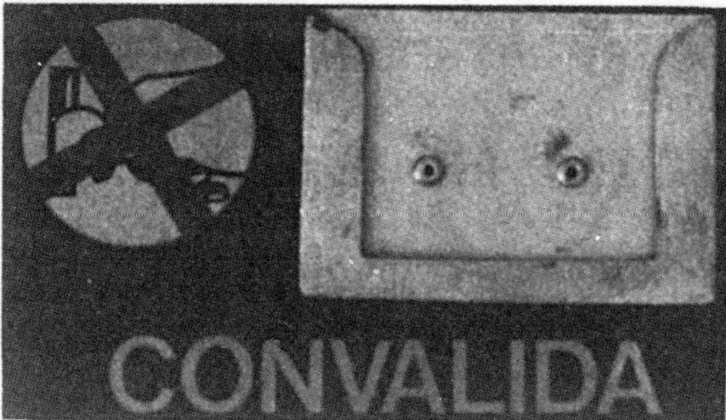

This sign is self-explanatory, and is found on buses with coin-operated ticket machines.

Some towns have private narrow-gauge railway systems linking them with the surrounding region; like the **Ferrovia Circumvesuviana** operating between Naples and the towns at the foot of the Vesuvius; and the **Ferrovia Nord Milano**, linking Milan with the 'Lake District' towns.

You will see the following signs on most buses:

SALITA	way in, from the verb **salire** to climb on
DISCESA	way out, from the verb **discendere** to step down

Street names

Italian street names are more obviously 'meaningful' than English ones. They are usually chosen from the names of other towns or regions; names of famous men and women from national, local or world history; and include a few historical dates (like **via Venti Settembre**, commemorating the fall of Rome to the Italian army in 1870). **Via** corresponds to 'street' in English; **viale** is wider than a **via** and is usually tree-lined; **vico** or **vicolo** is a narrow alleyway; **corso** is a main street, usually of particular architectural, historical or commercial importance. **Piazza, piazzale** and **largo** all refer to squares of different sizes. In Venice small urban squares are called **campo** or **campiello**; and a **rio terà** is a filled-in canal.

Your turn to speak

In this section you work with your cassette only. Marisa will prompt you.

1 You want to go to the tourist office; and so ask a passer-by for directions. Remember the expression: **a piedi,** on foot.

2 This time, *you* will be asked the questions – about buses.

Answers

Practise what you have learnt p. 71 Exercise **1** (**1**) a (**2**) a (**3**) a and b (**4**) c.

p. 71 Exercise **2** (**1**) b (**2**) b (**3**) b (**4**) a.

p. 71 Exercise **3** (**1**) b (**2**) a (**3**) b.

p. 72 Exercise **4** (**a**) all'angolo di (**b**) di fronte (**c**) esce/la prima a destra (**d**) deve attraversare.

p. 72 Exercise **5** a, e, and h are true.

Grammar p. 73 (**a**) formaggi (**b**) pubblici, parchi (**c**) valigie (**d**) analcoolici (**e**) archi.

Read and understand p. 74 Exercise 1 (**a**) a, b, c, d, g, (back) h (**b**) a, b, c, e, f, g, (back) h.

Exercise **2** 200 lira.

6 *Scusi, che ora è?*

What you will learn

- how to ask 'when' in simple statements
- how to ask what time it is
- how to tell the time
- how to understand announcements concerning delays
- days of the week
- some expressions of time

Before you begin

Remember some of the things you learned in Unit 5:

1 verbs
dovere must, ought to
devo, devi, deve, **dobbiamo, dovete, devono**
uscire to go out
esco, esci, esce, **usciamo, uscite, escono**

2 questions
scusi, come faccio per andare a . . .?
dove posso cambiare . . .?
dove posso telefonare?

3 locations
a destra, a sinistra, di fronte, davanti, dall'altra parte, fuori, all'angolo

Study guide

	Dialogues 1–4: listen straight through without the book
	Dialogues 1–4: listen, read and study one by one
	Dialogues 5–7: listen straight through without the book
	Dialogues 5–7: listen, read and study one by one
	Dialogue 8: listen straight through without the book
	Dialogue 8: listen, read and study notes
	Learn the *Key words and phrases* and how to tell the time
	Do the exercises in *Practise what you have learnt*
	Study *Grammar* and do the exercises
	Do *Read and understand*
	Read *Did you know?*
	Do the tape exercises in *Your turn to speak*
	Listen to all the dialogues again without the book
	Do the *Revision* section for Units 4–6 on p. 219.

Dialogues

1 *A traveller asks an information office employee at what time the train leaves*

Viaggiatore Il treno per Firenze a che ora parte?
Impiegato Alle quattro e diciassette.
Viaggiatore Quattro e diciassette?
Impiegato Sì.
Viaggiatore A che binario?
Impiegato Cinque.
Viaggiatore Grazie.
Impiegato Prego.

Firenze Florence

2 *Trains can be delayed, as this station announcement indicates*

Treno diretto proveniente da Roma Termini, Milano Centrale, per Briga, Losanna, Ginevra, Berna, atteso alle ore 7,50, viaggia con 60 minuti circa di ritardo.

proveniente da coming from (from **provenire**, same pattern as **venire**)
Briga, Losanna etc. Brig, Lausanne, Geneva, Bern
atteso expected (from **attendere** to expect)
viaggia is travelling (from **viaggiare** to travel)

3 *An airport announcement: the flight to London will be delayed*

La partenza del volo BA 529 per Londra sarà ritardata di circa 30 minuti a causa condizioni meteorologiche sull'aeroporto di Pisa.

sarà ritardata will be delayed (from **ritardare**, to delay)
condizioni meteorologiche weather conditions

4 *Giovanni asks the hotel receptionist when breakfast is served*

Giovanni A che ora è la colazione?
Portiere Senta, la colazione al mattino è dalle sette alle dieci, dieci e un quarto. E il ristorante è aperto dalle dodici alle due, e la sera dalle sette alle nove.
Giovanni Molte grazie.

senta well (lit. listen)
aperto open

1 ➧ **a che ora parte?** what time does it leave? The word for 'train', 'bus' etc. can also come *after* this phrase: **a che ora parte il treno per Firenze? a che ora parte l'autobus per Roma?**

alle quattro e diciassette at 4.17.

Note the feminine plural form **alle** because **ore** (hours) is understood.

parte leaves, is leaving; from **partire**, to leave. (See *Grammar* p. 86.)

2 ➧ **circa** about, approximately. **Circa** can be placed before or after the word to which it refers: **con 60 minuti circa/con circa 60 minuti di ritardo** about 60 minutes late. **Il treno è in ritardo** the train is late.

3 ➧ **a causa** because of; also: **a causa di . . .**

4 ➧ **dalle sette alle dieci** from seven o'clock to ten o'clock.

➧ **dieci e un quarto** a quarter past ten (lit. ten and a quarter). Minutes past the hour are also counted in this way: **le dieci e diciassette** 10,17; **le dieci e trenta** 10,30 or **le dieci e mezza** half past ten. After **le dieci e trentanove** 10,39 you could also count the minutes to the next hour; **le undici meno venti** twenty to eleven (lit. eleven less twenty), **le undici meno un quarto** a quarter to eleven etc.; but only when using the 12–hour clock. To ask the time say: **che ore è?** or **che ore sono?**

5 *Giovanni asks a lady how far away the famous Chartreuse of Pavia is from Milan*

Giovanni Signorina, quant'è lontana la Certosa di Pavia?
Signorina La Certosa di Pavia non è molto lontana. Sono venti minuti di autobus da qui. E gli autobus sono frequentissimi, con la frequenza di ogni mezz'ora, all'ora e alla mezz'ora, in partenza da Piazza Castello.
Giovanni Piazza Castello è vicina a qui?
Signorina Dieci minuti a piedi. Allora, Piazza Castello, ogni mezz'ora, ci sono i pullman che vanno a Pavia, e fermano vicino alla Certosa. La Certosa è chiusa il lunedì, mentre è aperta in giorno normale dalle 10 alle 12,30, dalle 14 alle 17.

frequentissimo very frequent
frequenza frequency
chiuso closed (from **chiudere**, to close)
mentre while
in giorno normale on normal days

6 *In the next two dialogues Giovanni is given bank and shop opening times*

Giovanni Quali sono gli orari di apertura delle banche?
Signorina Le banche qui a Milano sono aperte dalle otto e trenta alle – euh – tredici.
Giovanni Dalle 8,30 alle 13. E i negozi quando sono aperti?
Signorina Dalle 9 alle 12,30, 15,30–19,30 circa, con piccole variazioni.
Giovanni C'è un giorno di riposo alla settimana?
Signorina Il lunedì mattina i negozi sono chiusi per il riposo, poi la domenica è chiuso tutto il giorno.

orari di apertura opening times
negozi shops
con piccole variazioni with small variations
giorno di riposo closing day (lit. day of rest)

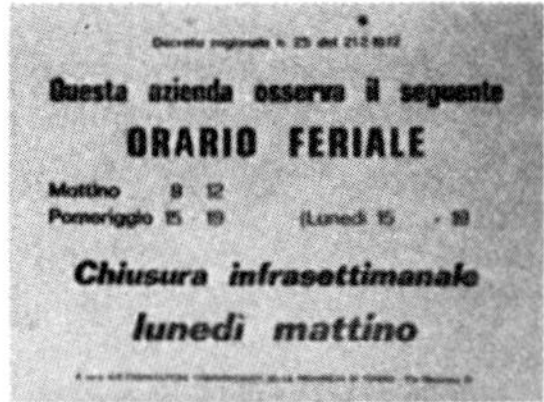

7

Signorina Il lunedì hanno orari diversi, perché, appunto, la mattina i negozi di generi alimentari sono aperti, mentre sono chiusi gli altri negozi. E il contrario: il pomeriggio i negozi di generi alimentari sono chiusi; sono aperti invece i supermercati e poi tutti gli altri negozi. Cioè lunedì hanno le loro chiusure, mattina o pomeriggio; mentre il sabato hanno una regolare apertura: 9–12,30, 15–19,30. Domenica chiusi, chiaramente.

orari diversi different times
appunto precisely, in fact, as a matter of fact
il contrario the other way round
invece instead
supermercati supermarkets
chiaramente clearly, of course

5 ➧ **quant'è lontana la Certosa?** how far is the Chartreuse? Other ways of asking the same question are: **quanto è distante la Certosa? a che distanza è la Certosa?** (lit. at what distance is the Chartreuse?).

sono venti minuti di autobus it's a twenty minute bus ride: but note that in Italian you use the plural form of the verb **essere, sono,** because it refers to the plural **minuti.**

all'ora e alla mezz'ora on the hour and on the half hour. Other similar expressions: **ai venti** twenty minutes past the hour; **ai quaranta** forty minutes past the hour etc.; **ogni ora** every hour; **ogni tre quarti d'ora** every three quarters of an hour.

➧ **il lunedì** on Mondays; **il venerdì** on Fridays; **la domenica** on Sundays. Note that days of the week have a small initial letter in Italian: for a full list see *Key words and phrases*, p. 83.

6 ➧ **quali sono?** which/what are? (See *Grammar* p. 86.)

alle tredici . . . quindici e trenta . . . diciannove e trenta . . . Many Italians also use the 24-hour clock, particularly in official notices (e.g. train stations) or announcements. Remember that the expressions **e un quarto, e mezza, meno venti** etc. are NOT used with the 24-hour clock. You have to use the full form and say **le quindici e trenta.**

➧ Of the names of the days of the week **lunedì** Monday, **martedì** Tuesday, **mercoledì** Wednesday, **giovedì** Thursday and **venerdì** Friday are all masculine and invariable (like all other nouns stressed on the last vowel). **Il sabato** and **la domenica** have plural forms: **i sabati** and **le domeniche** respectively. Note the following useful expressions: **lunedì** this Monday; **il lunedì** or **di lunedì** on Monday (in general); **tutti i lunedì, ogni lunedì** every Monday; **lunedì prossimo** next Monday (counting from today); **il lunedì successivo** or **il lunedì seguente** next Monday (counting from any other date). Workdays are called **giorni feriali** and Sundays and other holidays called **giorni festivi.** See also *Grammar* p. 87.

7 ➧ **la mattina** in the morning; **il pomeriggio** in the afternoon; also **la sera** in the evening. The word for 'morning' can also be masculine: **il mattino.**

hanno le loro chiusure they close (lit. they have their closures). **Chiusura** = closure, being closed.

hanno una regolare apertura they have regular opening times. **Apertura** = opening, being open.

8 *Aldo tells Giovanni about his plans for a week's holiday abroad*

Giovanni Dimmi un poco che cosa fai – euh – sabato prossimo.

Aldo Sabato ho intenzione di partire per – euh – fare una settimana di vacanza. La sera partiamo da Milano, poi ci fermiamo a Venezia e – euh – dormiamo la notte lì. Ripartendo il mattino dopo, arriviamo a Vienna, e, – euh – dopo qualche giorno di permanenza a Vienna, tappa a Budapest – euh – per tre giorni, e poi direttamente da Budapest ancora a Venezia.

Giovanni Come andate, andate in treno o . . .

Aldo Andiamo in automobile.

Giovanni E chi viene con voi?

Aldo Viene con – euh – con me viene Floriana e un altra coppia di amici, Paolo e Marcella.

dimmi un poco tell me (a little); **dire** = to tell
prossimo next
dormiamo we sleep; **dormire** to sleep (see *Grammar* p. 86)
ripartendo leaving again
permanenza sojourn, stay
tappa stop, stage in a journey
direttamente straight
ancora once more
un'altra coppia another couple

8

➧ **ho intenzione di partire** I intend to leave, I'm going to leave; a useful phrase which you can combine with other verbs, e.g. **ho intenzione di andare in Italia** I'm going to go to Italy; **ho intenzione di prendere il treno** I'm going to take a train; **che intenzioni hai**? what are you going to do? (lit. what are your intentions?).

per fare una settimana di vacanza for a week's holiday (lit. in order to take a week's holiday).

ci fermiamo we stop. When the verb **fermare** is used to mean that people themselves stop, as opposed to stopping someone or something else, it takes a 'reflexive' form (see Unit 3, p. 45) which in the present is as follows: **mi fermo, ti fermi, si ferma, ci fermiamo, vi fermate, si fermano.**
This can also happen with 'non-human' subjects: **l'autobus ferma/si ferma proprio davanti al negozio** the bus stops right opposite the shop.

➧ The verbs **aprire**, to open, and **chiudere**, to close, behave in the same way: **a che ora apre/si apre il museo? what time does the museum open? il negozio chiude/si chiude alle sette** the shop closes at seven.

➧ **il mattino dopo** the morning after; **dopo il lavoro** after work; **dopo un po'** after a little while. When **dopo** is followed by a verb, it is interchangeable with **poi**: **dopo/poi ci fermiamo a Venezia** then we stop in Venice.

in automobile in the car, by car. A more common, colloquial word for 'car' is **macchina**. Note **in treno**, by train; **in autobus**, by bus.

Key words and phrases

To learn

Time

che ora è? che ore sono?	what time is it?
a che ora . . .	at what time . . .
parte il treno?	does the train leave?
è la colazione?	is breakfast?
che intenzioni hai?	what are your intentions? what are you going to do?
ho intenzione di . . .	I intend to/I'm going to . . .
dopo	after, afterwards, later
dopo la colazione	after breakfast
parto dopo	I'm leaving later
il giorno dopo	the following day
dopo un po'	after a little while
oggi	today
domani	tomorrow
dopodomani	the day after tomorrow
la mattina	morning/in the morning
il pomeriggio	afternoon/in the afternoon
la sera	evening/in the evening
i giorni della settimana	the days of the week
lunedì	Monday
martedì	Tuesday
mercoledì	Wednesday
giovedì	Thursday
venerdì	Friday
sabato	Saturday
domenica	Sunday

Also, learn how to tell the time – look again at the note to dialogue 4, p. 79.

Distance

è lontano/lontana?	is it far?
è vicino/vicina?	is it near?
a che distanza è?	how far is it?

To understand

il negozio è aperto/chiuso	the shop is open/closed
il museo apre/chiude alle . . .	the museum opens/closes at . . .
dalle (due) alle (cinque)	from (two o'clock) to (five) o'clock
il treno è in ritardo	the train is late
ritarda di 50 minuti	it's 50 minutes late
la partenza è ritardata a causa delle condizioni meteorologiche	the departure has been delayed because of the weather conditions

Practise what you have learnt

1 On tape Giovanni asks five people what time it is. Number the five clock faces below in the order of the times mentioned. (Answers p. 90.)

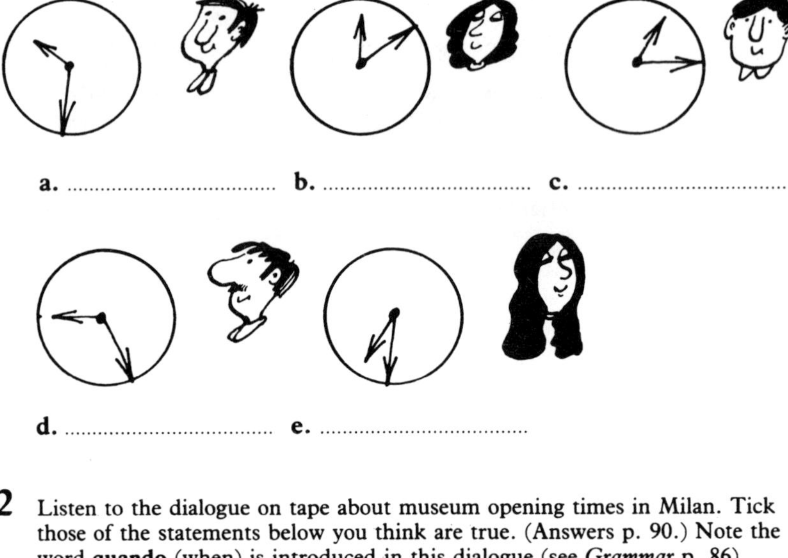

2 Listen to the dialogue on tape about museum opening times in Milan. Tick those of the statements below you think are true. (Answers p. 90.) Note the word **quando** (when) is introduced in this dialogue (see *Grammar* p. 86).

a. ☐ All museums are closed at lunch-time.

b. ☐ Some museums close between 12.30 and 2.30 p.m.

c. The Brera Museum opens

☐ (i) between 8 a.m. and 2 p.m.

☐ (ii) between 9 and 2 p.m.

d. ☐ The Pinacoteca (Picture Gallery) Ambrosiana can be visited during the lunch-time when other museums are closed.

3 The printer scrambled the programme of your week's holiday in Northern Italy. Listen to the tape, where the programme is given correctly and match the various visits and activities with the day reserved for them. (Answers p. 90.)

a. Escursione ai laghi di Como e Maggiore
b. Libero
c. Partenza da Londra (Gatwick) per Milano Malpensa, ore 14.10. Arrivo e sistemazione in albergo. Sera libera
d. Escursione alla Certosa di Pavia. Visita della città di Pavia
e. Visita guidata dei musei della città. Sera: opera al Teatro alla Scala
f. Mattino: visita della città in pullman. Pomeriggio libero. Sera: cena in un ristorante caratteristico
g. Escursione a Bergamo. Ore 19.30: partenza da Milano Malpensa per Londra (Gatwick)

mercoledì ....
giovedì ....
venerdì ....
sabato ....
domenica ....
lunedì ....
martedì ....

4 The printer has again scrambled the sentences in the following dialogue. Can you write them out on the dotted lines below in the right order? When you have done so, check by listening to the correct dialogue on your tape.

– Che autobus vuole prendere?
– Prego.
– La fermata del 63 è venti metri a destra all'angolo della strada.
– Il 63.
– Buon giorno, signorina. Scusi, dov'è la fermata dell'autobus più vicina?
– Molte grazie.

....
....
....
....
....
....
....
....

Grammar

Partire to leave

parto	I leave
parti	you leave
parte	he/she/it leaves you (polite) leave
partiamo	we leave
partite	you (pl.) leave
partono	they leave

Dormire to sleep

dormo	I sleep
dormi	you sleep
dorme	he/she/it sleeps you (polite) sleep
dormiamo	we sleep
dormite	you (pl.) sleep
dormono	they sleep

The verb **ripartire** to leave again, to start again, follows the same pattern as **partire**.

Quanto, quale, quando

qu- for 'question'! These two initial letters characterize a group of Italian question words (much in the same way as *wh-* are the initials of a similar English group: which?, where?, when?, what?).

You are already familiar with **quanto** how much, how many. When followed by a noun it behaves like a normal adjective:

quanti chili pesa? how many kilos does it weigh?
quante camere vuole? how many rooms do you want?

When it means 'how much' it does not change its form:
quanto pesa? quanto costa?

When it refers to an adjective indicating a dimension (time, length, distance or size) you translate it simply as 'how':
quanto è distante? how far is it?
quanto sono pesanti? how heavy are they?
quanto è grande? how big is it? etc.

quale what, which, which one:
quale camera vuole? which room do you want?
a quali ore? at what times?
qual'è? which one is it?
quali sono i musei più importanti? which are the most important museums?

quando when, is not to be confused with **quanto**:
quando apre il museo? when does the museum open?
quando parte il treno? when does the train leave?

Exercise 1

Fill in the gaps in the following questions with the appropriate **qu-** question word **quale, quando, quanto.** (Answers on p. 90.)

a. .... arriva il treno? —Alle 12,10.

b. A .... binario arriva? —Al binario 6.

c. .... valigie ha? —Ho due valigie.

d. .... pesano queste valigie? —Pesano venti chili.

e. Mi può dire .... parte l'autobus? —Parte alle nove.

f. .... autobus devo prendere per andare in centro?

—Deve prendere il numero 63.

g. .... è lontano il centro della città? —Dieci minuti in autobus.

h. .... mezzi posso prendere per andare in centro?

—Può prendere l'autobus e la metropolitana.

Other expressions of time

oggi today;
domani tomorrow;
dopodomani the day after tommorrow

} are all invariable

Oggi pomeriggio this afternoon: of the words specifying the periods of day, **pomeriggio** is the only one that may accompany **oggi**; **domani** and **dopodomani** can combine with **mattina** and **sera**, e.g. **domani mattina** tomorrow morning, **domani pomeriggio** tomorrow afternoon, **dopodomani sera** the day after tomorrow in the evening.
(Expressions indicating past time will be studied in Unit 13, p. 181.)

Exercise 2

Assuming that today is **giovedì 18**, how would you indicate the following times using one of the expressions above. (Answers p. 90.)

a. venerdì 19, ore 19,30 ....

b. sabato 20, ore 10,00 ....

c. venerdì 19, ore 9,30 ....

d. giovedì 18, ore 15 ....

e. sabato 20, ore 20 ....

f. venerdì 19, ore 14,30 ....

Read and understand

This is a page from the Lake Maggiore Passenger Boat Service timetable. Study it carefully and answer the following questions. (Answers on p. 90.)

NAVIGAZIONE LAGO MAGGIORE (Arona-Locarno) (Dal 5-IV al 27-IX) 170

170																									
ARONA ..p.					705		735	805	830	845	935	1000	1000	1025				1100			1215	1235	1320		
Angera ...					710		740	810	835	850	940	1005	1005	1030				1105			1220	1240	1335		
Meina					⚒		⚒	⚒	✠	900			③					♦15							
Ispra												②													
Lesa										920								*25			✠				
Belgirate										925								1130							
STRESA ....a.	⚒							▲	▲	950		1045	1045				▲	1155	▲		1415		Scolastica		▲
STRESA ....p.	640		715	830	920	△55	905	930	1020	955	1040	1050	1050	1100	1120		1140	1205	1240	1320				1400	1420
Isola Bella	645		725	840		1000	910	935	1025	1000	1045			1105	1125			1210	1246	1325				1405	1425
Isola Superiore	650		730			1005	915	940	1030	1005	1050			1110	1130		1145	1215	1250	1330				1410	1430
BAVENO	655		740			1015	925	950	1040	1015	1100	1055			1140		1150	1225		1340				1420	
Feriolo					dal 28-VI																Crocera Arona a. 1515				
Isola Madre ...	⚒		750				935	1000	1050	1025	1109	②			1150		1200	1235		1350				1430	1440
Suna																									
PALLANZA ...	710		755				940			1030		1101			1155			1240		1355				1435	
Villa Taranto ..			✝805				959			1040					1205			1250		1405				1445	
INTRA ....a.	725		815				959			1050		1105	1110		1215			1259		1414				1455	
INTRA ..... p.	740		820				1000			1100		1106	1115		1220			1300		1420		1415		1500	
LAVENO ... a.	800		840		929		1015			1120			③		1240			1320		1440				1520	
LAVENO ......p.					930																				
Ghiffa					938																	◊21			
Porto Valtr.					945								◊35									◊28			
Oggebbio					952																	◊35			
Cannero		749			958	959	1051									1240						1442			
LUINO ....a.		756				1005						1125	1200	②		1246						1449			
LUINO ....p.		757				1006						1130	1210	1245		1247		1400		1415		1450			
Maccagno		802				1012										1252		②		②		1456			
CANNOBIO ...a.		815				1020	1100						1229	1310		1300		1419				1503			
CANNOBIO ...p.													1230		1240			1420							
BRISSAGO ....a.												1145	1250		1300			1440							
BRISSAGO ....p.						905	1010		1130			1150	1300		1310		1340	1445						1520	
Isole Brissago .						920	1012		1135				③		1325		1355							1535	
Porto Ronco ...						915	①		1140						1320		1350	1455						1530	
Ranzo						935						②			⑤		⑥			1500				1550	
Gerra						940														1505				1555	
Ascona							1017		1200			1157			1340		1405	1510		⑦				1605	
S. Nazzaro						950	1022		1215								1420	②		1515					
Vira	⚒		⚒				1026									⑤	1430			1525					
Magadino	630		730	830	930		1028	1130		1230				1330	⑤	1430	1435			1530					
LOCARNO ....a.	650		750	850	950	1005	1035	1150	1230	1250		1205	1330	1350	1400	1450	1450	1530		1550				1625	

△ Carciano. ▲ Festiva fino 27-VI, giornaliera dal 28-VI. ③ Non si effettua il mercoledì. ⑤ Si effettua la domenica. ★ Ferma nei festivi. ◊ Ferma dal 28-VI.
② Si effettua il mercoledì. ① Sospeso mercoledì e domenica. ⑥ Sospeso la domenica. ✝ Ferma nei giorni di scuola. ♦ Ferma il martedì.

1. Supposing you are in Angera for the weekend and wish to meet a friend in Baveno at 11 a.m., which is the *latest* time you can leave?

....

2. At what time does the Sunday service to Locarno leave Brissago?

....

3. Supposing you wish to travel from Angera to Meina on a Monday. Is there any service you can use between 8.50 and lunch-time?

....

4. You are in Stresa and wish to visit the famous botanical gardens at Villa Taranto on a Sunday. Which is the earliest boat you can take?

....

5. Does the 14.00 boat from Stresa to Laveno stop at Suna?

....

6. How long does the 10 a.m. boat from Arona to Locarno stop at Luino on Fridays? ....

7. How long is the shortest journey from Cannero to Cannobio?

....

Did you know?

Business and leisure times

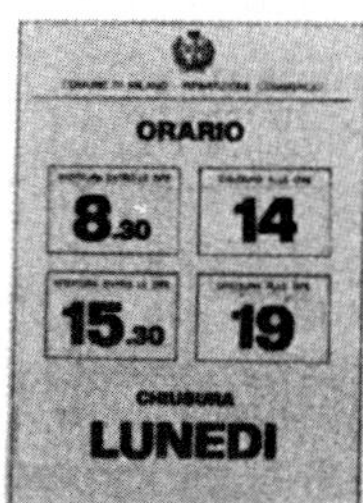

Italian shops and offices have, with very few exceptions, an **orario spezzato** (lit. broken timetable), which allows for a lunch-time closure, generally from 12,30 to 3 p.m. In Southern Italy shops may re-open as late as 4 or 4.30 in the afternoon, and may stay open until 8 p.m. Some offices in the North are tentatively moving towards **orario continuo**, with no lunch-time closure, but they are the exception. One of the consequences of the **orario spezzato** is that Italian towns have four **ore di punta**, rush hours, instead of two.

Meal times tend to be later in the South than in the North. **Il pranzo**, or midday meal, can start as late as 1.30 or 2 p.m. in the south. **La cena**, evening meal, ranges from 7 p.m. in the North to 9 p.m. in the South. Concerts, theatrical performances and last cinema shows begin much later than in Britain: about 8.30 p.m. for theatres and concerts, and 10.30 for cinemas. It is not uncommon for theatre or concert-goers to dine out after the performance ends: there will be plenty of restaurants still open.

Holidays

The following days are public holidays in Italy:
Capodanno New Year's Day
lunedì in Albis, or **lunedì dell'angelo** or **lunedì di Pasqua** Easter Monday
Anniversario della Liberazione to celebrate the freedom from Fascist rule achieved at the end of World War II, on April 25
Festa del lavoro May Day, on May 1st
Proclamazione della Repubblica to celebrate the proclamation of the Republic of Italy, on the 1st Sunday in June
Ferragosto August Holiday, on August 15
Ognissanti, or **Tutti i Santi** All Saint's Day, on November 1st
Immacolata Concezione the religious festival of the Immaculate Conception of the Virgin Mary, on December 8
Natale Christmas
Santo Stefano Boxing Day, or the feast of St. Stephen.

Whenever one of these public holidays falls on a Friday or a Tuesday, firms and public offices often grant their employees an extra day's holiday, called **il ponte**, bridge.

There is also a number of local and regional holidays, often centering on the festivity of the patron Saint of the town, or of a particular church: like the **Festa del Redentore**, the Feast of the Redeemer, in Venice (3rd Sunday in July), or the Festa dei Ceri (May 15), when heavy decorative structures symbolizing **ceri**, church candles, are paraded in a colourful procession through Gubbio.

There are also plenty of non-religious pageants, some of which, like the **Palio of Siena** the horse-race in Siena (which takes place twice a year, on July 2 and August 16); **il Gioco del Ponte** – lit. the Game on the Bridge, in Pisa (last Sunday in May), or the **Partita a scacchi**, the chess game played with live chessmen in a square in Marostica (September 9–10) are nationally and internationally famous.

Your turn to speak

1 In the first exercise you will practise asking questions about train departure and arrival times.

2 For this exercise, first look at the clocks below. You will be asked five questions about what time it is. Say the five times in the order shown on the clock faces. Use the 12-hour clock. The correct answers will be given on tape.

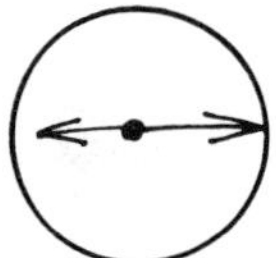

Revision

Next you should do a short revision section which goes over the language you have studied in Units 4–6. Turn to p. 219 for the written part of the exercises. The tape exercises follow straight after this unit on your cassette.

Answers

Practise what you have learnt p. 84 Exercise **1** (**a**) 3 (**b**) 2 (**c**) 5 (**d**) 1 (**e**) 4.

p. 84 Exercise 2 You should have ticked **b, c** (**ii**) and **d**.

p. 85 Exercise **3** mercoledì **c**, giovedì **f**, venerdì **a**, sabato **b**, domenica **d**, lunedì **e**, martedì **g**.

Grammar p. 87 Exercise **1** (**a**) quando (**b**) quale (**c**) quante (**d**) quanto (**e**) quando (**f**) quale (**g**) quanto (**h**) quali.

p. 87 Exercise **2** (**a**) domani sera (**b**) dopodomani mattina (**c**) domani mattina (**d**) oggi pomeriggio (**e**) dopodomani sera (**f**) domani pomeriggio.

Read and understand p. 88 (**1**) 8.50 because the 10 a.m. service from Angera stops at Baveno only on Wednesday (**2**) 13.10 (**3**) No, because the 11.05 stops at Meina only on Tuesdays (**4**) 9.05 because the 7.15 stops there only on schooldays (**5**) No (**6**) 10 minutes (**7**) 9 minutes.
si effettua is a formal way of saying 'runs'; **scuola** = school.

7 *Bene, lo compro!*

What you will learn

- how to buy things in shops:
  a baker's shop – various types of bread
  a newspaper kiosk – local and national newspapers
  a perfumery – perfumes
  a tobacconist's shop – Italian cigarettes.
- how to make simple comparative statements e.g. 'this is better, that's not so strong', etc.
- how to state prices in a shorter way

Before you begin

Points to remember from Unit 6:

1 verbs
partire to leave
parto, **parti**, **parte**, **partiamo**, **partite**, **partono**
ripartire, **dormire** and **aprire** are conjugated in the same way.

2 **qu-** words
quanto how much
quale which
quando when

3 Expressions of time
oggi today
domani tomorrow
dopodomani the day after tomorrow

Study guide

	Dialogues 1, 2: listen straight through without the book
	Dialogues 1, 2: listen, read and study one by one
	Dialogues 3, 4: listen straight through without the book
	Dialogues 3, 4: listen, read and study one by one
	Dialogues 5, 6: listen straight through without the book
	Dialogues 5, 6: listen read and study one by one
	Learn the *Key words and phrases* and the list of foods
	Do the exercises in *Practise what you have learnt*
	Study *Grammar* and do the exercises
	Do *Read and understand*
	Read *Did you know?*
	Do the tape exercises in *Your turn to speak*
	Finally, listen to all the dialogues again without the book

Dialogues

1 *A woman buys a loaf of white bread from the baker*

Fornaio Buon giorno, signora. Mi dica.
Cliente Mezzo chilo di pane di quello là in fondo.
Fornaio Nero o bianco?
Cliente No, no, bianco, però di quello normale.
Fornaio Tipo toscano, proprio.
Cliente Tipo toscano, hmm . . .
Fornaio Quattrocento, signora. Desidera altro?
Cliente No.
Fornaio Buon giorno, signora. Grazie signora. Buon giorno.

fornaio baker (man)
nero black (*see notes*)
bianco white
però but, however
proprio in fact

2 *Another customer asks the baker for wholemeal bread*

Cliente Un pane integrale, se non ti dispiace.
Fornaio Intero o mezzo?
Cliente Intero.
Fornaio Intero. Desidera altro, signora?
Cliente No.
Fornaio (*to his assistant*) Paolo, mi dai diecimila lire, per favore?
Paolo Eh?
Fornaio Mi dai 10.000 lire, per favore?
Ecco cinquanta di resto alla signora.
Buon giorno, signora. Grazie.

integrale wholemeal (speaking of bread)
intero (or **intiero**) whole, the whole piece

3 *At the newsstand (**edicola**) Giovanni inquires whether they sell any English newspapers and magazines*

Giovanni Signorina, ha dei giornali stranieri?
Giornalaia Sì, alcuni.
Giovanni Che giornali inglesi ha?
Giornalaia Giornali inglesi ci abbiamo il *Time*, *Newsweek*, *Express* . . .
Giovanni Mi da il *Times*?
Giornalaia Sì.
Giovanni Cioè, ha il *Time* o il *Times*?
Giornalaia Abbiamo il *Time*, la rivista e il *Times* il quotidiano.
Giovanni E il *Times* quotidiano.
Giornalaia Sì.
Giovanni Quanto costa il *Times* quotidiano?
Giornalaia Novecento lire.
Giovanni Novecento lire. Bene, lo compro.
Giornalaia Grazie.
Giovanni Grazie.

giornalaia newsagent (woman)
stranieri foreign
alcuni some, a few
cioè that is, I mean

1 ◆ **di quello là in fondo** that one there on the end/at the back. **In fondo** can mean both 'at the end', i.e. of a row, or 'at the back'.

mezzo chilo di pane half a kilo (about one pound) of bread. Bread in Italy is often bought by the weight.

nero o bianco? lit. black or white? Any bread not made of white flour (**farina bianca**), e.g. wholewheat, wholemeal, rye etc. is called **pane nero**.

tipo toscano Tuscan type, which unlike bread made in most other regions of Italy is unsalted.

◆ **desidera altro?** do you want anything else? **Desidera?** is sometimes used by shopkeepers as an opening, instead of **(mi) dica**. Customers can also use the verb **desiderare** in reply: **desidero mezzo chilo di pane nero**.

2 ◆ **un pane** lit. a bread, is the way to ask for 'a loaf' in Italian.

◆ **se non ti dispiace** if you don't mind. Note the colloquial **ti** instead of the formal **le** for 'you' (**se non le dispiace**). Longstanding customers of food shops often address the shop-keepers with the informal **tu**; but the shop-keeper tends to answer in the polite **Lei** form, particularly when talking to female customers.

intero o mezzo? a whole (loaf) or half? Larger loaves can be cut in half by the baker. There is a wide variety of types of bread in Italy, with names and shapes varying from region to region. **Panini**, rolls, are popular, as is **focaccia** a flat pizza-like bread coated with olive oil or with other savoury seasonings – usually eaten as a snack. If you want **focaccia** you would usually ask for **un pezzo**, a piece.

mi dai 10.000 lire per favore? (can you/will you) give me 10,000 lire, please? In Italian you simply use the present tense for 'can you/will you' in this type of sentence. The baker addresses his assistant in the **tu** form. **Dai** is from **dare** (to give).

◆ **ecco cinquanta di resto** here's 50 (lira) change. Besides being a stop-gap word, **ecco** is used when showing or pointing to something: **ecco il pane** here's the bread; **ecco il fornaio** here's the baker; **ecco le sigarette** here are the cigarettes, or simply **ecco** here you are.

3 ◆ **il giornale** (from **giorno**, day) is the standard word for daily paper. A less common word is **quotidiano** (lit. daily) which, unlike **giornale**, can be used as an adjective (**il pane quotidiano** daily bread). **Riviste**, magazines, reviews, can be **settimanali** weekly, or **mensili** monthly: these adjectives can also be used as nouns, e.g. ***Newsweek* è un settimanale americano**. If you want to talk in general terms about periodical publications use **la stampa periodica** or **i periodici**.

ci abbiamo we have. Often **ci** is used with forms of **avere** but it may be ignored in translation: **ci ha del pane?** have you got any bread? (lit. have you got any bread there?).

◆ **mi da . . .** (can you/will you) give me . . . Note the difference between this polite form and the **tu** form expression in the previous dialogue: **mi dai**.

lo compro I'll buy it (but note the use of the simple present tense in Italian). **Comprare** (occasionally **comperare**) = to buy. For **lo** see *Grammar* p. 101.

4 *At the post office: Giovanni wants to buy a stamp for a letter to England*

Giovanni Quanto costa un francobollo per l'Inghilterra, signorina?
Signorina Centocinquanta lire.
Giovanni Questo per lettera?
Signorina Per cartolina.
Giovanni E per lettera?
Signorina Duecentoventi.
Giovanni Me ne da uno, per favore?
Signorina Certo.
Giovanni Molte grazie.
Signorina Prego.

francobollo postage stamp
per for
lettera letter
cartolina postcard (**cartolina illustrata** picture postcard)

5 *The assistant in a perfumery tries to convince a customer to buy a perfume*

Commessa Senta un attimo questo. Questo è un bel profumino, eh? E non è eccessivamente caro . . . questo qui viene seimilatrè.
Cliente È caro.
Commessa È caro? No, non è caro. Normale va sulle dieci, dodicimila lire.
Cliente Prendo questo. Qual'è meglio, questo o quello?
Commessa Questo prenda! È più buono.

commessa shop assistant (woman)
eccessivamente excessively
➧ **caro** expensive, dear
normale used instead of **normalmente** normally
➧ **questo prenda!** (or **prenda questo!**) take this one! (polite)

4 **me ne da uno?** may I have one (lit. you give me one of them?) **Mi, ti, ci, vi** etc. (see p. 59) followed by **ne** and **lo, la** etc. (see *Grammar* p. 101) change their final **-i** to **-e**. **Ne**, meaning 'of . . . whatever has just been mentioned' is generally not translated into English, but is often found in Italian particularly in conjunction with numbers: **ne voglio tre** I want three; **ne compro uno** I'll buy one.

If you want to ask for a stamp of a given value, use **da** before its value: **un francobollo da trecento lire** a 300 lira stamp. **Da** is also used before the face value of banknotes, coins etc., and the rating of appliances etc., e.g. **un biglietto da diecimila** a 10,000 (lira) bill; **una lampadina da 240 volt** a 240 volt bulb; **un motore da trenta cavalli** a 30 HP engine (lit. **cavallo** = horse).

5 **senta un attimo questo** just smell this one. **Senta** is from **sentire** with the general meaning of 'to sense' and so it can be translated in more than one way according to the context, e.g.
to hear – **sente la musica?** can you hear the music?
to listen – **senta** (polite) or **senti** (informal) listen (as opening to a conversation)
to feel (reflexive) – **non mi sento bene** I don't feel well.

un bel profumino a nice little perfume. **Profumo** = perfume. Some Italian nouns may combine with one of a number of special endings which tend to slightly modify their meaning: **-ino** and **-etto** usually indicate smallness e.g. **pezzo** piece, **pezzetto** small piece; **pane** (loaf of) bread, **panino** bread roll. Sometimes two such endings may be combined: **pezzo** → **pezzetto** → **pezzettino** a very small piece.
In this dialogue **profumino** doesn't indicate size but is used because it's more emphatic.

viene seimilatrè it comes to 6300 (lire). Note the use of **venire** and **andare** when talking about prices: **quanto viene questo?** how much does this cost (come to)? **a quanto va?** how much is it going for? **va sulle dieci, dodicimila lire** it's about 10–12,000 lire. **Sulle . . .** followed by a price (**lire** is understood) indicates approximation. For **seimilatrè** instead of **seimila trecento** see *Practise what you have learnt*, Exercise 3, p. 100.

qual'è meglio? also **qual'è migliore?** which one is better? **Meglio** is invariable, **migliore** has a plural: **questi sono migliori** these ones are better. Alternatively, 'better', when speaking of things that can be tasted or smelled, can be **più buono**: **questi formaggi sono più buoni**.

6 *A tobacconist tells Giovanni about the various types of Italian cigarettes*

Giovanni Allora, come sigarette italiane abbiamo le . . .
Tabaccaia Le *Nazionali*, prima base. Dopo le *Esportazioni*, le *Super*, così . . .
Giovanni Queste sono piuttosto forti.
Tabaccaia . . . noo . . . ma non tanto, perché ci sono anche quelle col filtro, son meno forti. Dopo ci sono queste *Nazionali* qui col filtro, N80, vede. Costan quattrocencinquanta queste, e non sono molto forti.
Giovanni Non sono molto forti.
Tabaccaia No.
Giovanni E quelle leggere, ha detto che sono le . . . le *Lido*.
Tabaccaia Le *Lido*, molto leggere, le *Lido* e le *Gala*.
Giovanni E le *Gala*.
Tabaccaia Le *Lido*, e *Gala*.
Giovanni Le *Gala* hanno il doppio filtro.
Tabaccaia Sì, sì doppio filtro.

tabaccaia tobacconist (woman)
Nazionali, Esportazioni, Super, N80, Lido, Gala all names of Italian cigarettes
dopo then, afterwards
così and so on
filtro filter
quattrocencinquanta Tuscan dialect for **quattrocentocinquanta**
leggere mild, light
doppio double

6 **sono piuttosto forti** they're rather strong.
Note also the following expressions:
non tanto not so much e.g. **non sono tanto forti** they're not so strong
non molto not much, not too . . . e.g. **non sono molto forti** they're not too strong
queste sono meno forti these are less strong
sono molto leggere they're very mild
(For more about comparisons see *Grammar* p. 101.)

Note **son** and **costan** instead of **sono** and **costano**: the final **-o** is often dropped from the 'they' form, in speech.

ha detto che sono . . . you said that they are . . .

Key words and phrases

To learn

desidero . . .	I'd like . . .
mi da . . . ?	will you give me . . . ?
un chilo/mezzo chilo di . . .	a kilo/half a kilo of . . .
un pezzo/pezzetto di . . .	a piece/small piece of . . .
pane bianco	white bread
pane integrale	wholemeal bread
un francobollo da 300 lire	a 300 lira stamp
per l'Inghilterra	for England
per una lettera	for a letter
per una cartolina	for a postcard
un giornale inglese	an English newspaper
un quotidiano	a daily
un settimanale	a weekly
una rivista	a magazine
me ne da uno/due?	will you give me one/two of those?
se non le dispiace (polite) **se non ti dispiace (informal)**	if you don't mind
quanto viene?	how much does it come to?
qual'è meglio?	which one is better/best?
è caro?	is it expensive?
più	more, -er
meno	less
ecco	here you are

To understand

desidera altro?	do you require anything else?
ecco cinquanta di resto	here's fifty (lira) change
va sulle dieci, dodici mila lire	it's about ten to twelve thousand lira
prenda questo!	take this one!

Remember some of the vocabulary you have already met for food.

le uova (*sing.* **l'uovo)**

il formaggio

il prosciutto

il salame

Other useful words for food

Most fruit and vegetables are bought at the market (**mercato**), as they are cheaper and often fresher than in the shops. You can usually select what you want yourself and give it to the stallholder to weigh. Make sure you take your own shopping bag.

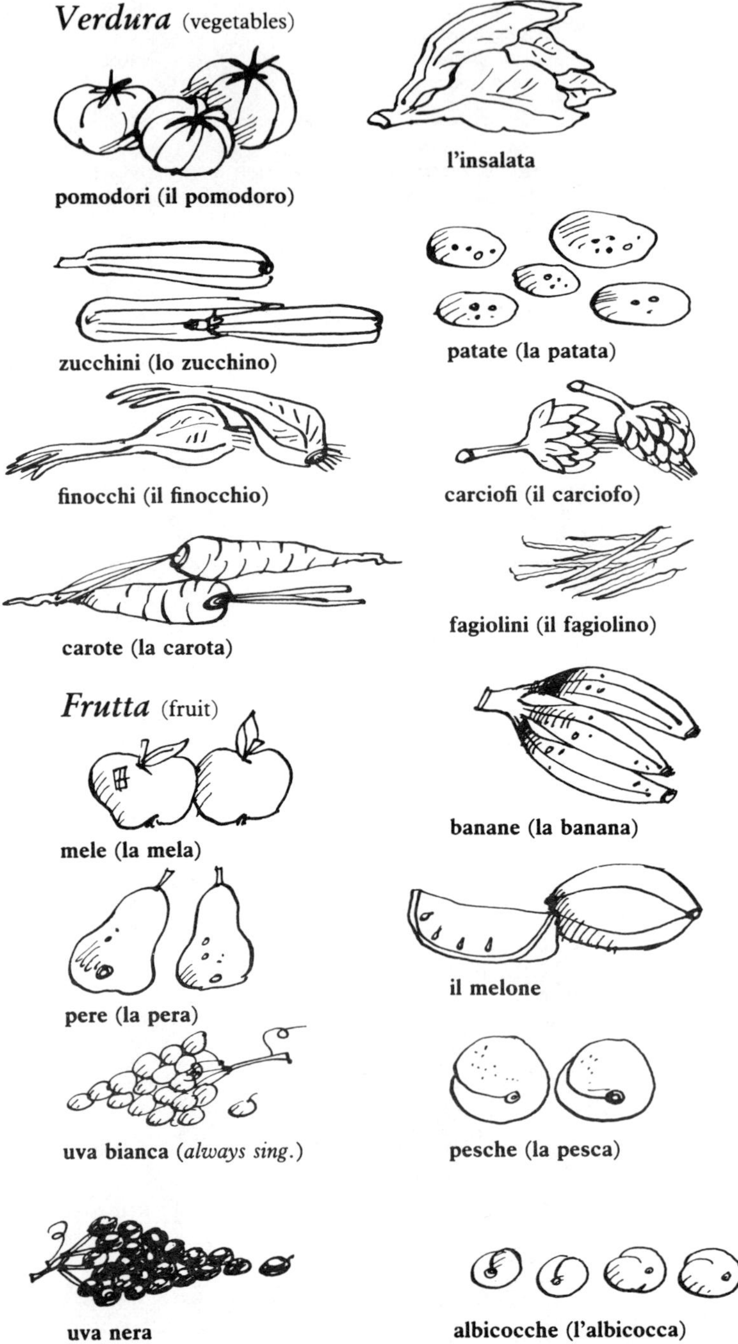

Practise what you have learnt

1 Giovanni asks the owner of a bread shop in Milan what types of bread she has for sale. Listen to your tape and tick the ones she mentions from the following list (you'll find that in other regions different names may be used). (Answers p. 104.)

a. ☐ francese, francesini (French bread)
b. ☐ ferrarese (Ferrara type bread)
c. ☐ pane di pasta dura (crusty bread)
d. ☐ pane integrale (wholemeal bread)
e. ☐ michette (round bread rolls)
f. ☐ banane (banana-shaped rolls)
g. ☐ tartine (sliced white bread)
h. ☐ fogliette (a type of bread roll)
i. ☐ grissini (bread sticks)
j. ☐ focaccia (flat savoury bread)

2 Listen to the short passage on tape about Italian newspapers and magazines. Try to get the gist of it, and tick the statements below you think are true. (Answers p. 104.)

a. ☐ *Il Corriere della sera* is a Milan evening paper.
b. ☐ *La Stampa* is a national paper published in Turin.
c. ☐ *Il Mattino* is a well-known national paper.
d. ☐ *Il Resto del Carlino* is published in Bologna.
e. ☐ *La Repubblica* is a weekly.
f. ☐ *L'Europeo* is a daily published in Naples.
g. ☐ *Panorama* and *L'Espresso* are two of the most important weeklies.

3 When quoting prices Italian shop assistants often omit **-mila** and **-cento**. **Seimila trecento** may become **seimila tre** or even **sei e tre**. Listen to the prices given on tape and write the appropriate price in the tag appended to each object depicted below. (Answers p. 104.)

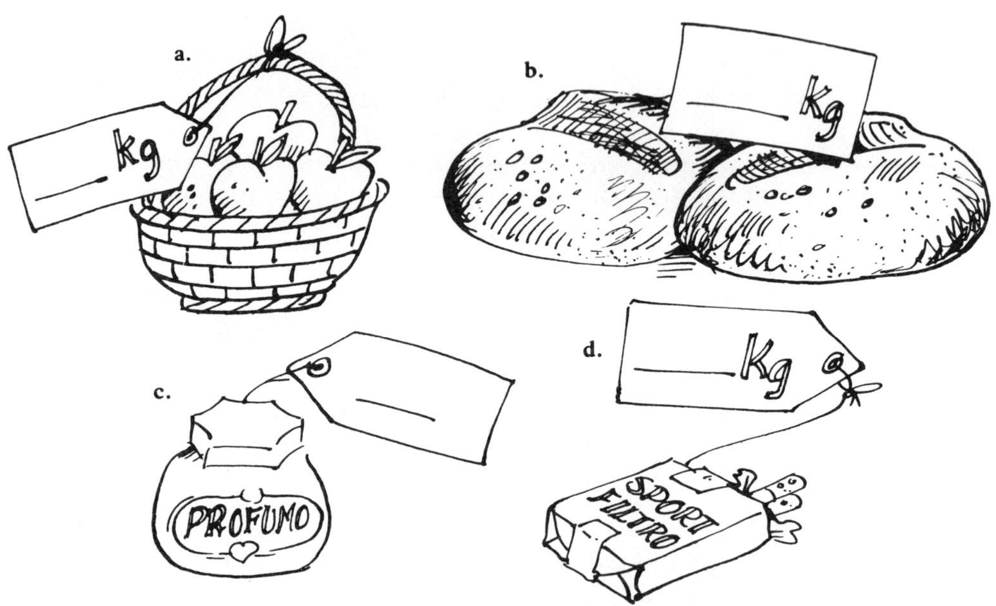

4 Write in the gaps in the sentences below the appropriate form for 'will you give me . . . if you don't mind', i.e.
informal – **mi dai . . . se non ti dispiace**
formal – **mi da . . . se non le dispiace**
Then check your answers by listening to the tape.

a. Paolo, ... cinquemila lire ....
.... ?

b. Signorina, ... la rivista *Time*, ...
.... ?

c. Ha delle sigarette americane? – Sì, abbiamo Camel, Lucky Strike, Marlboro. – Allora .... un pacchetto di Camel, ... ?

d. Rosanna, ... un pezzetto di focaccia, ...
.... ?

Grammar

Lo, la, li, le

These words are used as a translation of 'him', 'her', 'it' and 'them', e.g.

lo compro (**lo** replacing **<u>il</u> giornale**) **la compro** (**la** replacing **<u>la</u> rivista**)	I'll buy it
li compro (**li** replacing **<u>i</u> biglietti**) **le compro** (**le** replacing **<u>le</u> sigarette**)	I'll buy them

Note that they come in front of the verb.

Exercise 1 Fill in the appropriate word (**lo**, **la**, **li** or **le**) in the following dialogues. (Answers p. 104.)

a. – Signorina, ha dei giornali inglesi? – Ho solo il *Daily Express* ……… vuole? – Sì, ……… prendo.

b. – Ha sigarette americane? – Sì. – A quanto ……… vende?

c. – Ha maglie nere? – No signora, mi dispiace. Non ……… abbiamo nere, ……… abbiamo solo colorate.

d. – Dove sono i telefoni pubblici? – Non ……… vede? Sono proprio di fronte.

e. – Prende la colazione in camera? – Sì, ……… prendo in camera.

Comparisons

You will need the following expressions to make graded judgements. Study this basic sentence: **questo profumo è caro** this perfume is expensive.

meno less	**questo profumo è meno caro**
non . . . così **non . . . tanto** } not so	**questo profumo** { **non è così caro** **non è tanto caro**
non . . . molto not very	**questo profumo non è molto caro**
piuttosto rather	**questo profumo è piuttosto caro**
più more, -er	**questo profumo è più caro**
molto very	**questo profumo è molto caro**
tanto **così** } so	**questo profumo** { **è tanto caro** **è così caro**
troppo too (much)	**questo profumo è troppo caro**

Exercise 2 The following adjectives have opposite meanings:

forte strong	**caro** expensive	**grande** large
leggero light, mild	**economico** cheap	**piccolo** small

For each of the following sentences write another having the *same* meaning, but with the *opposite* adjective e.g. **questo profumo è più economico → questo profumo è meno caro.** (Answers p. 104.)

a. Queste sigarette sono meno forti. ……………………………

b. Questa camera è più cara. ……………………………

c. Questo albergo è meno grande. ……………………………

d. Questo profumo è meno leggero. ……………………………

Read and understand

1 There are on this photograph two shops whose signs you should be able to understand. What are they and what do they sell? (Answers p. 104.)

2 Here are more shop signs. Their English translations or explanation are given in the box below. By combining some judicious guessing with a process of elimination you should be able to understand all of them. (Answers p. 104.)

a. **ARTICOLI REGALO**

b. **FRUTTERIA**

c. **POLLERIA**

d. **BOTTIGLIERIA**

e. **FARMACIA**

f. **SUPERMERCATO**

g. **PANIFICIO**

h. **ALIMENTARI**

bottle shop, wine shop
general food store
fruit shop
bread shop, bakery
supermarket
poultry shop
chemist
souvenirs, gift shop

Did you know?

Shops

Like the England of old, Italy is still very much a nation of small shopkeepers, who somehow manage to resist the onslaught of supermarkets, with their greater purchasing power and consequently lower prices, by giving a really excellent personal service to their regular customers. Shop owners are often found behind the counter: unlike wage earners they have a real personal interest in gaining and retaining your custom, and are able to advise you on what will best suit your needs. They will also charge you what they think your purse will stand, which may not necessarily be the lowest possible price. That leaves a lot of scope for bargaining – mainly for regular customers. If you want **prezzi fissi**, fixed prices, you have to go to department stores or supermarkets.

If you pay by travellers' cheques, some shops will give you a discount: but make sure their rate of exchange is not less than that in the banks. Foreign currencies are rarely acceptable outside frontier towns. The acceptance of personal cheques is minimal, but the use of credit cards is slowly gaining ground. Customers in Italy do not enjoy as full a legal protection as in Britain: so the rule is still very much 'buyer beware!'

A few shop signs may be misleading to English-speaking tourists. **CONFEZIONI** is not a confectioner's but a clothes shop. In a **PASTICCERIA** you will find cakes and confectionery, not **pasta**. Spices, not drugs, are sold in a **DROGHERIA** together with the range of goods you would find at a grocer's. Chemists (**FARMACIA**) sell medical drugs, but they do not normally develop films: for that you will have to go to a specialized shop (**FOTO**, **FOTOGRAFIA** or **OTTICO**) dealing in cameras, films and optical goods (including spectacles). Tobacco goods, salt and postage stamps are a state monopoly, and they are sold from specially licensed outlets marked by the standard **T** sign illustrated opposite. These outlets are often combined with espresso bars: the advantage for the tourist is that stamps and cigarettes can be bought practically at every street corner. You can, of course, buy stamps at the post office, but this is less convenient as there are often long queues.

Watch out for sales, advertised by a variety of signs: **SALDI**, **SVENDITA**, **LIQUIDAZIONE**, **OCCASIONI**, **RIBASSI**, **PREZZI ECCEZIONALI**.

In many shops, and in all food shops (for reasons of hygiene) you do not pay the person who serves you, but the cashier. You either go to the cash till with your purchase and pay before going out, or get a stamped receipt, which you then show the attendant to obtain your purchase.

Your turn to speak

1 In the two exercises on tape you will practise ordering things in shops: first you are at a tobacconist's where you ask for stamps.

2 Here you are in a baker's shop, where you ask for a piece of **focaccia**.

Answers

Practise what you have learnt p. 99 Exercise **1** All except d, i, j. **Grissini** are the popular Italian breadsticks.

p. 99 Exercise **2** (**a**) false, it's a national paper (**b**) true (**c**) false, it's a local paper (**d**) true (**e**) false, it's a national paper (**f**) false, it's a weekly (**g**) true.

p. 100 Exercise **3** (**a**) 950 lire (**b**) 630 lire (**c**) 7500 lire (**d**) 1200 lire.

Grammar p. 101 Exercise **1** (**a**) lo . . . lo (**b**) le (**c**) le . . . le (**d**) li (**e**) la.

p. 101 Exercise **2** (**a**) Queste sigarette sono più leggere (**b**) Questa camera è meno economica (**c**) Questo albergo è più piccolo (**d**) Questo profumo è più forte.

Read and understand p. 102 Exercise **1** PROFUMERIA (perfumery); SALI E TABACCHI (tobacconist's shop, also known simply as a TABACCAIO).

p. 102 Exercise **2** (**a**) souvenirs, gift shop (**b**) fruit shop (**c**) poultry shop, **pollo** = chicken (**d**) bottle shop, wine shop (**e**) chemist (**f**) supermarket (**g**) bread shop, bakery (**h**) general food store.

8 Che tipo consiglia?

What you will learn

- more about shopping and comparing values
- how to ask for, and understand, advice on what to buy
- how to say you like something
- packaging
- weights and measures

Before you begin

Points to remember from Unit 7:

1 verbs
mi da . . .? (polite)
mi dai . . .? (informal) } (will) you give me . . .?

ha . . .? (polite)
hai . . .? (informal) } do you have . . .?

2 pronouns
lo prendo, la prendo I'll take it (m./f. sing.)
li prendo, le prendo I'll take them (m./f. pl.)
ne prendo due, tre etc. I'll have two, three (of them)

3 adverbs
meno less
più more
molto very
tanto so (much)
troppo too (much)
piuttosto rather

Study guide

	Dialogues 1–3: listen straight through without the book
	Dialogues 1–3: listen, read and study one by one
	Dialogues 4–6: listen straight through without the book
	Dialogues 4–6: listen, read and study one by one
	Learn the *Key words and phrases* and clothes vocabulary on p. 110.
	Do the exercises in *Practise what you have learnt*
	Study *Grammar*
	Do *Read and understand*
	Read *Did you know?*
	Do the tape exercises in *Your turn to speak*
	Finally, listen to all the dialogues again straight through

Dialogues

1 *At a bread shop in Milan, Giovanni asks the manageress whether she has any jam*

Giovanni Buon giorno, signora.
Fornaia Buon giorno.
Giovanni Ha marmellata?
Fornaia Sì.
Giovanni Che tipo ha?
Fornaia Fichi, prugna, ciliegie, pesche e . . . marroni.
Giovanni E quanto costa?
Fornaia Millecento.
Giovanni Me ne da una di . . . fichi, per favore.
Fornaia Va bene.

fichi figs
prugna plum
ciliegie cherries
pesche peaches
marroni chestnuts (also: **castagne**)

2 *Giovanni asks a grocer's advice on the most suitable kinds of* **pasta**

Giovanni Che tipo di pasta consiglia?
Droghiere Dipende quale . . . qualità preferisce, se pasta da minestrone, pasta per fare pastasciutta, o pasta al forno.
Giovanni Per fare della . . . della pastasciutta.
Droghiere A Milano usan gli spaghetti, però . . . va molto bene la pasta un po' più grossa: bucatini, e . . . tipo maccheroni, e . . . Così, dipende dal . . . dai gusti, dal cliente.
Giovanni E come pasta al forno, forse le . . . le penne.
Droghiere Pasta al forno, vanno . . . No, la . . . lasagne va di più. Le penne devono essere molto grosse.
Giovanni Hm . . . grazie.
Droghiere Prego.

droghiere (m.) grocer (man)
preferisce you prefer (polite) (See *Grammar* p. 115)
usa it's customary to use
grosso large, thick
spaghetti, bucatini, penne, lasagne types of pasta
dipende dai gusti it's a matter of taste (lit. it depends on the tastes)

1 ➧ **che tipo ha?** what kind do you have? This question could also be asked in the plural: **che tipi ha?** or **che gusti ha?** (remember Unit 4, dialogue 6). Similarly the manageress could have answered **prugne** in the plural.

2 ➧ **che tipo . . . consiglia?** what type . . . do you advise? **Consiglia** is from **consigliare** to advise (**il consiglio** advice, counsel). There are countless varieties of pasta (see *Did you know?*); and **pasta asciutta** or **pastasciutta** is the general name for pasta cooked in boiling water, drained and seasoned in many ways. **Pasta al forno** is the general name for all baked pastas, like **lasagne**.

minestrone a thick soup made with a large number of (mostly vegetable) ingredients. While the endings **-etto** and **-ino** (Unit 7) often indicate small size, the ending **-one** suggests large size: **spaghetti** actually means small **spaghi** (strings), **bucatini** small pasta pieces with a hole (**buco**), **cannelloni** large **cannelli** (tubes).

va di più sells more (lit. goes more).

3 *Another grocer describes the various types of coffee she stocks*

Giovanni Buon giorno, signora.
Droghiera Sì, dica.
Giovanni Vorrei del caffè. Che tipi di caffè ha?
Droghiera C'è *Suerte* in pacchettino, sottovuoto, macinato, e costa mille e sei. Questo è *Splendid*, caffè *Splendid*, che costa mille e sette, due etti, macinato, confezione in lattina.
Giovanni È buono?
Droghiera Sì, sì, è speciale. Questo è superiore al *Suerte*.
Giovanni Costa di più?
Droghiera Costa mille e sette.
Giovanni E il *Suerte* quanto costa, ha detto?
Droghiera Mille e sei.
Giovanni Ah, mille e sei. Quindi questo costa cento lire di più.
Droghiera Cento lire in più lo *Splendid*. Poi c'è ancora in lattina un caffè speciale, *Lavazza 'Oro'*, due etti, macinato, e quello costa duemila e seicento. È un caffè superiore.
Giovanni E tipo *Nescafé*?
Droghiera *Nescafé* c'è *Grand'Aroma*, che costa settecento lire. Sono bustine, da dieci grammi ogni bustina, sono dieci bustine. E poi c'è *Faemino 'Tranquillo'*, settecento lire. Sono pure dieci bustine. E poi c'è in vasetto, vasetto in vetro *Grand'Aroma*, duemila.
Giovanni Signora, io prendo un pacchetto di *Splendid*, allora.
Droghiera Grazie.

droghiera grocer (woman)
Suerte, Splendid, Lavazza 'Oro', Nescafé 'Grand'Aroma', Faemino 'Tranquillo' brands of coffee and instant coffee
➧ **pacchettino** a small packet (**pacco→pacchetto→pacchettino**)
sottovuoto vacuum packed (lit. under vacuum)
➧ **macinato** ground (from **macinare**, to grind)
ha detto? did you say?
bustine sachets (lit. small envelopes)
pure also
➧ **vasetto** jar, small pot (**vaso→vasetto**)
di vetro (of) glass

4 *In a fashion shop the assistant describes the colour range to a customer, who is not sure whether to buy separates or a dress*

Commessa Queste esistono anche in altri colori, se non le piace questa tinta qui: giallo, rosa e viola. Sono rimaste soltanto colorate, ma il bianco è finito. Non so se il tessuto le piace più o meno. Ci sono altri colori e altri modelli. Invece in questo qua; signora, no. Il modello è classico e cambia soltanto la tinta.
Signora Ho capito.
Commessa Centrotrentamila, questo.

queste (camicette) these (blouses)
esistono exist (from **esistere**)
tessuto material
modelli styles
invece on the other hand
ho capito I see (lit. I have understood)

3 **vorrei . . .** I'd like . . . This is a form of **volere** to want; you use it when asking for things, e.g. **vorrei una camera** I'd like a room, **vorrei partire questa sera** I'd like to leave tonight, **vorrei telefonare** I'd like to 'phone, etc. (See also Unit 14.)

confezione in lattina packed in a tin. 'Tin' is also **latta. Confezionare** has the general meaning of 'to prepare things for sale; hence the various possible uses of **confezione** meaning, e.g. ready-made clothes, as in **confezioni maschili** (a shop sign corresponding to gentlemen's outfitters), or packaging, as in **confezione regalo** gift-wrapped.

due etti 200 grams. In Italy weights are reckoned in **chili** (**un chilo** being just over 2 lbs), **etti** (100 grams, or about 3½ ounces) and **grammi**. The 10 gram sachets of instant coffee weigh about 1/3 ounce each.

è buono? is it good? **è di buona qualità?** is it (of) good quality? **costa di più?** does it cost more? These are some of the questions you may like to ask shopkeepers. And here are some possible replies:
è speciale it's special: **è superiore all'altro tipo** it's better than the other type; **costa cento lire di più** (or **in più**) it costs 100 lira more; **costa cento lire di meno** (or **in meno**) it costs 100 lira less.

4 **colore** colour; **tinta** colour (i.e. shade or hue). The Italian names for colours fall into two categories: those whose endings change just like those regular adjectives: **bianco** white, **giallo** yellow, **rosso** red, **verde** green, **nero** black, e.g. **la casa bianca** the white house, **i campi verdi** the green fields; and those that are invariable (because they are in origin names of flowers or fruits): **rosa** pink, **viola** violet, **arancio** orange (also **arancione**), **marrone** brown; and **blu** blue (which like all monosyllables is invariable), e.g. **un vestito rosa** a pink dress, **scarpe marrone** brown shoes.

se non le piace . . . if you don't like . . . **Non so se . . . le piace**. I don't know if you like . . . From **piacere** to please, which in Italian is used to mean 'to like' (see *Grammar* p. 115).

sono rimaste soltanto colorate there are only coloured ones left.

è finito is out of stock (lit. finished). **Sono finiti** they're out of stock.

5 *Another shop assistant helps an undecided customer*

Commessa È molto bella anche questa. È un classico, insomma.
Cliente Gonna e . . .
Commessa Gonna e camicetta; quindi è come un abito. Il colore sta molto bene, eh?

gonna skirt

6 *In a perfumery the assistant compares two perfumes*

Commessa Questa è una lavanda, non è nemmeno una colonia: è una lavanda. Senta un attimo, eh? Questa è più leggera come profumazione eh? . . . A me come profumo piace più la colonia della lavanda: è meno persistente, meno noioso . . .
Cliente Queste quanto vengono?
Commessa Lo stesso: settemilacinque, signora, anche quella. Settemilacinque, poi facciamo sempre un pochino di sconto: settemila. Altrimenti qualcosa di più dolce, anche, meno classico, più profumo. Può andare, guardi, questo. Questo è un pochino più dolce.

lavanda lavender (water)
profumazione (f.) type of scent
persistente long lasting
noioso annoying (*sometimes* boring, dull)
altrimenti otherwise
dolce sweet
più profumo more of a perfume, more like a perfume

5 ◆ **è come un abito** it's like a dress. **Come** is used in comparisons: **è bella come quella** it's as nice as the other one; **è leggero come seta** it's as light as silk; **questo profumo non è buono come quello** this perfume is not as good as that one.

◆ **sta molto bene** suits (you) very well. This is similar to **va bene** but it's more frequently used when speaking of clothes and can also mean 'it fits' **(le) sta molto bene** it fits (you) very well; **mi stanno bene?** do they fit me? **stanno benissimo l'una e l'altra** they both fit you perfectly.

Here are some more useful phrases and vocabulary for buying clothes:

◆ **taglia** size; **che taglia ha?**
◆ **portare** to wear; **porto la quaranta** I take size 40
◆ **provare** to try on; **posso provare**? can I try it on?

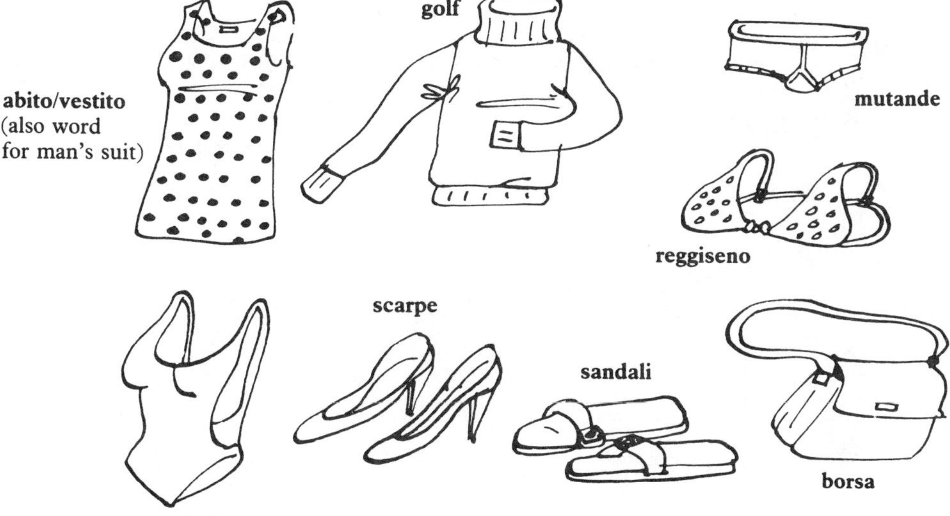

6 **non è nemmeno una colonia** it's not even a cologne. Other examples of this phrase: **non è nemmeno caro** it's not even dear; **non mi sta nemmeno bene** it doesn't even fit/suit me; **non voglio nemmeno questo** I don't want this either.

◆ **a me piace** (or **mi piace**) **più la colonia della lavanda** I like cologne better than lavender. In most comparisons 'than' is **del** (**dello, della** etc.), e.g. **questa gonna mi va meglio dell'altra** this skirt fits me better than the other one; **il caffè *Suerte* costa meno dello *Splendid*** *Suerte* coffee costs less than *Splendid*.

◆ **poi facciamo sempre un pochino di sconto** then we always give (you) a little discount. You may wish to use this expression yourself: **mi fa un poco (→pochino→pochettino) di sconto?** will you give me a little discount?

può andare, guardi, questo look, this one is all right (lit. can go).

Key words and phrases

To learn

che tipo ha? che tipi ha?	what kind do you have?
che gusti ha?	what flavours do you stock?
che tipo di . . . consiglia?	what kind of . . . do you advise?
vorrei . . .	I'd like . . .
un vasetto di marmellata	a pot of jam
un pacchetto di caffè	a packet of coffee
una lattina di sardine	a tin of sardines
è buono? è di buona qualità?	is it good? is it good quality?
(questa marmellata) è buona come quella?	is (this jam) as good as that one?
costa di più o di meno?	does it cost more or less?
porto la (quaranta)	I take size (40)
posso provare?	can I try it on?
sta bene, mi sta bene	it fits, it fits me
questa, camicetta mi sta meglio dell'altra	this blouse fits me better than the other one
mi piace	I like it
(questo profumo) mi piace di più	I like (this perfume) best/better
mi fa un pochino di sconto?	will you give me a little discount?

Colours (colori)

bianco	white
nero	black
marrone	brown
blu	blue
verde	green
giallo	yellow
arancio(ne)	orange
rosso	red
rosa	pink
viola	violet

To understand

in pacchetto	in a packet
in lattina/latta	in a tin
in vasetto	in a small pot
macinato	ground
è speciale	it's special
è superiore	it's better quality
le piace?	do you like it?
non le piace?	don't you like it?
è finito/sono finiti	it's/they're out of stock
che taglia ha?	what's your size?
dipende	it depends

Practise what you have learnt

1 Listen to the grocer's wife telling Giovanni about the jams she has in stock, and answer the following questions. (Answers p. 118.)

a. What types of jam does she stock?
- ☐ chestnut
- ☐ mango
- ☐ cherry
- ☐ peach
- ☐ fig

b. How much does a jar cost?
- ☐ 1100 lire
- ☐ 1010 lire
- ☐ 1110 lire

c. What jam does Giovanni buy?
- ☐ fig
- ☐ chestnut

2 Fill in the grid below with the information on the packaging, weight (**peso**) and cost (**prezzo**) of the various kinds of coffee mentioned in dialogue 3. Refer back to it either on p. 108 or on tape: this is not a memory exercise. Some boxes are already filled in to help you.

Tipo	**caffè macinato**					
Marca	Suerte	Splendid	Lavazza 'Oro'	Nescafé 'Grand'Aroma'		Faemino 'Tranquillo'
Confezione	pacchetto				vasetto	
Peso			200 g.		/	
Prezzo		L.1700				

And now, referring to the grid above, complete the following sentences, using the words in the box below (each once), as appropriate. Then listen to the tape where you will hear the correct sentences.

a. Il caffè *Splendid* è meno .... del caffè *Suerte*.

b. Il caffè *Suerte* è meno .... del *Lavazza 'Oro'*.

c. Il caffè *Suerte* è confezionato in pacchetti da 200 grammi

.... il caffè *Splendid*.

d. Il *Nescafé 'Grand'Aroma'* in bustine .... come il *Faemino 'Tranquillo'*.

e. Il caffè .... caro di tutti è il *Lavazza 'Oro'*.

costa	più	economico	caro	come

3 You are in a grocer's shop and wish to buy several things. Fill in the dialogue with the missing words jumbled below and check by listening to the complete dialogue on tape.

Droghiere Buon giorno.

Cliente Un .... di marmellata, per favore.

Droghiere .... la vuole?

Cliente Di ....

Droghiere .... signorina. Altro?

Cliente Sì. .... di spaghetti, e poi del

....

Droghiere Che .... di caffè?

Cliente ....

Droghiere Abbiamo questa confezione in .... da 250 grammi, qualità ....

Cliente Va bene. Me .... da uno. Quanto ....?

Droghiere Marmellata mille e cinque, spaghetti mille e quattro e cinquanta, caffè ...., viene .... in tutto.

duemila e due · ecco · cinquemila cento e cinquanta · pacchetti · un chilo · vasetto · macinato · tipo · come · superiore · vengono · caffè · ciliegie · ne

4 Gina wants to buy some other things at the grocer's. Listen to her reading out her shopping list on tape and see if you can label the groceries in the pictures below with their Italian name. (Answers p. 118.)

a. .... b. .... c. ....

d. .... e. .... f. ....

Grammar

All the grammar notes in this unit concern verbs.

Past participle

This is the name of the verb form which, both in Italian and in English, can be used as an adjective (as in *ground* coffee, from 'to grind'; or *sliced* ham, from 'to slice'). Italian past participles belong to two groups:

- verbs ending in **-are** and **-ire** form the past participle by replacing **-re** in their ending with **-to** (or **-ta**, **-ti**, **-te**)
  affettare to slice **affettato** sliced
  capire to understand **capito** understood
- some past participles, however (a few from **-are** and **-ire** verbs and all those from **-ere** verbs) cannot be easily formed from their **-re** ending. These will be given when necessary. Here are a few to begin with:

avere to have **avuto** had
dire to say **detto** said
fare to do, to make **fatto** made
prendere to take **preso** taken

Present tense of most verbs in -ire

Only a small number of verbs in **-ire** is conjugated like **partire** and **dormire** (Unit 6). Some have **-isc-** in the middle. When an **-ire** verb is introduced we'll tell you whether it is conjugated like **partire** (Unit 6) or like **finire** (see below).

finisco I finish
finisci you finish
finisce you (polite) finish
he/she finishes
finiamo we finish
finite you (pl.) finish
finiscono they finish

Capire (to understand) is conjugated like **finire** above. Can you work out its present tense? Write it on a piece of paper and then check it on p. 118.

How to say 'I like'

There is *no* Italian verb meaning 'to like'. Italians use **piacere** meaning 'to please'.

Therefore in order to say 'I like coffee', 'I like spaghetti', you have to say 'coffee pleases me' **il caffè mi piace**; 'spaghetti pleases me' **gli spaghetti mi piacciono**. Only two forms of this verb, **piace** (sing.) and **piacciono** (pl.) are therefore usually needed. When asking questions you say:

ti piace il tè? do you (informal) like tea? (lit. to you pleases tea?)
le piace il tè? do you (polite) like tea?
ti piacciono i pomodori? do you like tomatoes? (lit. to you please tomatoes?)
vi piace viaggiare? do you (pl.) like travelling? (lit. to you pleases travelling?)

Note that **mi dispiace** which you have already met in Unit 3 does *not* mean 'I dislike' but 'I'm sorry, I regret' (though the verb **dispiacere** is conjugated like **piacere**). To say 'I don't like' you say **non mi piace**.

Read and understand

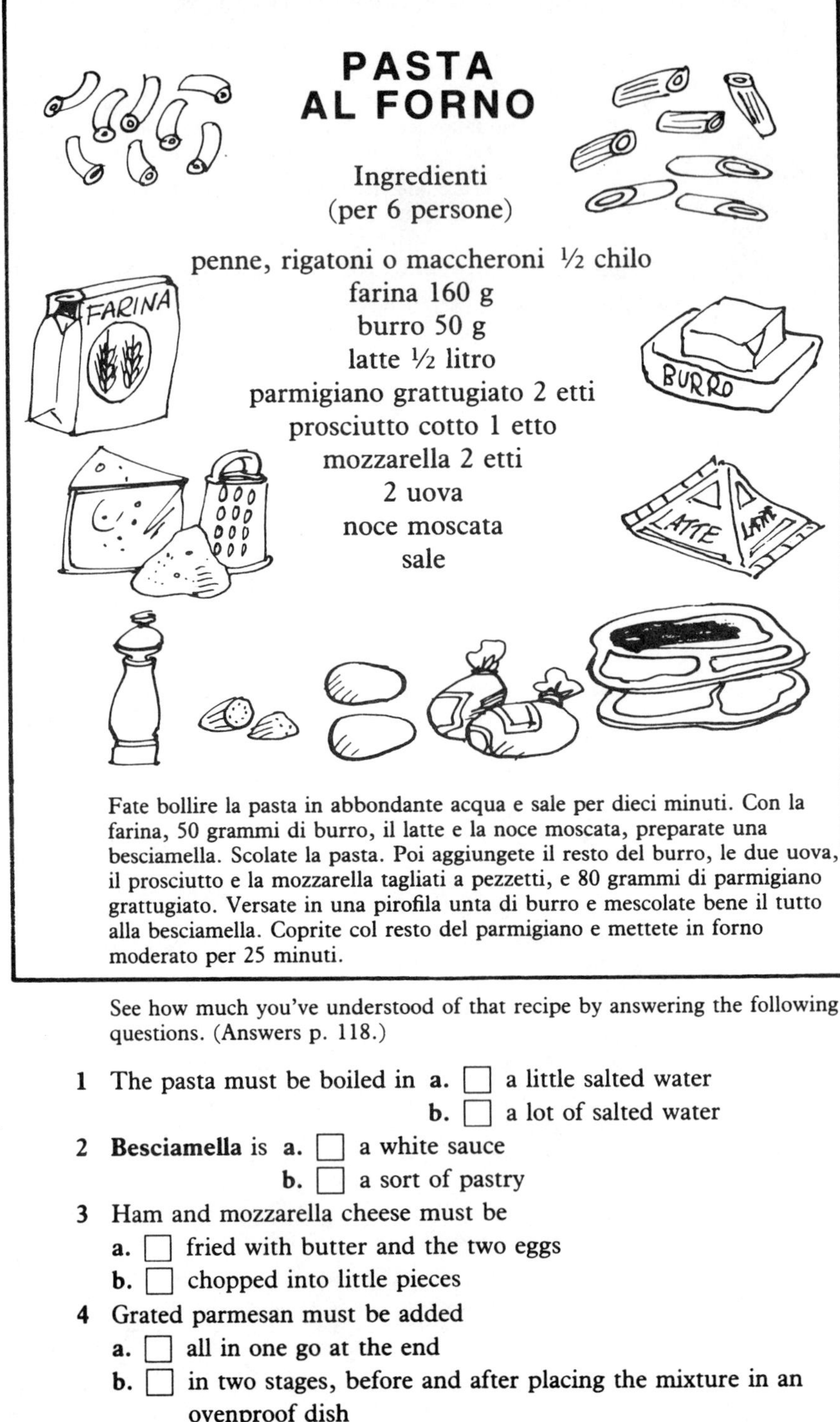

PASTA AL FORNO

Ingredienti
(per 6 persone)

penne, rigatoni o maccheroni ½ chilo
farina 160 g
burro 50 g
latte ½ litro
parmigiano grattugiato 2 etti
prosciutto cotto 1 etto
mozzarella 2 etti
2 uova
noce moscata
sale

Fate bollire la pasta in abbondante acqua e sale per dieci minuti. Con la farina, 50 grammi di burro, il latte e la noce moscata, preparate una besciamella. Scolate la pasta. Poi aggiungete il resto del burro, le due uova, il prosciutto e la mozzarella tagliati a pezzetti, e 80 grammi di parmigiano grattugiato. Versate in una pirofila unta di burro e mescolate bene il tutto alla besciamella. Coprite col resto del parmigiano e mettete in forno moderato per 25 minuti.

See how much you've understood of that recipe by answering the following questions. (Answers p. 118.)

1 The pasta must be boiled in **a.** ☐ a little salted water
b. ☐ a lot of salted water

2 **Besciamella** is **a.** ☐ a white sauce
b. ☐ a sort of pastry

3 Ham and mozzarella cheese must be
a. ☐ fried with butter and the two eggs
b. ☐ chopped into little pieces

4 Grated parmesan must be added
a. ☐ all in one go at the end
b. ☐ in two stages, before and after placing the mixture in an ovenproof dish

Did you know?

The metric system

In Italy, as in all countries of continental Europe, the metric system is used. It was devised in 1791 to end the absurd situation of almost every town or region having its own system of weights and measures often incompatible with those of neighbouring areas. The metric system became standard in France in 1801 and was adopted internationally in 1875.

The more commonly used units are the following:

Length **chilometro** (1000 metres), **metro, centimetro** (1/100 of metre)
Area **ettaro** (100 square metres), **metro quadrato** (square metre)
Volume for solids: **metro cubo, centimetro cubo** (one millionth of a cubic metre); for liquids: **litro** (1000 cc)
Weight **tonnellata** (metric ton = 1000 kilos), **quintale** (100 kilos), **chilo, etto** (1/10th of a kilo = 100 grams), **grammo** (1/1000th of a kilo).

Pasta

It is thought that pasta may have been imported into Western Europe and Italy from the Far East at the time of Marco Polo's journey (end of 13th century) or even earlier. **Maccheroni** and **ravioli**, seasoned with parmesan cheese, are mentioned in a story by Boccaccio (14th century). Nowadays there are hundreds of different varieties of pasta in all shapes and sizes.

They fall into five main types:

small pasta (**pastina**), as small as rice grains, shaped like stars, alphabet letters, squares, triangles etc., to be used in soups or cooked in meat or vegetable stock (in which case it is called **pasta in brodo, pastina in brodo**);
string-shaped pasta called, in decreasing order of thickness, **vermicelli, spaghetti, spaghettini, capelli d'angelo** (angel's hair);
ribbon-shaped pasta called, in decreasing order of width, **lasagne, tagliatelle, fettuccine, fresine, bavette;**
tube-shaped pasta of which the basic varieties are **cannelloni, maccheroni, rigatoni** and **penne** (with a slanted cut);
stuffed pasta of various shapes, such as **ravioli** (square), **agnolotti** (half circle), **cappelletti** (hat-shaped) and **tortellini** (ring-shaped);
frilly and fancy shaped pasta like **farfalle** and **farfallette** (butterfly-shaped), **fusilli** (coil-shaped), **conchiglie** and **conchigliette** (pasta shells).

Home-made pasta can be bought in a special shop called a **PASTIFICIO**. You can often watch it being made on the premises. Be careful when cooking home-made pasta as it is ready in a flash.

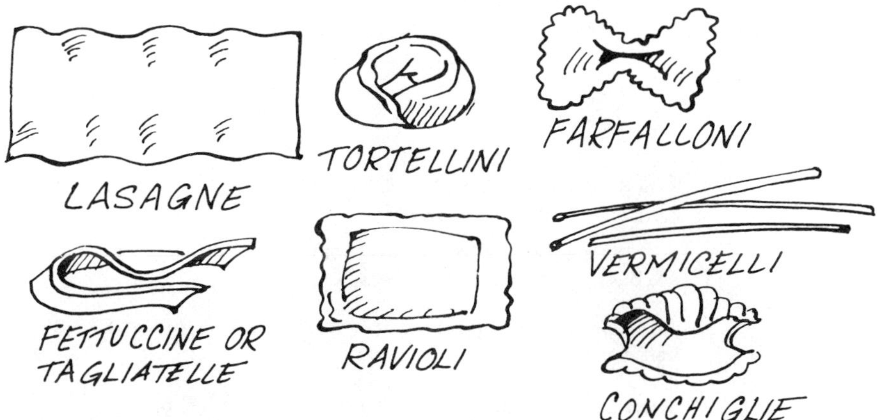

Your turn to speak

1 First you're going shopping in a grocer's, you want to buy some ingredients for **pasta al forno**. Whenever you use weights, remember that 100 grams = **un etto**.

2 This time you're in a **PROFUMERIA**, buying perfume to take home as a present. It's quite expensive so you try to get a discount.

Answers

Practise what you have learnt p. 113 Exercise **1** (**a**) chestnut, cherry and peach (**b**) 1100 lire (**c**) chestnut.

p. 114 Exercise **4** (**a**) burro (**b**) pomodori (**c**) formaggio parmigiano (**d**) biscotti (**e**) salamino (**f**) sardine.

Grammar p. 115 **capire**: capisco, capisci, capisce, capiamo, capite, capiscono.

Read and understand p. 116 (**1**) b (**2**) a (**3**) b (**4**) b.
scolare = to drain; **una pirofila unta** = greased ovenproof dish.

9 *Due, seconda, andata e ritorno*

What you will learn

- how to buy railway tickets
- how to ask for and understand information about train journeys
- more ways of saying 'one needs . . .', 'one must . . .'
- how to form adverbs from adjectives

Before you begin

Points to remember from Unit 8:

1 verbs
finire to finish
finisco, finisci, finisce, finiamo, finite, finiscono
preferire, to prefer, is conjugated like **finire**

2 how to say: 'I like'
mi piace il vino bianco
mi piacciono le lasagne

3 past participle
verbs in **-are** **comprare** > **comprato, -a, -i, -e**
verbs in **-ire** **capire** > **capito, -a, -i, -e**

4 comparisons **questa marmellata è più buona di quella**
questo vino è migliore di quello
questo modello è elegante come quello

Study guide

	Dialogues 1, 2: listen straight through without the book
	Dialogues 1, 2: listen, read and study one by one
	Dialogues 3, 4: listen straight through without the book
	Dialogues 3, 4: listen, read and study one by one
	Dialogues 5, 6: listen straight through without the book
	Dialogues 5, 6: listen, read and study one by one
	Learn the *Key words and phrases*
	Do the exercises in *Practise what you have learnt*
	Study *Grammar* and do the exercises
	Read *Did you know?* (this time before *Read and understand*)
	Do *Read and understand*
	Do the tape exercises in *Your turn to speak*
	Listen to all the dialogues again without the book
	Do the *Revision* exercises for Units 6–9 on p. 221

Dialogues

1 *Two travellers buy tickets for Livorno at the ticket office of Pisa railway station*

Viaggiatore Livorno!
Impiegato Solo andata?
Viaggiatore Andata e ritorno.
Impiegato Cento lire le avete per favore?
Viaggiatore Cento? No.

2º Viaggiatore Due andata e ritorno Livorno.
Impiegato Due?
2º Viaggiatore Sì.

solo only

2 *Two travellers ask for tickets to La Spezia*

Viaggiatrice Due per La Spezia, andata, seconda. Finisce alla Spezia?
Impiegato Finisce alla Spezia.

3º Viaggiatore La Spezia, andata e ritorno.
Impiegato Tremiladuecento.

3 *At the information office a woman asks how to get to Susa*

Signora Mi scusi, devo andare a Susa. . .
Impiegato Undici e quarantacinque treno per Modane, binario dodici, cambia a Bussoleno per Susa.
Signora Mm. Non si può andare direttamente?
Impiegato Sì, c'è un treno locale alle dodici e cinquanta.
Signora E che binario?
Impiegato Binario tredici.
Signora Ah va bene, binario tredici, grazie.

Modane name of station (on Italian-French border)

1 ♦ **Livorno!** You could use a more complete sentence, such as **mi da un biglietto per Livorno** can you give me a ticket for Livorno, but in fact many intending travellers simply say the name of the station they want to go to.

♦ **andata** one way (from **andare**). A return ticket is **andata e ritorno**.

♦ **due . . . Livorno** If you want more than one ticket begin your request with the number of tickets you want, i.e. the number of persons travelling (you may be issued one ticket for all of them).

2 ♦ **seconda** second class; if you don't specify the class, it will be assumed that's what you want. Otherwise say: **prima**.

♦ **finisce alla Spezia?** does (the train) terminate at La Spezia? You might also want to ask: **ferma a Genova?** does it stop at Genoa?

3 **devo andare a Susa. . .** I've got to go to Susa.

♦ **cambia a Bussoleno per Susa** you change at Bussoleno for Susa. If you want to know whether you must change, you can ask: **devo cambiare?** (see also next dialogue).

♦ **non si può andare direttamente?** can't I (lit. one) go directly? (i.e. without changing).

4 *Giovanni asks the information office clerk how to go to Siena*

Giovanni Vorrei andare a Siena.
Impiegato Per Siena, verso che ora?
Giovanni Nel pomeriggio.
Impiegato Ecco, ci sarebbe un treno alle quattordici e quarantacinque.
Giovanni A che ora arrivo a Empoli?
Impiegato A Empoli arriva alle quindici e diciannove.
Giovanni A Empoli bisogna cambiare: e a che ora ho la coincidenza?
Impiegato La coincidenza ce l'ha alle quindici e cinquantanove, e a Siena arriva alle diciassette e tredici.
Giovanni Molte grazie.
Impiegato Prego.

coincidenza connection

5 *Giovanni asks the information office clerk about the types of train used in the Italian Railway system*

Giovanni Che tipi di treno viaggiano sulle ferrovie italiane?
Impiegato Abbiamo treni rapidi, treni espressi, diretti e locali.
Giovanni Per viaggiare sui rapidi ci vuole un supplemento?
Impiegato Per viaggiare sui rapidi ci vuole un supplemento. Ci sono rapidi ordinari dove basta solo il supplemento, e rapidi speciali dove, oltre al supplemento normale, ci vuole anche la prenotazione del posto.
Giovanni E questa prenotazione si fa all'atto dell'acquisto del biglietto?
Impiegato Si fa all'atto dell'acquisto del biglietto. Possibilmente farlo qualche giorno prima.

viaggiano travel (from **viaggiare**, to travel)
oltre, -a besides
all'atto dell'acquisto at the time (lit. on the act) of purchase
possibilmente possibly
farlo (one should) do it

6 *You really need very few words to book a ticket, if you let the booking clerk do all the talking!*

Impiegato Partenza quando?
Signorina Oggi.
Impiegato Seconda classe?
Signorina Sì.
Impiegato Una persona?
Signorina Sì.
Impiegato Valido cinque giorni. Ordinario. Diciannovemila e duecento.

valido valid

4 ➧ **verso che ora?** about what time? Or remember **a che ora?** at what time? If you don't want to be too specific in your reply say **verso le due**, about two o'clock, **verso le tre** etc.

ci sarebbe un treno . . . lit. there should be a train, but the clerk does not imply that he is uncertain, merely that Giovanni *could* take that train.

➧ **bisogna cambiare** you (one) must change. **Bisognare** is one of a number of verbs used only in the 3rd person. It is equivalent to **si deve**. Other examples: **bisogna partire alle tre** you (one) must leave at three; **non bisogna prendere il treno delle 12, 03 se si vuole andare direttamente** you must not take the 12.03 train if you want to travel on a through train. (See also *Grammar* p. 127.)

la coincidenza ce l'ha . . . you have the connection at . . . This is the same as **ha la coincidenza**. When the object is placed for emphasis *before* the verb in Italian, the appropriate form of **lo**, **la**, **li**, **le** must be added: **il caffè lo prende?** (= **prende il caffè?**); **il viola lo porta molto bene** (= **porta il viola molto bene**); **le vacanze le facciamo in Italia** (= **facciamo le vacanze in Italia**) we take our holidays in Italy.

5 **che tipi di treno?** what types of train? You should already be familiar with the four types of train from Unit 2.

➧ **ci vuole un supplemento** a surcharge is payable (lit. it is necessary a supplement). **Ci vuole . . . ci vogliono . . .** and **basta . . . bastano . . .** are used only in the 3rd person: **ci vogliono due ore per andare alla Spezia** it takes two hours to go to La Spezia; **basta solo il supplemento** only the surcharge is needed; **bastano mille lire** a thousand lire is enough. (See also *Grammar* p. 127.)

la prenotazione del posto seat reservation; **prenotare** to book; **posti prenotati** reserved seats.

6 **ordinario** ordinary. Other types of ticket are **ridotto** or **biglietto a riduzione** reduced price (e.g. for children); **festivo** issued on Sundays and holidays; **familiare** for families travelling together; **circolare** round trip (i.e. returning through a different route). See also *Did you know?* p. 129.

Key words and phrases

To learn

Livorno, (solo) andata	(just) a single to Livorno
andata e ritorno	a return
due andata e ritorno	two returns
seconda	second (class)
prima	first (class)
vorrei andare a . . .	I'd like to go to . . .
direttamente	on a through train
verso le (quattordici)	around (two) p.m.
devo cambiare?	do I have to change?
il treno ferma a . . . ?	does the train stop at . . . ?
questo treno finisce a . . . ?	does this train terminate at . . . ?
c'è la coincidenza?	is there a connection?
a che ora ho la coincidenza?	at what time do I have a connection?
ci vuole il supplemento?	does one/do you need to pay a surcharge?
ci vuole la prenotazione?	does one/do you need a reserved seat?

To understand

bisogna cambiare a . . .	one/you must change at . . .
prende il treno dopo	you take the next train
basta solo il supplemento	you only need a surcharge
ci vuole anche la prenotazione	you also need a reserved seat
il biglietto è valido cinque giorni	the ticket is valid for five days

Practise what you have learnt

1 Listen to the four people on tape booking their train tickets, then answer the following questions. (Answers p. 132.)

a. Which travellers book a return ticket?
- ☐ the 1st and 3rd
- ☐ the 2nd and 4th

b. How much does a return ticket to Pontedera cost?
- ☐ 600 lire
- ☐ 800 lire
- ☐ we are not told

c. Which traveller asks for more than one ticket?
- ☐ the one going to Florence
- ☐ the one going to Livorno

2 Listen to an information office clerk giving information to a woman wishing to travel from Pontedera to Santo Stefano di Magra, and answer the following questions. (Answers p. 132.)

a. When does the woman wish to travel?
- ☐ the same day in the afternoon
- ☐ the next day in the afternoon

b. Is there a through train?
- ☐ yes, in the morning
- ☐ no

c. How long is the shortest journey?
- ☐ 1 hour 45 minutes
- ☐ 2 hrs 15 mins
- ☐ 2 hrs 18 mins

d. Travelling at the time she eventually decides, how often will she have to change?
- ☐ once
- ☐ twice

e. Will she complete the journey by train?
- ☐ yes
- ☐ no, by a connecting bus service

3 Select the correct answers to the questions from the phrases in the box below to complete the dialogue. Then check your version on tape.

Impiegato Per quando il biglietto?

Viaggiatore ....

Impiegato Andata e ritorno?

Viaggiatore ....

Impiegato Per quante persone?

Viaggiatore ....

Impiegato Che classe?

Viaggiatore ....

Impiegato Duemila seicento. Cento lire le ha?

Viaggiatore ....

Impiegato Ecco quattro di resto

Viaggiatore ....

Solo andata **Grazie** **No** **Per dopodomani** **Seconda** **Due**

4 Fill in the puzzle, using the sentences below as clues. (Most of the words can be found in the *Key words and phrases*.) (Answers p. 132.)

1. Il treno delle 14 —— a Pontedera? (5)
2. Tre andata e —— per Roma, per piacere. (7)
3. Per Roma deve —— a Firenze, c'è la coincidenza. (8)
4. Ritorna oggi? – No, no, ovoglio solo ——. (6)
5. Per la —— classe ci vuole la prenotazione sul rapido speciale. (5)
6. Che tipo di treno è? (8)
7. Che classe? —— per piacere. (7)

Grammar

Third person phrases

In a large number of commonly used phrases, the verbs are used only in the third person:

basta . . . **basta cambiare una volta** it's enough to change once
bisogna . . . **bisogna pagare un supplemento** it's necessary to pay a surcharge
ci vuole . . . **ci vuole la prenotazione** you need a reserved seat
mi piace . . . **mi piace il treno rapido** I like the fast train

The third person is singular or plural according to what it refers to. (Infinitives are treated as singulars.) Study these examples:

mi piace viaggiare in treno I like travelling by train (lit. travelling by train pleases me)
le pizze mi piacciono molto I like pizzas very much (lit. pizzas please me very much)
ci vuole più tempo one needs more time (more time is required)
ci vogliono tre ore it takes three hours (three hours are required)

Exercise 1 Complete the following sentences with the appropriate third person expression chosen from the box below. (Answers p. 132.)

a. Nella pasta al forno .... la besciamella.
b. Si può andare da Pontedera a Santo Stefano senza cambiare, ma .... partire la mattina.
c. I vini italiani .... molto.
d. Per viaggiare in questo rapido speciale .... il supplemento e la prenotazione.
e. Questa gonna verde è bella ma quella rossa .... di più.
f. Vuole provare un'altra camicetta? – No, grazie .... questa.

basta	bisogna	mi piace	ci vogliono	ci vuole	mi piacciono

Adverbs

You have already come across several adverbs. They are those invariable words usually linked to adjectives (**molto buono** very good) or verbs (**andare direttamente a . . .** to go straight to . . .). They belong to two main categories: (cont. on p. 128).

- adverbs which are, or look like, the masculine or common form of adjectives:
  queste sigarette sono <u>piuttosto</u> forti these cigarettes are rather strong
  sono rimaste <u>solo</u> colorate only coloured ones are left
- adverbs ending in **-mente**. This ending is added to the feminine or common form of the adjective:
  eccessivo → eccessivamente
  non è eccessivamente caro it's not excessively expensive
  frequente → frequentemente
  vado a Siena frequentemente I go to Siena frequently

  Adjectives ending in **-le** or **-re** drop the final **-e** before adding **-mente**:
  possibile → possibilmente
  possibilmente prenotarsi qualche giorno prima
  normale → normalmente
  normalmente questo treno parte alle tre

Exercise 2 Fill in the gaps with a suitable adverb formed from the adjectives in the box below. (Answers p. 132.)

a. .... bisogna cambiare a Empoli, ma con questo treno non è necessario.

b. Voglio andare .... a Bagni di Lucca.

c. Con questo treno espresso si viaggia più ....

d. *Il Telegrafo* non è un giornale nazionale. Si pubblica .... a Livorno.

e. Il caffè mi piace .... a colazione.

rapido	ordinario	locale	speciale	diretto

Did you know?

Where to get information

Before you go to Italy you will, of course, consult your travel agent, but they may not know all the detailed local information you may wish to have. Here are some useful addresses:

ENIT (Italian State Tourist Office) 201 Regent St, London W1R 8AY; 47 Merrion Sq., Dublin 2.

Alitalia (Italian national airline) 251 Regent St, London W1.

It's also a good idea to write direct to Italy. In every province there is an **Ente Provinciale del Turismo**. Holiday resorts with a lot of tourists may also have an **Azienda Autonoma di Soggiorno**: both are tourist offices with particular interest in travel, sightseeing and accommodation in their specific area (addresses available from **ENIT**). They will advise you about the opening times of museums, etc.; send you lists of addresses of hotels and boarding houses with recommended prices, and often provide you with timetables of local bus services which never seem to find their way to tourist offices and travel agents abroad.

In large towns your hotel will provide you with free weekly handouts of the *What's on* type, detailing the main events (concerts, theatres, cinemas, exhibitions etc.). Similar information will be displayed on posters and flysheets on street corners, and advertised in the local papers, or in the local editions of the national papers.

Public telephones

You can telephone in most hotels either from your room or from telephone booths near the reception: in both cases the cost will be debited to your account.

It is usually cheaper to use a public payphone. Look out for the sign of a yellow disc with a telephone handset (see below). The words **TELESELEZIONE** or **INTERURBANO AUTOMATICO** mean that you can make trunk calls (not all public telephones have this facility).

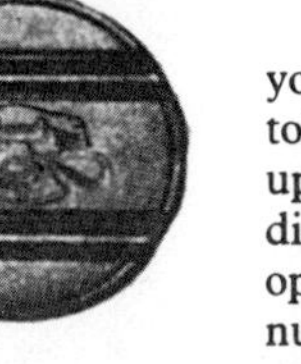

Most public telephones take special **gettoni** or telephone tokens, which you can get from kiosks, bars and a few automatic dispensers. You put the tokens in before dialling. Any unused tokens are returned when you hang up. At least, that's the theory. In practice it is not unknown for tokens to disappear without a connection being made. It's no good appealing to the operator (**centralino**), you will not be connected without payment. A number of new push-button telephones are available in mainline stations and other public places. Some take coins, and some take magnetic cards which can be bought from the **Ufficio dei Telefoni**, and from some newspaper kiosks in main stations.

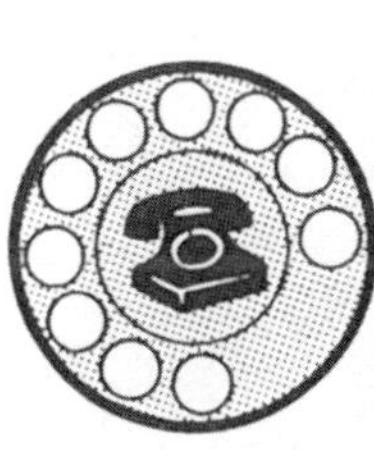

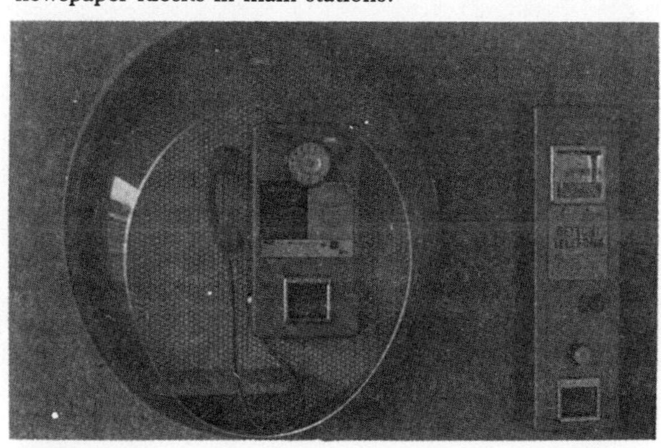

Read and understand

There are many kinds of railway tickets, of various colours, shapes and sizes, but here you have two of a type issued by computerized booking offices. The illustrations opposite are face and reverse side of the same ticket: the one below is the face of a different ticket. Both tickets refer to the same journey. Examine them carefully, and see how many of the following questions you can answer. (Answers p. 132.)

1. Where were the tickets issued? ....
2. What was the destination? ....
3. Give the date of the journey, the number and time of the train.

   ....
4. How many people were travelling? ....
5. In what class? ....
6. The ticket opposite was issued not for the whole journey but for a specific purpose, identified by the abbreviation CC. What was it for? ....
7. What was the ticket below for? ....
8. Knowing that the ticket below was compulsory for that journey, what was the type of train used? ....

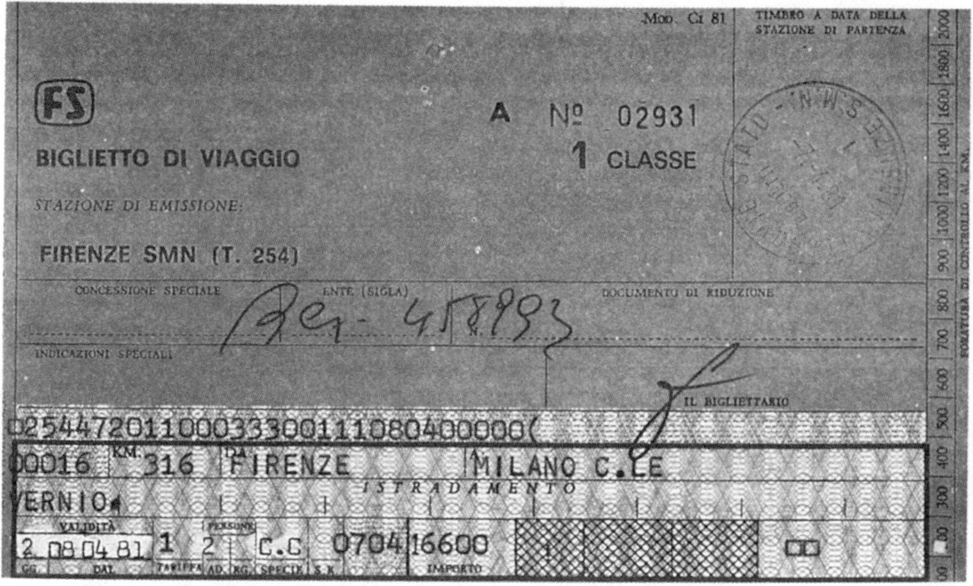

MOD. Ci 81

TIMBRO A DATA DELLA STAZIONE DI PARTENZA

FS

BIGLIETTO DI VIAGGIO

A N° 02931

1 CLASSE

STAZIONE DI EMISSIONE:

FIRENZE SMN (T. 254)

CONCESSIONE SPECIALE | ENTE (SIGLA) | DOCUMENTO DI RIDUZIONE

INDICAZIONI SPECIALI

IL BIGLIETTARIO

02544720110003330011108040000 0(

00016 | KM. 316 | DA FIRENZE | A MILANO C.LE

ISTRADAMENTO

VERNIO

VALIDITÀ GG.	DAL	TARIFFA	PERSONE AD.	RG.	SPECIE	S.K.	IMPORTO
2	08 04 81	1	2		C.C	0704	16600

FORATURA DI CONTROLLO AL KM.

00 | 200 | 300 | 400 | 500 | 600 | 700 | 800 | 900 | 1000 | 1200 | 1400 | 1600 | 1800 | 2000

AVVERTENZE

I biglietti di corsa semplice rilasciati per viaggi di percorrenza fino a 250 km. scadono alla mezzanotte del giorno di validità, ma consentono al viaggiatore che abbia iniziato il viaggio prima della mezzanotte di proseguirlo fino a destinazione senza fermate intermedie.

La non utilizzazione del biglietto, per avere titolo al rimborso nei casi ammessi, deve essere certificata dal personale di servizio.

Il biglietto deve essere riconsegnato, prima del termine del viaggio, al personale del treno incaricato del ritiro.

SPECIE DEL VIAGGIO

Per i biglietti concessionali, nella casella SPECIE è stampato il numero o la lettera della Concessione.

ABBREVIAZIONI DELLE SPECIE

ORD = Ordinario
LOC = Locale
FAM = Comitiva familiare
FST = Comitiva festiva
T.A = Tessera di autorizzazione
T.M = Trasporti militari
ECC = Concessione eccezionale
SR = Solo supplemento rapido
CON = Congiunzione
C.C. = Cambio di classe
C.T. = Compimento tariffa

Your turn to speak

1 In this first exercise you will be booking tickets, but unlike other exercises in this section, you will not be prompted. The booking-office clerk will ask you some questions (rather like those in dialogue 6) and you will give him the following information:
- you're going with a friend
- you're going to Turin
- you want second-class tickets
- you want a return

2 This time you're booking the same tickets but Marisa will prompt you. You'll then carry on the conversation with the clerk.

3 In this exercise you will be asking for information on train timetables, connections etc., for getting from Milan to Salsomaggiore Spa. Marisa will prompt you as usual.

Revision

Next do the short revision section which goes over the language you have studied in Units 7–9. Turn to p. 221 for the written part of the exercises. There is one tape exercise which follows straight after this unit on your cassette, but read all the instructions on p. 221 before you start it.

Answers

Practise what you have learnt p. 125 Exercise **1** (**a**) the 1st and 3rd (**b**) 800 lire (**c**) the one going to Livorno.

p. 125 Exercise **2** (**a**) the next day in the afternoon (**b**) yes, in the morning (**c**) 1 hour 45 minutes (**d**) twice (**e**) no, by a connecting bus service.

p. 126 Exercise **4** (**1**) FERMA (**2**) RITORNO (**3**) CAMBIARE (**4**) ANDATA (**5**) PRIMA (**6**) ESPRESSO (**7**) SECONDA.

Grammar p. 127 Exercise **1** (**a**) ci vuole (**b**) bisogna (**c**) mi piacciono (**d**) ci vogliono (**e**) mi piace (**f**) basta.

p. 128 Exercise **2** (**a**) ordinariamente (**b**) direttamente (**c**) rapidamente (**d**) localmente (**e**) specialmente.

Read and understand p. 130 (**1**) Florence (**2**) Milan (**3**) 8th April, Train 78, 14h23 (**4**) two (**5**) first (**6**) change of class (**cambio di classe**) (**7**) a seat reservation (**8**) a **rapido**.

10 *Ci abbiamo tante specialità*

What you will learn

- how to order a meal in a restaurant
- the names of the various courses
- the way in which they have been prepared

Before you begin

Points to remember from Unit 9:

1 verbs, used in the third person
bisogna one needs, it's necessary
basta one needs only . . ., it's enough
ci vuole . . . ci vogliono . . . . . . is/are required, it takes . . .
mi piace . . . mi piacciono . . . I like

2 adverbs formed from adjectives (English *-ly* = Italian **-mente**)
vero true **veramente** truly
facile easy **facilmente** easily

3 how to book railway tickets e.g.

number of travellers	*town*	*class*	*single or return*
due	**Pisa**	**seconda**	**andata e ritorno**

NB In this unit, there are a lot of useful words in the notes to the dialogues.

Study guide

	Dialogues 1, 2: listen straight through without the book
	Dialogues 1, 2: listen, read and study one by one
	Dialogues 3–5: listen, straight through without the book
	Dialogues 3–5: listen, read and study one by one
	Dialogues 6, 7: listen straight through without the book
	Dialogues 6, 7: listen, read and study one by one
	Learn the *Key words and phrases*
	Do the exercises in *Practise what you have learnt*
	Study *Grammar* and do the exercise
	Do *Read and understand*
	Read *Did you know?*
	Do the tape exercise in *Your turn to speak*
	Finally, listen to all the dialogues again without the book

Dialogues

1 *The head waiter describes his restaurant's menu to Giovanni. He begins with the first courses*

Giovanni Come primi che cosa avete?
Cameriere Come primi ci sono delle penne da fare . . . come vuole Lei. All'arrabbiata, al ragù, al pomodoro.
Giovanni Come sono all'arrabbiata?
Cameriere Le penne all'arrabbiata sono fatte con sugo di pomodoro, prezzemolo, prezzemolo crudo . . . che dà un buon profumo, e del peperoncino rosso. Vengono molto piccanti.
Giovanni Ah, ecco. No, allora forse no. Non le prendo perché salto il primo.

penne type of pasta (see Unit 8 p. 117)
sugo di pomodoro tomato sauce/juice
prezzemolo parsley
crudo (*here*) fresh, (*normally*) raw
peperoncino chilli
piccante hot, spicy

2 *Next an unusual meat course*

Giovanni Poi come secondo il . . . che cos'è il carpaccio?
Cameriere Carpaccio. Sì. È un . . . piatto di carne cruda tagliata sottile. Carne magrissima dev'essere. Possibilmente filetto.
Giovanni Ah, ecco.
Cameriere Possibilmente. Poi va condita con olio e limone, e pepe, e sopra uno strato di . . . grana. Sfogliettine di grana, capito?
Giovanni Ah, di formaggio parmigiano . . .
Cameriere . . . Formaggio parmigiano.

carne(f.) meat
tagliata sottile sliced thinly (from **tagliare**, to slice)
filetto fillet steak
pepe(m.) pepper
strato layer
sfogliettine flakes

1 ◆ **come primi che cosa avete?** what do you have as first (courses)? The word for 'course', omitted in the Italian question, is **piatto** (which also means dish and plate): **primo piatto** first course (pasta, soup etc.), **secondo piatto** second course.

da fare to be specially prepared (lit. to be made) i.e. not immediately ready (look back at Unit 4, for use of **da** + infinitive). **Pronto, -a** means 'ready'.

all'arrabbiata, al ragù, al pomodoro describe the various ways of preparing **penne**, which in an English menu might be translated as 'hot and spicy', 'bolognaise', 'with tomato sauce'. **Arrabbiato** (from **arrabbiarsi**, to get angry) suggests that the chilli sauce is hot enough to make you rage; **ragù** meat sauce is the Italianization of the French word **ragout**, stew. Methods of preparation are introduced by **a**, e.g. **spaghetti alla carbonara** spaghetti in the coalmen's fashion, **scaloppine al Madera** escalopes in Madeira sauce, etc.

◆ **come sono . . .? come sono fatti/fatte?** how are they prepared? A useful phrase if you wish the waiter to explain an unfamiliar name. In the singular the question would be: **com'è . . .? com'è fatto?**

◆ **salto il primo** I'll skip the first course (from **saltare** to jump): a very useful phrase for weight watchers!

che dà un buon profumo which gives a pleasant odour.

2 **carne magrissima** very lean meat. **Magro**, thin, lean, applies both to steak and to living beings (**una donna molto magra** a very thin woman).

Note that in some cases the word for the animal and its meat is the same in Italian: **vitello** is both 'calf' and 'veal'. Other meats are: **maiale** pig, pork; **pollo** hen, chicken; **manzo** bullock, beef.

dev'essere it should be. **Dev'** is short for **deve** (from **dovere**).

va condita con olio e limone it should be seasoned/dressed with (olive) oil and lemon (juice). This use of **andare** followed by the past participle is very common as a translation of 'must' or 'should': **la pasta va bollita per dieci minuti** pasta should be boiled for ten minutes, **il prosciutto va tagliato sottile** ham must be sliced thinly. Note that the English word 'condiment' has the same origin as **condire.**

grana is another word for parmesan cheese.

3 *The waiter describes a few more second courses*

Cameriere E poi – euh – ci son delle trotelle da fare ai ferri. Poi c'è la *paillard*, la costata, la cotoletta, il nodino! . . .
Giovanni Cos'è la *paillard*?
Cameriere La *paillard* è una bistecca di carne bianca. Dovrebbe essere di vitello, ma molti imbroglioni ci danno anche quella di maiale, perché è più bianca e più saporita. Ah, ah! capito?

trotelle nice little trout (**trota** + **-ella**)
costata rib steak
cotoletta cutlet
bistecca (beef) steak
dovrebbe essere it ought to be
saporita tasty, full of flavour

4 *How do you want your meat cooked?*

Giovanni Come si dice per ordinare la carne . . .?
Cameriere Ben cotta.
Giovanni Ben cotta.
Cameriere Sì. Una costata ben cotta. Una costata poco cotta.
Giovanni Non si dice 'al sangue'?
Cameriere No.
Giovanni Ah ah.
Cameriere Si dice: ben cotta, giusta, poco cotta.
Giovanni Quindi: ben cotta, giusta, poco cotta. Benissimo.

5 *And now for some vegetables to go with the meat*

Cameriere Di verdura cotta abbiamo degli spinaci e dei rapini.
Giovanni Mi fa un misto spinaci e rapini.
Cameriere Sì.
Giovanni Benissimo.
Cameriere Li vuole già saltati o da condire?
Giovanni No, da condire.
Cameriere Con un po' di limone?
Giovanni Con un po' di olio e limone, sì.
Cameriere Va be', grazie.

cotta cooked
spinaci spinach
rapini turnip tops
va be' = va bene

3 ai ferri grilled (lit. on the irons), also **alla griglia**. Other names for the basic ways of preparing food: **al forno** baked; **al vapore** steamed (**vapore** steam); **arrosto** roast(ed); **bollito, -a**, or **lesso, -a** boiled; **fritto, -a** fried; **in umido** stewed; **saltato, -a** sautéed, lightly fried.

paillard veal cutlet. Even in Italy some of the cookery terms are French.

nodino veal loin rolled with fillet and cut into cutlets.

molti imbroglioni ci danno anche quella di maiale a lot of crooks also give us pork (lit. that of pork). **Imbrogliare** = to deceive.

4 **come si dice per ordinare la carne?** what do you say to order meat?

bencotta well done (lit. well cooked);
giusta medium (lit. just right); **poco cotta** rare.

al sangue (lit. with blood) is in fact used in some parts of Italy to mean 'rare' for meat.

5 **la verdura** (from **verde** green) is a general word for vegetables including even a few, like carrots which are by no means green. If you want a salad, ask for **insalata** or **insalata mista** (mixed salad) which normally includes tomatoes. **Verdura** is part of the **contorno** (lit. surround), which is anything placed in your plate beside a main course.

mi fa un misto will you make me a mixture.

li vuole già saltati o da condire? do you want them already lightly fried or ready to dress? **Condire** means 'to season' or 'to dress' for vegetables, salads etc. Vegetables are often dressed with oil and vinegar like salads, or they might be **saltati**, tossed in butter over a low flame.

con un po' di limone with a little lemon. Lemon juice is also used instead of vinegar as a dressing. Remember also **senza**, without: **senza olio** without oil, **senza aglio** without garlic.

6 *Finally a sweet course to round off the meal.*

Giovanni E . . . come dolce che cosa avete?

Cameriere Ci abbiamo tante specialità. La zuppa inglese, prima di tutto. Zuppa inglese, che è un misto di crema e cioccolata con biscotti oppure Pan di Spagna im . . . imbevuto un po' di liquore. Poi c'è la *crème caramel*, c'è la torta di mele, c'è la crostata di ricotta e frutta candita (anche quella una specialità). Poi c'è la torta di cioccolato e noci. Quella è una specialità del Balanzone, sì, veramente. Eh, i dolci li fa tutti lui.

specialità (f.) specialities (see *Grammar* p. 143)
prima di tutto first of all, to begin with, above all
Pan di Spagna a sort of sponge cake (lit. Spanish bread)
imbevuto di . . . soaked with . . .
liquore (m.) liqueur
ricotta a type of very mild cream cheese
frutta candita candied peel, crystallized fruit
noci walnuts

7 *Let's not forget the wine list!*

Giovanni Come vini, avete . . .

Cameriere Vini del Piemonte, della Toscana, dell'Emilia, tipo il Trebbiano, il Sangiovese, il Lambrusco secco e il Lambrusco amabile. Euh – poi ci son tutti gli altri vini. Dei vini bianchi, tipo Pinot grigio, tipo Verdicchio, tipo Soave. Il Soave è buono, secco, *molto* buono. E poi ci sono i vini sfusi della casa.

Giovanni Vini sfusi. In caraffa . . .

Cameriere . . . in caraffa. Quartino, mezzo litro, e un litro.

Piemonte, Toscana, Emilia wine growing regions in Italy
Trebbiano, Sangiovese etc. names of wines
secco dry
tipo like
grigio grey
caraffa carafe, jug

6 **dolce** (from **dolce**, sweet) sweet course. Sweets like bonbons, chocolates etc., are **caramelle.**

zuppa inglese (lit. English soup) is like trifle. Note that **crema** in the recipe is not 'cream' (**panna** in Italian) but 'custard'.

In some parts of Italy *crème caramel* is called **latte alla portoghese** (lit. milk in the Portuguese fashion). Crèmes, mousses, jellies and blancmanges belong to the category **budini** puddings (but excluding savoury puddings). **Torta** also has no exact equivalent in English, since it covers cakes, pies and tarts: **torta di mele** is generally an apple tart. **Crostata** is any tart (usually latticed) made with a short pastry base; whereas **sfogliata** would be one with a puff pastry base. **Ricotta** (lit. re-cooked) is a sort of curd cheese.

è una specialità del Balanzone Balanzone is the name of the owner-chef of the restaurant who takes his name from **il dottor Balanzone**, a character in the **Commedia dell'Arte** pantomime associated with Bologna.

i dolci li fa tutti lui he makes all the desserts himself.

7 **amabile** (lit. lovable) or **abboccato** describe medium-dry wines with a hint of sweetness. Besides being **secco** or **amabile**, Lambrusco is also **frizzante**, slightly fizzy.

i vini sfusi della casa the house wines; **sfuso** applies to anything sold loose or unpacked, from beans out of a sack, to wine out of a cask. **Un quartino**, a quarter-litre carafe, contains two large glasses. House wines can be very good, and are normally much less expensive than bottled wines (**vini in bottiglia**).

Key words and phrases

To learn

che cosa ha/avete come . . .	what do you have in the way of . . .
primi/secondi (piatti)	first/main courses
contorno	vegetables (lit. to go with the main course)
dolce	sweet course, dessert
vini	wines
che cosa è (il carpaccio)?	what is (*carpaccio*)?
com'è fatto?/come sono fatti?	how is it made?/are they made?
salto il primo	I'll skip the first course
con un po' di olio/aceto/limone	with a little (olive) oil/vinegar/lemon juice
senza limone/parmigiano	without lemon juice/parmesan cheese
prendo un misto di . . .	I'll have a mixture of . . .
voglio la costata/bistecca . . .	I want my chop/steak . . .
poco cotta	rare
giusta	medium
ben cotta	well done
vorrei – un vino della casa	I'd like some house wine

And remember how to ask for the bill:

il conto, per favore	the bill, please

To understand

la costata è da fare	the chop (rib-steak) is to be prepared to order
le scaloppine al Madera sono da fare	the escalopes in Madeira sauce are to be prepared to order
va condita/vanno condite con . . .	it/they must be dressed (seasoned) with . . .
al pomodoro	with tomato
al burro e formaggio	with butter and cheese
ai ferri	grilled
fritto, -a	fried
al vapore	steamed
al forno	baked
in umido	stewed
arrosto, -a	roast(ed)
bollito, -a / **lesso, -a**	boiled
saltato, -a	sautéed, lightly fried
vino amabile, abboccato	medium dry wine
vino secco	dry wine

Practise what you have learnt

1 Listen to the head-waiter of the *Ristorante Il Balanzone* in Milan describing yet another mouth-watering list of first courses. Then tick the statements below you think are true. (Answers p. 146.)

Before you start, study this list of new words:

gnocchi similar to small dumplings, served like pasta
tortelloni di zucca large ravioli stuffed with pumpkin
raviolini small ravioli
fondo dei carciofi artichoke hearts
pancetta bacon
frutti di mare shellfish
fegatini chicken livers (**fegato** = liver)
in bianco plain

a. You can have **i.** ☐ green gnocchi
ii. ☐ gnocchi served with meat sauce.

b. ☐ The **tortelloni di zucca** are served with butter.

c. The **raviolini** are **i.** ☐ factory made
ii. ☐ served with a cream sauce.

d. ☐ The **maccheroncini alla carciofara** are so-called because they are boiled with artichoke hearts.

e. **Maccheroncini all'amatriciana** are served
i. ☐ with bacon and parsley
ii. ☐ with bacon and tomato.

f. ☐ The waiter describes 13 different types of risotto.

g. ☐ **Risotto alla paesana** is made with vegetables.

h. ☐ **Risotto alla parmigiana** is rice simply seasoned with butter and parmesan.

2 Listen to a man and a woman ordering a meal on tape. When you have fully understood the dialogue answer the following questions. (Answers p. 146.)

a. What does the woman choose as first course?
☐ spaghetti bolognaise
☐ she skips the first course

b. Does she like parmesan on her **carpaccio**?
☐ yes ☐ no

c. What does she choose as **contorno**?
☐ spinach with butter
☐ turnip tops, with oil and lemon

d. Does the man want parmesan on his **gnocchi** with cream sauce?
☐ yes ☐ no

e. How does he want his rib steak? ☐ well done
☐ medium
☐ rare

f. What does he choose as **contorno?** ☐ sautéed turnip tops
☐ spinach with oil and lemon

g. Do they drink bottled wine? ☐ yes
☐ no

h. How do they want their mineral water? ☐ natural ☐ fizzy

3 Decide which type of preparation (in the box below) is appropriate to which dish and write it in the space provided. You won't need your tape recorder. (Answers p. 146.)

a. ravioli ....

b. maccheroni all'arrabbiata ....

c. costata ....

d. patate ....

e. spinaci ....

f. torta di mele ....

con olio e limone	**alla panna e pomodoro**	**conditi con prezzemolo, peperoncino e pomodoro**
al forno	**ai ferri**	**fritte**

4 Listen to the tape where a woman is ordering lunch and tick what she orders on the menu below. You will hear a new word **pesce**, fish. When you have done this write her order, in English, in the space provided. (Answers p. 146.)

....

....

....

Grammar

How to translate 'very . . .' into Italian

Besides using **molto** you can translate 'very' into Italian by replacing the ending of the adjective with the ending **-issimo, issima, -issimi, -issime**:

magro lean	**magrissimo, -a** very lean
buono good	**buonissimo, -a** very good
possibile possible	**possibilissimo, -a** very likely

This ending may also be used with those adverbs which do not end in **-mente**:

bene well	**benissimo** very well
giusto right	**giustissimo** quite right

Of course, **-issimo** forms may also be translated into English by means of expressions like 'extremely . . .' 'terribly . . .' etc.

Exercise Complete the following sentences by using an appropriate **-issimo** word, formed from the adjectives or adverbs in the margin.

saporito
forte
bello
caro
poco
molto
bene
sottile

a. Questo vestito le sta davvero ....
b. In questo ristorante si mangia bene e si spende ....
c. Questo minestrone è ....
d. 75.000 lire questo profumo? Ma è ....!
e. La carne per il carpaccio va tagliata a fette ....
f. Prende un dolce? No, salto il dolce. Ho già mangiato ....
g. Queste sigarette sono .... Preferisco sigarette più leggere.
h. Mi piace molto questa gonna. È ....

Shortened words

As in English, some Italian words may also be used in a shortened form:

- verbs may lose the final **-e** of their infinitive or the final **-o** of their 'we' and 'they' forms:
  delle penne da far come vuole Lei (fare)
  ci son tante specialità (sono)
  vengon molto piccanti (vengono)
- **bene** may be shortened to **ben** or even **be'**:
  una costata ben cotta   va be', grazie

You shouldn't try to shorten words like this yourself, at least not at first, but learn to recognize and understand them. Remember however that, as a rule:

- **buono** becomes **buon** before all nouns that could be preceded by **un**:
  un giorno   un buon giorno
  un profumo   un buon profumo
- nouns which are the shortened form of longer nouns are invariable i.e. they don't change their endings:
  la motocicletta motorbike → **la moto, le moto**
  l'automobile motorcar → **l'auto, le auto**
- nouns ending in **-tà** originate from nouns ending in **-tade** which permanently lost the **-de** a few centuries ago. They are all invariable:
  una specialità della casa   tante specialità
  una possibilità   molte possibilità

Read and understand

Barolo is a small town in Piedmont which has given its name to one of the best and best known Italian wines. Look at the wine label below and answer the following questions:

a. Where was the wine produced? ☐ in Barolo territory
☐ in the surrounding area

b. Who bottled the wine? ☐ the distributors
☐ the producer

c. Was the production of the wine in this bottle subject to any quality controls? ☐ yes
☐ no

d. How big was the bottle? ☐ ¾ litre
☐ one litre

e. What degree of alcoholic content does the wine have? ☐ 10%
☐ 13.5%

Did you know?

Italian restaurants

You may still find the word **Ristoratore** over the door of a few station restaurants, probably kept because of its old-fashioned flavour; but the most common word for a restaurant is **Ristorante**. Italian **ristoranti** range from the sublime to the average: it is on the whole difficult to blunder into one which is irredeemably bad. Italians are far more food-conscious than English-speaking people, and standards of preparation and service are correspondingly higher. That applies also to convenience food, which can be had from places called **Self-Service, Snack Bar** or **Tavola Calda** (Hot Table), where chefs miraculously manage to keep large quantities of pasta constantly on the ready in steaming trays – without overcooking it.

The best reasonably priced food can often be eaten in unpretentious working-class establishments, also called **Trattoria** or **Osteria** or bearing the name of the chef-owner, e.g. **Da Luigi**. Their degree of success in pleasing customers can be judged by the number of locals eating there. In these restaurants you may find the owner and family actively involved in cooking and serving the food. **Trattoria** and **Osteria** are names used also by luxury restaurants disguised as country inns; that applies particularly to establishments calling themselves **Hostaria**, which you should approach as guardedly as you would somewhere called 'Ye Olde Countrie Inne'. Hotel restaurants tend to be more standardized and anonymous, but you may still find pleasant surprises and enjoy memorable meals, especially in small country hotels.

Italian waiters often know quite a lot about cooking and are able to give reliable advice: they will sometimes talk you out of a particular choice if they think that, for whatever reason, it is not up to the restaurant's usual standard. Variations from the published menu (e.g. if you want your dish without its particular sauce, or your vegetables prepared differently) are readily granted. If you can't attract the waiter's attention with the usual **senta!** or **scusi!** you may call out **cameriere!** Waitresses are usually called **signora** or **signorina** according to their apparent age.

At the end of your meal ask for the bill (**il conto**) and check it: not only for possible mistakes but to find out whether the service charge (**servizio**) is included or left to your discretion (say 12%). Most bills include a small fixed charge (**coperto**) but bread and additional condiments, like olive oil and parmesan cheese, are free.

And so, **buon appetito!** as the Italians wish each other before beginning their meals.

Your turn to speak

Practise ordering a meal in Italian. The exercise is in three parts: first course and drinks, second course, and the dessert. Occasionally you will not be told exactly what to order, but will be given a general prompt (e.g. to order the meat course, or the second choice), so pay attention to what the waitress is telling you.

You will also hear the word **gelato**, ice-cream.

Answers

Practise what you have learnt p. 141 Exercise **1 a** (**i**) true (**ii**) false, they are served with tomato, cream sauce and parmesan **b**. true **c**. (**i**) false, they are home made (**ii**) true **d**. false, they are sautéed with artichoke hearts **e**. (**i**) false (**ii**) true **f**. false, he describes 4 types **g**. true **h**. true.

p. 141 Exercise **2** (**a**) she skips the first course (**b**) no (**c**) spinach with butter (**d**) yes (**e**) rare (**f**) sautéed turnip tops (**g**) no (**h**) fizzy.

p. 142 Exercise **3** (**a**) ravioli alla panna e pomodoro (**b**) maccheroni all'arrabbiata conditi con prezzemolo, peperoncino e pomodoro (**c**) costata ai ferri (**d**) patate fritte (**e**) spinaci con olio e limone (**f**) torta di mele al forno.

p. 142 Exercise **4** She orders: spaghetti al ragù, manzo lesso, carote, frutta e vino rosso. English translation: spaghetti with meat sauce, boiled beef, carrots with oil and lemon, an apple and a quarter litre of red wine.

Grammar p. 143 (**a**) benissimo (**b**) pochissimo (**c**) saporitissimo (**d**) carissimo (**e**) sottilissime (**f**) moltissimo (**g**) fortissime (**h**) bellissima.

Read and understand p. 144 (**a**) in the Barolo territory (**b**) the producer (**c**) yes (**d**) $\frac{3}{4}$ litre (**e**) 13.5%.

11 *Che cosa preferisce?*

What you will learn

- how to express likes or dislikes
- how to ask others what they prefer
- more about food, tastes and flavours
- how to describe the position of hotel rooms
- the names of some flowers

Before you begin

Remember some of the key points in Unit 10:

1 What you will find on a menu
piatti pronti o da fare
primo: **pasta asciutta, minestre varie** (choice of soups), **risotti**
secondo: **carne o pesce con contorno di verdura cotta o insalata**
dessert: **dolce o formaggio**
frutta
vino: **in bottiglia o sfuso, bianco o rosso, secco o amabile**
acqua minerale: **naturale o gasata**

2 words ending in **-tà** don't change in the plural
la specialità, le specialità

3 another way of saying 'very . . .'
buono good **buonissimo** very good
dolce sweet **dolcissimo** very sweet

Study guide

	Dialogues 1, 2: listen straight through without the book
	Dialogues 1, 2: listen, read and study one by one
	Dialogues 3, 4: listen straight through without the book
	Dialogues 3, 4: listen, read and study one by one
	Dialogue 5: listen straight through without the book
	Dialogue 5: listen, read and study notes
	Learn the *Key words and phrases*
	Do the exercises in *Practise what you have learnt*
	Study *Grammar* and do the exercise
	Read *Did you know?* (this time before *Read and understand*)
	Do *Read and understand*
	Do the tape exercises in *Your turn to speak*
	Finally, listen to all the dialogues again without the book

Dialogues

1 *A waiter tells Giovanni what starters are available*

Cameriere Mi dica, cosa posso offrirle da mangiare, cosa preferisce.
Giovanni Ha degli antipasti?
Cameriere No, non c'è una grossa scelta come antipasti.
Giovanni Che cosa c'è?
Cameriere Antipasto della casa, fatto con del prosciutto nostro, toscano, saporito. Eh, è abbastanza salato il prosciutto toscano. Salame e un misto di sottolii.
Giovanni Hm, hm.
Cameriere Se vuole ci possiamo aggiungere anche due crostini. . . di pane abbrustolito; e poi ci mettiamo una salsa sopra.
Giovanni No. Un antipasto della casa, eh? Ma senza . . .
Cameriere . . . senza i crostini . . .
Giovanni . . . senza crostini e salsa. Semplice. Semplicemente prosciutto, salame e . . .
Cameriere . . . e questo misto di sottolio . . .
Giovanni . . . di sottolio, sì.

toscano Tuscan
salato salty
aggiungere to add (past part. **aggiunto**)
crostino toast (**la crosta** = crust)
abbrustolire to toast (*also* **tostare**)

2 *Giovanni decides on a main course*

Giovanni E dopo cosa . . . cosa c'è? Cosa . . . cosa avete?
Cameriere C'è arrosto . . . c'è del buon prosciutto di maiale al forno.
Giovanni Ah ah.
Cameriere O del vitello. Se vuole le facciamo un misto, l'uno e l'altro . . .
Giovanni . . . no, preferisco, preferisco solo vitello. E come contorno che cosa avete? Avete verdure cotte?
Cameriere Ci sono rapini, spinaci, bietole. Fagioli senz'altro ci sono.
Giovanni Sì. Avete del vino della casa, anche non in bottiglia?
Cameriere C'è il vino rosso o bianco, come lo preferisce.
Giovanni Mi dia un, un mezzo di . . . vino rosso e mezzo di . . . acqua minerale.
Cameriere Gasata o naturale l'acqua . . .?
Giovanni Gasata, gasata.

bietole spinach beet

1 ➧ **cosa preferisce?** what do you prefer? The waiter might also have asked **che cosa sceglie?** what's your choice? what do you choose? (from **scegliere**, see below).

➧ **ha degli antipasti?** do you have any starters? **Antipasto** is the Italian for a starter (lit. before the meal, **pasto** = meal) i.e. the course eaten before the **primo**.

non c'è una grossa scelta there's not a big choice. **Scelta**, choice, is from the verb **scegliere** to choose (past part. **scelto, -a**), see *Grammar* p. 155.

prosciutto divides into two categories: **prosciutto cotto** ham, and **prosciutto crudo** Parma ham (but in fact widely manufactured outside Parma; the best is said to come from Friuli, the region north-east of Venice).

sottolio (or **sott'olio**) is anything preserved in oil, like **carciofini** small artichokes, or **funghi** mushrooms; **sottaceti** are pickles (**sotto** = under).

ci mettiamo una salsa sopra we'll put a sauce on top. When speaking about tomato sauce Italians use both **salsa** and **sugo**; **sugo**, however, is the juice naturally coming out of food (e.g. **il sugo della carne** meat juice); **salsa** is a prepared sauce. The words **salsa, salame, i salumi** (a general word for preserved meats like hams, salami etc., from which **salumiere**, a dealer in salumi, something between a pork butcher and a grocer), **le salsicce** sausages, are all related to **il sale**, salt.

2 ➧ **fagioli senz'altro ci sono** we definitely have beans (lit. beans definitely there are). **Senz'altro** is probably short for **senz'altro dubbio** without further doubt. In general it is used to confirm things: **vieni questo pomeriggio? senz'altro!** will you come this afternoon? of course!; **questo vino in bottiglia è senz'altro migliore** this bottled wine is certainly better.

➧ **come lo preferisce** as you prefer (it), as you like. (For the conjugation of **preferire** see Unit 8.) Other expressions with this verb are: (**che**) **cosa preferisce?** what would you like? **preferisco solo vitello** I'd rather have veal on its own; **preferisce veder le camere?** would you rather see the rooms?

mi dia please could I have (lit. give me). Although short, this Italian expression is very courteous and can be used instead of **mi da**.

un mezzo . . . whether you use **un mezzo** or **una mezza** depends on whether you are thinking of **un mezzo (litro)** or **una mezza (bottiglia)**.

3 *Two friends discuss their favourite flowers*

Roberto Ti piacciono i giacinti o preferisci le violette?
Alda Io preferisco le violette. E il tuo fiore preferito qual'è?
Roberto A me piacciono molto i narcisi . . . e il tuo preferito?
Alda Il mio invece è la rosa.

giacinti hyacinths
violette violets
narcisi narcissus, daffodils
rosa rose

4 *The hotel receptionist offers Giovanni a choice of rooms*

Portiere Se vuol veder le camere . . . preferisce vederle?
Giovanni No, se può chiamarmi qualcuno che mi aiuti con le valigie.
Portiere Volentieri. Chiamo subito il facchino, così vi mandiamo nelle camere, eh?
Giovanni Molte grazie.
Portiere Le camere sono al primo piano, non so . . .
Giovanni . . . sono al primo piano . . .
Portiere . . . le preferisce sul dietro, perché sono più tranquille. . .
Giovanni . . . eh, dietro, magari sì, sul dietro sono un po' più tranquille. . .
Portiere . . . ecco, io gli faccio vedere tutt'e due, quale Lei preferisce.

volontieri certainly, willingly
facchino porter
mandare to send

5 *Some Italian students tell Giovanni what they think of English food*

Giovanni Allora, Enza, ti piace l'Inghilterra?
Enza Eh, mi piace abbastanza. Unica cosa che non mi piace dell'Inghilterra è il cibo.
Giovanni Il cibo?
Cesarina Per noi Italiani è un po' un problema, più che altro . . .
Enza . . . quei sapori tipo agrodolce che noi . . . in Italia non usiamo.
Claudio I sapori sono molto diversi, anzi, sono diversi perché troviamo salato e dolce molte volte assieme. Non si separa il salato dal dolce come in Italia.
Enza Siamo abituati a un'alimentazione molto diversa, e . . .
Giovanni Insomma, non mi pare che andate matti per la cucina inglese, eh?

cibo food
più che altro rather, more than anything
anzi in fact (*filler word*)
assieme (or **insieme**) together
non si separa one doesn't separate (from **separare**)
siamo abituati a . . . we're used to
alimentazione (f.) way of eating
insomma so
non mi pare che. . . it doesn't seem to me that . . ., I don't think
cucina cooking

3 ▸ **il tuo fiore preferito qual'è?** (Also: **qual'è il tuo fiore preferito?**) what's your favourite flower? Note that Alda addresses Roberto informally with **tuo** instead of **suo** (see *Grammar*, p. 155). Past participles of both **-isco** and ordinary **-ire** verbs end in **-ito**: **preferito, partito**.

▸ You will find the names of a few more common flowers in the *Key words and phrases* section. If you buy flowers you may also need the phrase **un mazzo di. . .** a bunch of. . . .

▸ **a me piacciono. . .** I like. . . For the difference between **a me piacciono** and **mi piacciono**, see *Grammar*, p. 156.

4 ▸ **preferisce vederle?** would you rather see them?

se può chiamarmi qualcuno che mi aiuti if you can call me someone to help me (lit. who can help me).

▸ **le preferisce sul dietro** would you rather have them at the back. Other possible locations: **sul cortile** facing onto/overlooking the courtyard; **sul davanti** at the front; **sulla strada** overlooking the street; **sul giardino** overlooking the garden; **sul mare** overlooking the sea.

▸ **magari** perhaps, maybe. A different use of this word is to express an unrealized wish, rather like 'if only!' in English: **non sono tranquille, le camere? magari! sono rumorosissime** aren't the rooms quiet? I wish they were!/(if only they were!) they're extremely noisy.

gli faccio vedere tutt'e due I'll show you both.

quale Lei preferisce whichever you prefer, i.e. you can choose . . . whichever you prefer.

5 ▸ **mi piace abbastanza** I quite like it (lit. I like it enough). Other examples: **è abbastanza buono** it's rather/quite good; **ancora patate? no grazie, ne ho abbastanza** more potatoes? no thank you, I have enough; **questa bistecca non è abbastanza cotta** this steak is not cooked enough.

quei sapori tipo agrodolce those kind of sour-sweet flavours. The sharp distinction between flavours in Italian cooking is mirrored in the language, which, as you have seen in Unit 10, does not contain words like 'pudding' or 'pie' referring to both sweet and savoury foods. The basic flavours in Italian are: **agro** or **aspro** sour, **acido** acidy, **amaro** bitter, **dolce** sweet, **salato** salty.

▸ **andate matti per . . .** you're mad about . . . (lit. you go mad about). You can use this phrase to express strong preference or liking: **ti piace la cassata? ne vado matto** do you like cassata? I'm mad about it.

Key words and phrases

To learn

che cosa preferisce?/sceglie?	what do you prefer?/choose?
come lo preferisce?	how do you prefer it?
preferisco/scelgo. . .	I prefer/choose. . .
una camera sul davanti	a room at the front
sul dietro	at the back
sul cortile	overlooking the courtyard
sulla strada	overlooking the street
sul giardino	overlooking the garden
sul mare	overlooking the sea
qual'è il tuo piatto preferito?	what's your favourite dish?
il mio piatto preferito è . . .	my favourite dish is . . .
mi piace abbastanza	I quite like it
ho abbastanza verdura	I have enough vegetables
ne vado matto	I'm mad about it
vado matto per . . .	I'm mad about . . .
senz'altro!	of course! no doubt, without fail
magari	perhaps, if only!

To understand

antipasto	hors d'oeuvre, starter
basic flavours	
acido	acidy
agro/aspro	sour
salato	salty
amaro	bitter
dolce	sweet
common flowers	
la rosa	rose
la margherita	daisy
la viola / **la violetta**	violet
il garofano	carnation
il giglio	lily
il ciclamino	cyclamen
il crisantemo	chrysanthemum
la primula	primrose

Practise what you have learnt

1 Listen to a couple ordering starters in a restaurant. From the list below write in the spaces the items chosen by the woman and by the man. (Answers p. 160.)
New word: **russa** = Russian

Antipasti

a. prosciutto cotto
b. prosciutto crudo del Friuli
c. salame toscano
d. carciofini sott'olio
e. funghi sott'olio
f. sottaceti vari
g. olive nere
h. olive verdi
i. insalata russa
j. paté di Borgogna e crostini

....	....
....	....
....	....
....	....
....	....

2 Who likes what? In the dialogue on tape a couple discuss the alternatives on the menu. Get the gist of what they are saying, then fill in the spaces below with the initials M, for the man's choice, and W, for the woman's choice. If they both choose the same dish, put M/W. (Answers p. 160.)

. . . . menu turistico
. . . . menu à la carte
. . . . piatti pronti
. . . . piatti da fare
. . . . antipasto
. . . . niente antipasto
. . . . primo piatto
. . . . niente primo
. . . . minestra
. . . . pasta asciutta
. . . . pizza
. . . . risotto
. . . . carne
. . . . pesce
. . . . verdura cotta
. . . . insalata
. . . . formaggio
. . . . dolce

3 Describe the position of the rooms in the hotel illustrated on facing page 155. Complete the sentences using *two* phrases chosen from the box below: the first the direction the room faces, the second the floor it's on. You won't need your tape recorder. (Answers p. 160.) The first has been done for you.

a. Il ristorante è sul davanti, al piano terreno

b. La camera 101 è ...., ...

c. La camera 206 è ...., ...

e. La camera 231 è ...., ...

f. La camera 110 è ...., ...

sul davanti	**sulla strada**	**sul giardino**
sul dietro	**sul cortile**	**sul mare**
al primo piano	**al piano terreno**	**al secondo piano**

4 Describe the food and drink below with one of the words on the right. You won't need your tape recorder. (Answers p. 160.)

a. Campari soda ....

b. prosciutto del Friuli ....

c. limone ....

d. torta di mele ....

e. marmellata di fichi ....

f. salame toscano ....

g. sottaceti ....

h. vino Soave ....

i. caffè expresso senza zucchero ....

dolce
amaro
aspro
salato
acido
secco

Grammar

Scegliere to choose

The present tense of this verb is as follows:

scelgo	I choose	**scegliamo**	we choose
scegli	you choose	**scegliete**	you (pl.) choose
sceglie	you (polite) choose he/she chooses	**scelgono**	they choose

Its past participle is **scelto, -a**.

Togliere to remove, to take away, (past part. **tolto**) is conjugated like **scegliere**.

Possessives my, mine, your, yours etc.

Look at the Italian possessives listed below (you have already met some of them in previous units).

m. sing.	*f. sing.*	*m. pl.*	*f. pl.*		*m. sing.*	*f. sing.*	*m. pl.*	*f. pl.*	
mio	**mia**	**miei**	**mie**	my, mine	**nostro**	**nostra**	**nostri**	**nostre**	our(s)
tuo	**tua**	**tuoi**	**tue**	your(s)	**vostro**	**vostra**	**vostri**	**vostre**	your(s)
suo	**sua**	**suoi**	**sue**	his/her(s) your(s) polite	**loro**	**loro**	**loro**	**loro**	their

Note that except for the first three masculine plurals (**miei** etc.) and **loro** (which stays the same), they all behave like normal **-o, -a** adjectives. (Cont. p. 156.)

Remember three basic differences between English and Italian possessives:

- possessives tend to be omitted in Italian when there is no doubt as to whose things you're speaking of, and are therefore used less frequently:

  metto la gonna marrone I'll put on my brown skirt
  la coincidenza è alle 11, 23 your connection is at 11.23
  voglio la bistecca poco cotta I want my steak underdone

- like all adjectives they agree with the noun they qualify, not with their owner. There is no distinction between his and her(s):

  il suo ombrello his/her umbrella
  la sua valigia his/her suitcase

  If you must distinguish, then you have to specify, e.g. **la valigia di Giorgio, l'ombrello di Maria** etc.

- when you do use the possessives, they are nearly always preceded by articles:

  le mie valigie my suitcases
  una mia valigia one of my suitcases

Exercise Replace the English possessives in brackets with the appropriate Italian forms. Do not forget to combine prepositions, where they occur, with the required article. (Answers p. 160.)

a. Qual'è .... (your) valigia? Questa è ....
(my) valigia.

b. .... (Their) albergo è l'Albergo Vittoria.

c. Dov'è .... (her) passaporto?

d. La Banca Commerciale è proprio fuori di .... (our) ufficio.

e. .... (Your: informal) carta d'identità è in .... (my) camera.

f. .... (Your: polite) treno parte alle 19,40.

Mi piace, a me piace

Both these phrases mean 'I like', but the second one is more emphatic and it should be used when there is a contrast, e.g.

a me piace la verdura cotta, ma a Giorgio non piace
I like cooked vegetables, but Giorgio doesn't like them

io preferisco gli anemoni, ma a lei piacciono le giunchiglie
I prefer anemones, but she likes jonquils

Did you know?

Italian cuisine

'Italy is a ham-shaped peninsula surrounded by five seas called Barolo, Chianti, Lambrusco, Frascati and Cirò [a Calabrian wine]' wrote Riccardo Morbelli in 1967, 'and is divided into two main regions: Butter Italy in the North and Oil Italy in the South, otherwise known as Rice Italy and Pasta Italy.' He formally warned travellers never to ask for spaghetti in the North or risotto in the South, unless they wanted to be served wallpaper glue in either case. Today one need not give such a warning. Greater social mobility and internal migrations in the past twenty years or so have changed a situation where cuisine was, like everything else in Italy, intensely parochial, and where regional specialities did not travel at all well. Since then Tuscan innkeepers have set up **trattorie** in Naples, Apulian farmers have opened Apulian eating houses in Milan, and Sicilian pastry-cooks and confectioners have given a new meaning to the Roman '**dolce vita**'.

And yet regional specialities are still well worth tasting in their homeland. Tourists without much time or money for expensive restaurant food (and especially self-catering campers) can, and should, enjoy something of the regional flavour of Italian cuisine simply by buying local cheeses, hams and salamis (far too many to allow even a passing mention), and by visiting the local vegetable market. There they will discover the common round lettuce is only one, and not the tastiest, among dozens of varieties of salad, and that there are many more vegetables to go with one's meat than carrots, peas and potatoes.

Since most of these specialities have a regional or even a dialectal name, Italians from other areas are no wiser than you; when it comes to buying, they too have to point to the thing, ask **come si chiama?** and even **come si mangia?** (how do you eat it ?). Furthermore Italian has only recently become a viable national language, and so it still lacks standard names for vegetables. What in some areas are called **bietole** and **cavolo** (cabbage), in others are called **coste** and **verza**; and what people actually mean by **cicoria** (chicory) varies from place to place. Names of fish are also mostly local or dialectal. The same can be said of the names of birds, plants and flowers, apart from the most common ones. This difficulty with giving things that are part of one's everyday experience generally understandable and acceptable names, may be one of the causes of the rather widespread ignorance of Italians about birdlife and gardening, and the slow development in the country of nature-lovers' societies.

Read and understand

Read the restaurant bill opposite and answer the following questions. (Answers p. 160.)

1 Where was the restaurant?
- ☐ in Florence
- ☐ in Rome

2 How many people went there for a meal?
- ☐ one
- ☐ two
- ☐ three

3 Was the bill for:
- ☐ a fixed charge 'Tourist' meal?
- ☐ an 'à la carte' meal?

4 Did anybody skip the main course?
- ☐ yes
- ☐ no

5 Was the wine:
- ☐ bottled wine?
- ☐ carafe wine?

6 Was a service charge included in the bill?
- ☐ yes
- ☐ no

7 Is the bill:
- ☐ an informal receipt for the customer's record only?
- ☐ a legally valid statutory document?

8 Is the total:
- ☐ correct
- ☐ incorrect

Ristorante Esperia

di NATALUCCI GIANCARLO

VIA FIRENZE, 16 - 17 — ☎ 48.65.62 — ROMA

Cod. Fisc. NTL GCR 44M07 H501J

lì 16/9/81 N° 4114

quantità	DESCRIZIONE	prezzo
2	Coperto	800
1	Antipasto	900
1	Primo piatto	1100
	Secondo piatto: carne . .	
2	» » pesce . .	5700
2	Contorno	1800
1l.	Vino	2700
	Birra	
1/2	Acqua minerale	900
	Bibite	
1	Frutta	500
1	Dolce	1000
	Pranzo Turistico . .	

Tip. EgR di E. Militano - Via Onorato, 46 PALERMO - Aut. n. 380405 - 28.1.1980

Copia per il Cliente

RICEVUTA FISCALE
MOD. XAR

№ 147214 80

Importo L.	15400
Servizio L.	1850
Totale L.	17250

Your turn to speak

1 In this exercise you are ordering in a restaurant and you have to express your preferences. You won't be prompted, but when the waiter offers you two choices, refuse the first by saying **non mi piace** (or **non mi piacciono**), and agree to the second by saying **preferisco. . .** Here is an example:

Waiter **Come antipasto abbiamo prosciutto e salame, oppure un misto di sottoli.**
You **Il prosciutto e il salame non mi piacciono. Preferisco il misto di sottoli.**

Pause the tape after the waiter's question to give yourself time to speak aloud, and then start it again and you will hear the correct answer.

2 In this exercise you will be discussing preferences with someone you have just met – asking her what she likes best. Remember to use the polite form **Lei** etc. This time Marisa will prompt you as usual.

Answers

Practise what you have learnt p. 153 Exercise **1** **Signora**: b, c, f, g **Signore**: e, f, g, j.

p. 153 Exercise **2** menu à la carte M/W; piatti pronti M/W; antipasto W; niente antipasto M; primo piatto M; niente primo W; minestra M; pesce M/W; verdura cotta M; insalata W; formaggio W; dolce M.

p. 154 Exercise **3** (**b**) sul davanti/sulla strada, al primo piano (**c**) sul giardino, al secondo piano (**d**) sul mare, al secondo piano (**e**) sul dietro, al secondo piano (**f**) sul cortile, al piano terreno.

p. 154 Exercise **4** (**a**) amaro (**b**) salato (**c**) acido (**d**) dolce (**e**) dolce (**f**) salato (**g**) aspro (**h**) secco (**i**) amaro.

Grammar p. 156 (**a**) la tua (*or* la sua), la mia (**b**) il loro (**c**) il suo (**d**) al nostro (**e**) la tua, nella mia (**f**) il suo.

Read and understand p. 158 (**1**) in Rome (**2**) two (**3**) an 'à la carte' meal (**4**) no (**5**) carafe wine (**6**) yes (**7**) a legally valid statutory document (**8**) correct.

12 *Già che ci sei, fai anche il pieno*

What you will learn

- how to ask for petrol and for basic car maintenance
- how to talk about the weather and understand weather forecasts
- more ways of talking about future events
- talking about the past
- seasons and months of the year

Before you begin

Points to remember from Unit 11:

1 conjugation of **scegliere** (and other verbs ending in **-gliere**)
scelgo, scegli, sceglie, scegliamo, scegliete, scelgono

2 expressions of preference
che cosa preferisce . . . ? preferisco . . .
il mio fiore preferito è . . . e il tuo?/il suo?
a me piace . . ., e a te/Lei?

3 possessives
il mio ombrello, la tua valigia, i suoi documenti
le nostre camere, il vostro albergo, le loro specialità

Study guide

	Dialogues 1, 2: listen straight through without the book
	Dialogues 1, 2: listen, read and study one by one
	Dialogue 3: listen straight through without the book
	Dialogue 3: listen, read and study notes
	Dialogue 4: listen straight through without the book
	Dialogue 4: listen, read and study notes
	Dialogue 5: listen straight through without the book
	Dialogue 5: listen, read and study notes
	Learn *Key words and phrases*
	Do the exercises in *Practise what you have learnt*
	Study *Grammar* and do the exercise
	Do *Read and understand*
	Read *Did you know?*
	Do the tape exercises in *Your turn to speak*
	Listen to all the dialogues again straight through
	Do the *Revision* section for Units 10–12 on p. 222

Dialogues

1 *Listen to a local radio advertisement about all the checks a motorist should do in winter*

È inverno, amico automobilista. Una ragione in più per salvaguardare il perfetto funzionamento del motore della tua auto. Hai pensato all'antigelo? E alla sostituzione dell'olio con quello di gradazione invernale? E alle candele? Hai controllato le condizioni dei pneumatici?

amico, -a friend
automobilista (m./f.) motorist
una ragione in più one more reason
antigelo antifreeze
candele spark plugs (lit. candles)
pneumatici tyres (*also* **le gomme**)
(more car vocabulary on p. 168.)

2 *The advertisement offers further advice*

E allora, amico automobilista, per la messa a punto della tua auto, recati alla stazione di servizio Roma, dove del personale altamente specializzato ti consiglierà sulla gradazione giusta del lubrificante invernale e dell'antigelo, e sul tipo di candele adatte alla stagione.

E se devi riparare o sostituire le gomme, Roma mette a tua disposizione le migliori marche di pneumatici esistenti sul mercato.

E magari di' che ti mando io, lo speaker della radio. Vedrai, rimarrai soddisfatto.

Ah, dimenticavo. Già che ci sei, fai anche il pieno.

recati go (lit. take yourself), from **recarsi**
stazione (f.) di servizio service station
personale altamente specializzato highly qualified personnel
giusto, -a right, correct
lubrificante (m.) lubricant, lubricating oil
adatto, -a suited, suitable
riparare to repair, to mend
mette a tua disposizione puts at your disposal
esistente existing
mercato market
speaker della radio radio presenter, disc jockey

1 **è inverno** it's winter. The adjective 'winter' is **invernale** as in the phrase which comes later **olio di gradazione invernale,** winter grade oil. The names of the other seasons (and related adjectives) are: **la primavera** (**primaverile**) spring; **l'estate** (**estivo**) summer; **l'autunno** (**autunnale**) autumn. The first two are feminine nouns.

salvaguardare il perfetto funzionamento del motore making sure the engine is in perfect working order (lit. to safeguard the perfect functioning of the engine).

Funzionamento is related to **funzionare** to function, to work (used of machines, not of people). This verb comes in many phrases you may find useful: **non funziona** it isn't working, **non funziona bene** it isn't working well, **guardi se funziona** see whether it works.

hai pensato a . . . have you thought/did you think about . . ., and later **hai controllato** have you checked/did you check. (See *Grammar* p. 171.)

la sostituzione the replacement, from **sostituire** (present: **sostituisco**) to replace, to substitute. More usual: **il cambio dell'olio,** from **cambiare** to change.

2 **la messa a punto** overhaul, general check-over. **Messo, -a** is the past participle of **mettere; mettere a punto il motore** to tune the engine.

ti consiglierà will advise you; and, further on, **vedrai** you'll see, and **rimarrai soddisfatto** you'll be (remain) satisfied, are all forms of the future tense, for which see *Grammar*, p. 171.

le migliori marche di pneumatici the best brands of tyres.

di' che ti mando io tell (them) I'm sending you.

dimenticavo I forgot. This past tense will be explained later in Unit 13. **Dimenticare** also means 'to leave something behind': **ho dimenticato il passaporto** I've left my passport behind.

già che ci sei, fai anche il pieno while you're at it (lit. since you're there) fill it up. Speaking of yourself you would say **già che ci sono,** while I'm at it.

3 *A garage attendant explains to Giovanni why foreign motorists and Italian garage attendants need not talk to each other*

Giovanni E quando viene da Lei un turista straniero, Lei gli parla? E che cosa dice?

Garagista Non . . . serve parlare . . .

Giovanni Ma Lei offre, non so, il cambio dell'olio, il controllo delle gomme?

Garagista No, quelle cose lì no. Lo salutiamo, buon giorno, buona sera, e poi . . . l'automobilista da sé dirà se, se vuole . . . quanta benzina vuole, vuole il pieno . . .

Giovanni Ah, ecco . . .

Garagista . . . o vuole, mettiamo, cinque, diecimila . . . ha capito?

Giovanni Mm, mm.

Garagista Poi generalmente lo straniero che viene qui ci ha la macchina a noleggio, allora farà sempre il pieno. Poi ci sono quelli che non parlano neppure, non dicono neppure una parola in italiano, allora chiedono solo benzina . . .

Giovanni Si va a gesti . . .

Garagista E poi, eh, a gesti, esatto. Poi sa, generalmente quando viene uno straniero, parte da casa già tutto bene organizzato, tutto tranquillo per il viaggio; quindi fa il cambio dell'olio prima di partire . . .

Giovanni Eh già . . .

Garagista . . . la macchina la fa riguardare dall'officina laggiù di sua fiducia, come si fa noi italiani se si va all'estero.

Giovanni Eh, già.

garagista (m.) garage attendant
da Lei to you
turista straniero foreign tourist
non serve parlare there's no need to talk
offre from **offrire** (past part. **offerto**) to offer
benzina petrol, fuel
mettiamo say, let's say (by way of example)
farà will have (lit. will do)
non . . . neppure not even (like **non . . . nemmeno**, Unit 8)
parola word
chiedono from **chiedere** (past part. **chiesto**) to ask for
si va a gesti you use sign language
bene organizzato well organized

4 *Giovanni and Aldo talk about the weather*

Giovanni Pfff! Come fa caldo qui in Italia. E com'era il tempo durante le tue vacanze in Inghilterra?

Aldo Alcune giornate di sole. Il resto ventoso e nuvoloso.

Giovanni Questo in che mese?

Aldo Agosto.

Giovanni Pioggia?

Aldo No.

Giovanni Meno male, perché quando in Inghilterra piove, eh? piove sul serio! Qui, invece, guarda che bel tempo oggi!

com'era il tempo? how was the weather?
durante during
ventoso windy (**vento** = wind)
nuvoloso cloudy (**nuvola** = cloud)
pioggia rain (**piovere** to rain, past part. **piovuto**)
sul serio in earnest
invece on the other hand

3 **lo salutiamo** we greet him (he is assuming the motorist is male!) from **salutare** to greet, to welcome. The word is related to **la salute**, health. You already know the main greetings and you should also learn how to say goodbye: **arrivederci** (lit. until we meet again).

da sé dirà himself will say. Another future, this time of the verb **dire** (see p. 171.)

il pieno lit. full (tank). If you want to fill your tank up, say: **mi fa il pieno, per favore**. Or you may ask, as the attendant suggests, for petrol up to a given sum: **mi da ventimila lire di benzina** give me 20,000 lira's worth of petrol.

la macchina a noleggio a hired car; **noleggiare** = to hire; look out for the signs **NOLEGGIO MACCHINE** or **SI NOLEGGIANO MACCHINE** CAR HIRE. If you want to hire a car, say: **vorrei noleggiare una macchina**.

prima di partire before leaving. Note that **prima di . . .** is followed by verbs in the infinitive: **prima di mangiare** before eating, or by nouns: **prima del pranzo** before lunch.

eh già is another 'filler' expression equivalent to 'yes, that's right'.

la farà riguardare will have it seen to.

dall'officina (laggiù) di sua fiducia by his trusted garage. **Officina** is a garage where repairs are done. **Laggiù** means literally 'down there', the attendant means 'abroad' i.e. in the driver's own country.

come si fa noi italiani se si va all'estero as we Italians do if we go abroad.

4 **fa caldo** it's hot; **fa freddo** it's cold. Generally **è caldo, è freddo** is used when there is a subject: **il clima è caldo** the climate is hot; **com'è oggi il mare? è freddo** how's the sea today? it's cold.

alcune giornate di sole a few sunny days (**il sole** = the sun). **Giornata** is the word for 'day' when you're thinking of what you do or what it was like, whereas **il giorno** is the calendar day or number of days e.g. **due giorni**.

in che mese? in what month?

agosto August. The names of the other months are in *Key words and phrases* p. 167. Note that they don't have a capital letter in Italian.

meno male! thank goodness! This is a very common way of expressing relief: **il treno è puntuale: meno male!** or **meno male che il treno è puntuale!** thank goodness the train's on time!

che bel tempo! what fine weather! **che brutto tempo, che tempo orribile!** what bad, awful weather! **fa brutto, piove e tira vento** the weather's bad, it's rainy and windy.

5 *Here's a weather forecast from the radio*

TEMPO PREVISTO PER DOMANI.
Sulle regioni occidentali della penisola e sulle isole maggiori, poco nuvoloso durante il pomeriggio. Sul settore nord-occidentale e sul versante adriatico nuvolosità variabile con locali precipitazioni anche temporalesche, che andranno trasferendosi da nord verso sud. Temperatura in lieve diminuzione sulle regioni orientali della penisola. Senza variazioni su quelle occidentali.

previsto past part. of **prevedere** to foresee, to forecast
settore (m.) sector, area
versante adriatico the Adriatic slope, the side of the Apennines sloping towards the Adriatic sea
variabile variable
temporalesco stormy (**temporale (m.)** storm)

5 **regioni occidentali** western regions. Here are the four compass points and related adjectives: **nord** north, **settentrionale** northern; **ovest** west, **occidentale** western; **est** east, **orientale** eastern; **sud** south, **meridionale** southern. South, east and west are also called **mezzogiorno**, **oriente** and **occidente** respectively; **il Mezzogiorno** (lit. midday) is a very common name for Southern Italy.

la penisola the peninsula i.e. Italy; **le isole maggiori** the larger/major islands i.e. Sardinia and Sicily. There is a tendency in Italian weather forecasts to prefer a rather artificial and roundabout language to direct concrete expressions: to say **nuvolosità** cloudiness, **precipitazioni** precipitations, **rilievi montuosi** mountainous uplands, instead of **nuvole** clouds, **pioggia** rain or **neve** snow, and **montagne** mountains. Also expressions like **temperatura in lieve diminuzione** simply mean **la temperatura diminuirà leggermente** temperatures will fall slightly.

andranno trasferendosi da nord verso sud will slowly move from north to south.

Key words and phrases

There are a lot of useful words in this section. They are all worth learning, but you can also refer back to them whenever you want. (They continue on p. 168.)

Seasons

primavera	spring
estate	summer
autunno	autumn
inverno	winter

Months of the year

gennaio	January
febbraio	February
marzo	March
aprile	April
maggio	May
giugno	June
luglio	July
agosto	August
settembre	September
ottobre	October
novembre	November
dicembre	December

The weather

fa caldo/fa freddo	it's hot/it's cold
il tempo è bello/brutto	the weather's fine/bad
piove	it's raining
tira vento	it's windy
c'è il sole	it's sunny
c'è un temporale	there's a storm
è nuvoloso	it's cloudy
nevica	it's snowing

The compass points

nord (settentrionale)	north
sud (meridionale)	south
est (orientale)	east
ovest (occidentale)	west

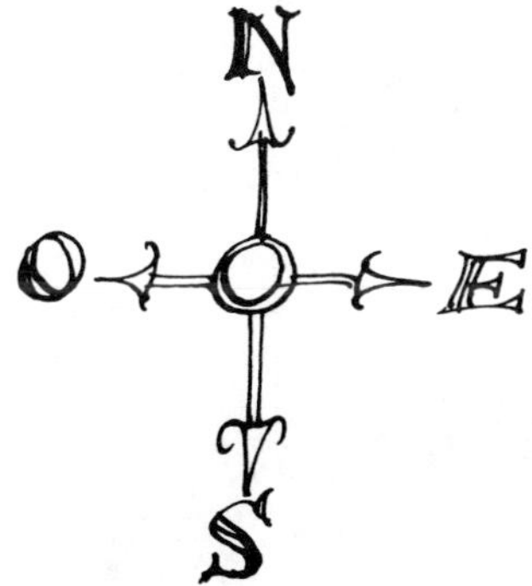

For your car

l'auto(mobile) / **la macchina**	car
il motore	engine
la carrozzeria	bodywork
il parabrezza	windscreen
i tergicristalli	windscreen wipers
le sospensioni	suspension
il volante	steering wheel
lo sterzo	steering mechanism
le gomme / **i pneumatici**	tyres
i freni	brakes
le candele	spark plugs
l'olio	oil
la benzina / **il carburante**	petrol
. . . non funziona	(it) doesn't work
. . . non funzionano	(they) don't work
mi fa . . .	would you . . .
il pieno (di normale/super)	fill it up (with 2-star/4-star)
il controllo delle gomme	check the tyres
il cambio dell'olio	change the oil
mi da (venti) litri di (super)	would you give me (20) litres of (4-star)

Other useful expressions

arrivederci	goodbye
meno male!	thank goodness!
già che ci sei/che ci siamo	while you/we're at it etc.
ho dimenticato . . .	I left . . . behind

Practise what you have learnt

1 Listen to the weather forecast on tape and answer the following questions. (Answers p. 174.)

a. Where is the weather going to be cloudy?
- ☐ northern regions
- ☐ centre-south and Adriatic coast

b. Is rain
- ☐ nearly certain?
- ☐ only possible?

c. Is the weather
- ☐ likely to improve?
- ☐ likely to get worse?

2 Complete the following sentences about cars and motoring with a suitable phrase taken from the box below. There are a couple of words you have not seen before, but you should have no difficulty in guessing what they mean. Then check by listening to the sentences on tape.

a. La mia auto ha .... a quattro cilindri.

b. Ogni 15000 chilometri bisogna .... e fare un controllo generale.

c. Prima di partire per l'estero è meglio .... la macchina da un'officina di fiducia.

d. D'inverno bisogna .... nel radiatore.

e. Non ho quasi più benzina. Devo ....

far riguardare	un motore	fare il pieno
mettere l'antigelo	cambiare l'olio	

3 Place the correct caption from box below with each scene. You don't need your tape recorder. (Answers p. 174.)

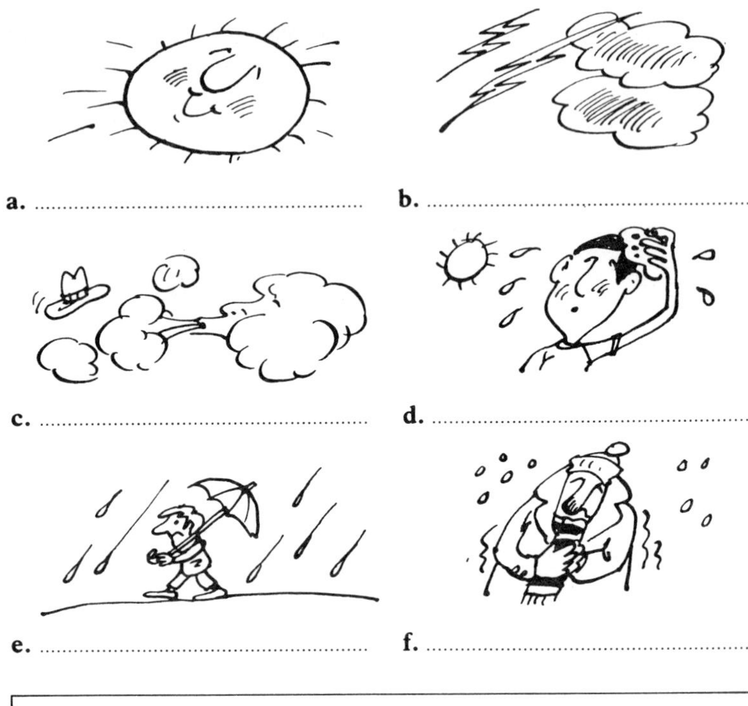

a. .... b. ....

c. .... d. ....

e. .... f. ....

piove	c'è il sole	fa freddo
tira vento	c'è un temporale	fa caldo

4 You may like to know the jingle Italians use to remember which months of the year have thirty and which thirty-one days.

> Trenta giorni ha novembre
> con aprile, giugno e settembre;
> di ventotto ce n'è uno,
> tutti gli altri ne han trentuno (han = hanno)

Listen to the tape where Gina will read it out to you, then write the Italian names of:

a. the month mentioned in the third line of the jingle ....

b. the autumn month with thirty-one days ....

c. the month in which spring begins ....

d. the month in which Christmas falls ....

(Answers p. 174.)

Grammar

Future

To form the future you take away the final **-e** of the infinitive (for **-are** verbs you also change **-ar-** to **-er-**) and add the endings as shown below. Note the stress on 1st and 3rd person singular and that the endings are the same for **-are**, **-ere** and **-ire** verbs.

consigliare
to advise

consiglierò	I'll advise	**consiglieremo**	we'll advise
consiglierai	you'll advise	**consiglierete**	you'll advise
consiglierà	you'll advise (polite) he/she'll advise	**consiglieranno**	they'll advise

mettere
to put

metterò	I'll put	**metteremo**	we'll put
metterai	you'll put	**metterete**	you'll put
metterà	you'll put (polite) he/she'll put	**metteranno**	they'll put

partire
to leave

partirò	I'll leave	**partiremo**	we'll leave
partirai	you'll leave	**partirete**	you'll leave
partirà	you'll leave (polite) he/she'll leave	**partiranno**	they'll leave

As in English, you can use both the present tense and the future: I'm going to the cinema *or* I'll go to the cinema. The future expresses greater deliberation, and is therefore more appropriate in the radio advertisement than the present.

The following verbs, all in frequent use, form their future in a slightly different way, with a shortened 'stem'. The endings are the same.

andare to go	**andrò**	**essere** to be	**sarò**	**vedere** to see	**vedrò**
avere to have	**avrò**	**potere** can	**potrò**	**venire** to come	**verrò**
dovere must	**dovrò**	**rimanere** to remain	**rimarrò**	**volere** to want	**vorrò**

How to talk about things in the past

There are two different past tenses in Italian. In this unit you will study the 'perfect', used when talking about specific events at a definite time in the past. It is formed by combining the present of **avere** or **essere** with the past participle (see Unit 8, p. 115) of the verb in question. You just have to learn which verbs take **avere** and which use **essere** as you meet them, but in general, verbs that can take a direct object (see *Grammar glossary* p. 227) form their perfect with **avere**, e.g.

ho dimenticato il passaporto I left my passport behind
hai pensato all'antigelo? did you remember (lit. think about) the antifreeze?
abbiamo bevuto un vino eccellente we drank an excellent wine

Verbs that cannot take a direct object, and *all* reflexive verbs (see Unit 3 p. 45) use **essere**. Some of the most common are 'verbs of movement', e.g. **venire**, **andare**, **arrivare**, **partire** etc.

è partita alle tre she left at three; **siete rimasti soddisfatti?** are you (lit. have you remained) satisfied?; **ci siamo trattenuti cinque giorni** we stayed five days

Note that when using **essere**, the past participle has to 'agree' with the subject of the verb, i.e. add an **-e** when referring to a feminine singular subject, an **-i** when referring to a plural subject etc.

Read and understand

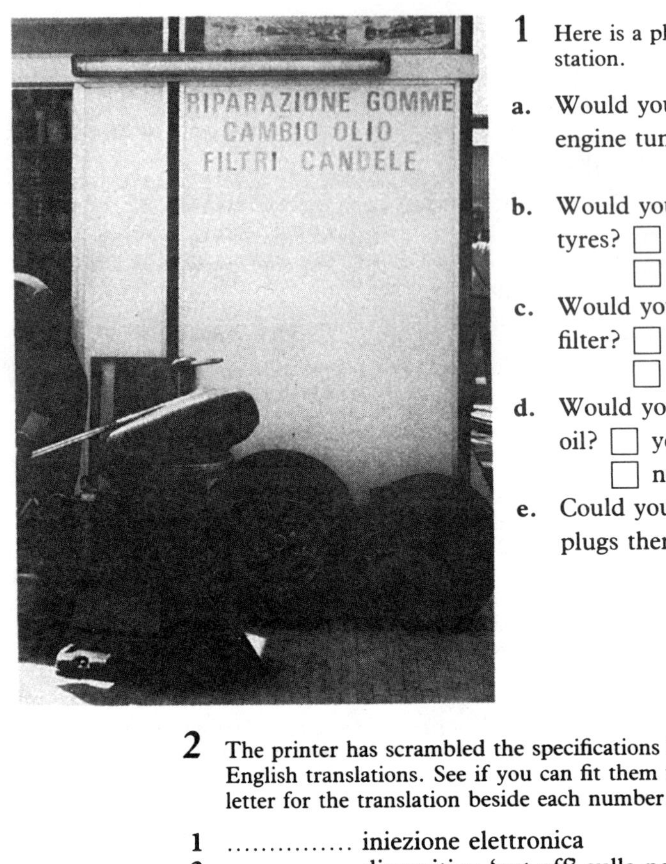

1 Here is a photograph of a small service station.

a. Would you go there to have your engine tuned? ☐ yes ☐ no

b. Would you ask them to mend your tyres? ☐ yes ☐ no

c. Would you ask them to fit a new oil filter? ☐ yes ☐ no

d. Would you ask them to change the oil? ☐ yes ☐ no

e. Could you buy a new set of spark plugs there? ☐ yes ☐ no

2 The printer has scrambled the specifications for a new Italian car and their English translations. See if you can fit them together again. Put the correct letter for the translation beside each number.

1 .... iniezione elettronica
2 .... dispositivo 'cut off' sulla pompa di iniezione per economizzare il carburante
3 .... cambio a cinque marce
4 .... servosterzo
5 .... parabrezza stratificato
6 .... tergicristalli anteriori a due velocità
7 .... tergicristallo posteriore
8 .... antenna radio incorporata nel parabrezza
9 .... condizionatore d'aria

a. two-speed windscreen wipers
b. five-speed gearbox
c. radio aerial incorporated into the windscreen
d. automatic cut-off on fuel injection pump for greater fuel economy
e. rear wiper
f. power steering
g. air conditioning
h. laminated windscreen
i. electronic fuel injection

(Answers to both exercises p. 174.)

Did you know?

Motoring in Italy

Any good motoring guidebook will give you most of the information you need to know before setting out to Italy by car. Of those traffic signs that give written instructions you are sure to be able to guess the meaning of **DEVIAZIONE, PARCHEGGIO, LAVORI IN CORSO**. Less obvious signs are **RALLENTARE, STRADA DISSESTATA, CADUTA MASSI** – though it's doubtful whether you could do much about the last one! (you'll find translations for all these signs at the end of this section). On another sign the words **SOCCORSO STRADALE** precede the telephone number of the rescue service which, with luck, you'll never need.

There are however a few tips you may not find in the normal guidebooks. Italians do not, on the whole, drive at higher speeds than drivers elsewhere, but they accelerate and manoeuvre faster. In a column of cars held up by a red traffic light, Italian drivers will watch not the car in front but the traffic lights: as a consequence the whole column will move forward as the lights change with little or no delay. Zebra crossings mark spots where traffic authorities thought it would be convenient *for motorists* that crossing pedestrians should be channelled, *not* places where pedestrians (**pedoni**) have priority. Try therefore not to stop suddenly to let a pedestrian through at a zebra crossing: the driver behind you will not expect it, and may bump into you. Do *not* use any of the flashing headlights signals you may be familiar with, nor expect to recognize any. Quick flashes in succession usually mean 'get out of my way!' Nobody makes hand signals: drivers or passengers dangling arms out of car windows are simply cooling themselves or throwing out cigarette ends. Country roads at night, particularly in the Northern plains, are plagued by invisible cyclists, riding around with the faintest of lights or no lights at all. Sometimes you'll come across one bicycle with lights on, accompanying another couple without lights.

You can now go from one end of Italy to the other on a network of superb motorways (**autostrade**); but it is likely that what you save in fuel costs is spent on toll fees; and you will most certainly miss all the picturesque, interesting and welcoming towns which ordinary roads pass through, each one of which could make your Italian holiday a most rewarding experience.

What the signs mean . . .
DEVIATION, PARKING, ROAD WORKS AHEAD, SLOW, UNEVEN ROAD SURFACE, FALLING STONES.

Your turn to speak

1 In the first exercise you are at a service station in Italy and you need some petrol, and also some small checks on your car. Look back at the *Key words and phrases* before you start. You'll need the word **tergicristalli** (windscreen wipers).

2 In this exercise you are telling someone about the weather in England, so revise the weather phrases before you start.

Revision

Before you go on to Unit 13, complete the revision section for Units 10–12 at the back of the book on p. 222. There is one revision exercise on tape which comes directly after this unit.

Answers

Practise what you have learnt p. 169 Exercise **1** (**a**) centre-south and Adriatic coast (**b**) only possible (**c**) likely to improve.

p. 170 Exercise **3** (**a**) c'è il sole (**b**) c'è un temporale (**c**) tira vento (**d**) fa caldo (**e**) piove (**f**) fa freddo.

p. 170 Exercise **4** (**a**) febbraio (**b**) ottobre (**c**) marzo (**d**) dicembre.

Read and understand p. 172 Exercise **1** (**a**) no (**b**) yes (**c**) yes (**d**) yes (**e**) yes.

p. 172 Exercise **2** (**1**) i (**2**) d (**3**) b (**4**) f (**5**) h (**6**) a (**7**) e (**8**) c (**9**) g.

13 *Tanti anni fa . . .*

What you will learn

- talking about things in the past (both at a definite point in time and happening over a period of time)
- some expressions of time
- giving information about yourself and your town
- asking this information of others
- talking about the languages you know

Before you begin

Remember the main points from Unit 12:

1 regular future
prenderò, prenderai, prenderà, prenderemo, prenderete, prenderanno
finirò, finirai, finirà, finiremo, finirete, finiranno

2 future with shortened 'stem'
avrò (from **avere**), **avrai, avrà, avremo, avrete, avranno**
verrò (from **venire**) **verrai, verrà, verremo, verrete, verranno**

3 perfect
with **avere**:
ho capito, hai capito, ha capito
abbiamo capito, avete capito, hanno capito
with **essere**:
sono andato/a, sei andato/a, è andato/a,
siamo andati/e, siete andati/e, sono andati/e

Study guide

	Dialogues 1, 2: listen straight through without the book
	Dialogues 1, 2: listen, read and study one by one
	Dialogue 3: listen straight through without the book
	Dialogue 3: listen, read and study notes
	Dialogue 4: listen straight through without the book
	Dialogue 4: listen, read and study notes
	Dialogue 5: listen straight through without the book
	Dialogue 5: listen, read and study notes
	Learn the *Key words and phrases*
	Do the exercises in *Practise what you have learnt*
	Study *Grammar* and do the exercise
	Read *Did you know?* (this time before *Read and understand*)
	Do *Read and understand*
	Do the tape exercises in *Your turn to speak*
	Finally, listen to all the dialogues again straight through

Dialogues

1 *Giovanni asks two women about their visits to England*

Giovanni È mai stata in Inghilterra?
1ª Signorina Ma, in Inghilterra sono stata esattamente vent'anni fa!
Giovanni Dov'è stata?
1ª Signorina Proprio a Londra. Ho soggiornato un anno circa a Londra.
Giovanni Le è piaciuto?
1ª Signorina Allora, sì. A me piaceva tanto.
Giovanni È rimasta a Londra per imparare l'inglese?
1ª Signorina Sì, sì, esatto.
Giovanni (*turning to the second young lady*) E Lei fa la turista qualche volta per conto suo?
2ª Signorina Sì, ma cerco di non fare il turista. Sono stata a Londra – euh – ho chiesto il materiale d'informazione, poi ho cercato di scoprirla un po' da sola, di conoscer la città personalmente.

esattamente exactly
Londra London
soggiornare to stay
un anno circa (*or* **circa un anno**) about one year
rimasto past participle of **rimanere** to remain
chiesto past participle of **chiedere** to ask
da sola by myself, on my own
personalmente personally, in person, by myself

2 *Giovanni asks a young woman about her stay in Canada*

Giovanni Signorina, quanto tempo è stata nel Canada?
Signorina Eh, in Canada quasi sette anni, e un anno in America anche.
Giovanni E che cosa faceva?
Signorina Eh, in Canada ho lavorato per un po' di tempo in un grande magazzino; poi ho lavorato in ospedale anche.
Giovanni E in che città del Canada è stata Lei?
Signorina Io ero . . . euh – nel nord del Canada, una città piccola chiamata Yellowknife.
Giovanni E . . . faceva freddo d'inverno?
Signorina Oh sì, tanto freddo! Sì.

quasi nearly, almost
ospedale (m.) hospital

1 **è mai stata . . .?** have you ever been? **Mai** means 'ever' and **non . . . mai** means 'never' and is used like **non . . . neppure, non . . . nemmeno** etc. e.g. **non vado mai in Italia** I never go to Italy; **non sono mai stata in Francia** I've never been to France.

vent'anni fa twenty years ago. **Fa** is used like 'ago' in English in these types of expression: **una settimana fa** a week ago, last week; **due giorni fa** two days ago; **un mese fa** a month ago etc.

le è piaciuto? did you like it? **Piaciuto** is the past participle of **piacere**.

allora sì. A me piaceva tanto at the time, yes. I was having such a good time. **Piaceva** (also from **piacere**) is a form of the other past tense mentioned in Unit 12, called the 'imperfect'. The different use of the perfect and imperfect doesn't exist in English. For the moment, just note how it occurs in these next dialogues and then look at the explanation in *Grammar* p. 184.

qualche volta sometimes, a few times. **Qualche** (invariable) is always followed by a singular noun: **qualche turista** a few tourists, **qualche giorno** a few days.

per conto suo on your (polite) own account, by yourself (or, in a different context, on his/her own account, by him-/herself). Other examples: **per conto mio preferisco vivere in Italia** as far as I'm concerned I'd rather live in Italy; **pago anche per conto del mio amico** I'm paying also on behalf of my friend.

ho cercato di scoprirla (i.e. **la città di Londra**) I tried to discover it. Note how the pronoun **la** (it) is added to the infinitive, which drops its final **-e**. **Cercare** (to look for, to try) is used in several common phrases: **cerca di arrivare puntuale** try to arrive on time; **ti ho cercato oggi pomeriggio** I looked for you this afternoon.

2 **quanto tempo è stata nel Canada?** how long (lit. how much time) were you in Canada?

che cosa faceva? what were you doing? Here is another example of the imperfect tense. He could also have asked: **che cosa ha fatto**? what did you do?

ho lavorato I worked. First she worked in a department store, then in a hospital. **Lavorare** = to work.

io ero I was. This is part of the imperfect of **essere**, see *Grammar* p. 184.

faceva freddo d'inverno? was it cold in winter? Here Giovanni is asking was it cold, in general. If he had wanted to know about a specific period he would have said, e.g. **ha fatto molto freddo due anni fa?** was it very cold two years ago?

3 *Giovanni talks to a young man who came to Plymouth to study English*

Giovanni E dove è stato l'anno scorso?
Signore Pluimun.
Giovanni Gli inglesi in realtà dicono 'Plymouth'.
Signore E va bene, io lo pronuncio come posso.
Giovanni Si è trovato bene?
Signore Abbastanza.
Giovanni Ha imparato l'inglese?
Signore Più che altro la grammatica.
Giovanni Ma lo parla l'inglese adesso?
Signore Sì, ma piccoli discorsi, cioè frasi che terminano dopo . . . massimo un minuto o due.
Giovanni Be', quanto tempo è stato?
Signore Eh, venti giorni.
Giovanni Non si può imparare di più in venti giorni, no? È già stato abbastanza bravo a imparare così tanto!

in realtà in fact
adesso now
piccoli discorsi short sentences
frasi phrases, sentences
terminare to end
(al) massimo at the most

4 *A waiter describes his work*

Giovanni C'è molto da lavorare in questo ristorante?
Cameriere Eh, uno che lavora qua, deve sacrificarsi. Far le pulizie, riordinare, preparare, servire.
Giovanni E Lei da quanto tempo lavora?
Cameriere Ho lavorato sempre da ragazzo. Tutti i migliori ristoranti, grandi alberghi; e son felice d' averlo fatto per tanti anni. Ho avuto un bel ristorante anch'io. Io ho avuto una 'Botte d'Oro' che veramente, anche oggi che l'ho venduta, è rimasta botte d'oro, in tutti i sensi.

qua here
sacrificarsi to sacrifice oneself
far le pulizie to clean
riordinare to tidy up
preparare to prepare, to get things ready
servire to serve

3 **l'anno scorso** last year. Also: **la settimana scorsa** last week; **il mese scorso** last month. 'Next' is **prossimo: l'anno prossimo, la settimana prossima, il mese prossimo.**

io lo pronuncio come posso I pronounce it the best I can. **La pronuncia** = pronunciation.

si è trovato bene? were you all right? how did you like it? If you asked a woman the same question you would say: **si è trovata bene?** Other expressions: **come si trova in quell'albergo?** how do you find that hotel? **mi trovo bene** I'm quite happy with it, I find it quite comfortable; **vi troverete bene in quel ristorante** you'll be OK in that restaurant.

è gia stato abbastanza bravo a imparare così tanto you've already been quite clever to learn so much. **Bravo** may be translated in a variety of ways: **un bravo ragazzo** a good boy; **un pianista molto bravo** a very good pianist; **brava gente, brave persone** nice people. It does *not* mean 'brave'.

4 **e Lei da quanto tempo lavora?** how long have you been working? (lit. you, since how long are you working?) Note the use of the present tense in Italian in this type of phrase: **lavoro da cinque anni in Italia** I've been working in Italy for the past five years (and still do); **abito con Giorgio da un mese** I've been living with Giorgio for a month. If Giovanni had wanted to imply that the waiter was no longer working, he would have asked: **per quanto tempo ha lavorato?**

sempre da ragazzo always since I was a boy (lit. since boy). A woman would have said **da ragazza**, since I was a girl.

un bel ristorante a beautiful restaurant. Before nouns that take **il** as a definite article (e.g. **il ristorante**) **bello** and **quello** are shortened to **bel** and **quel**, e.g. **il bel posto, quel giorno**. Before a noun beginning with a vowel, their final **-o** is replaced by an apostrophe: **un bell'albergo, quell'albergo.**

'Botte d'Oro' Golden Cask, was the name of the waiter's own restaurant, which still makes a lot of money, and therefore is still a barrelful of gold, **in tutti i sensi**, in all senses of the word.

l'ho venduta I've sold it. **Venduto** is the past participle of **vendere**, to sell. When the perfect is preceded by **lo** or **la** they are both reduced to **l'**, and the past participle has to 'agree'. Here it's **venduta** because the waiter is thinking of **la Botte d'Oro**, not of **il ristorante**.

5 *Enrico and Cesarina tell Giovanni about the places they come from, Palombaro and Suzzara*

Giovanni Che posto è Palombaro?
Enrico Eh, è un piccolo paesino di collina. Si trova molto vicino alla catena degli Appennini, alla Maiella, no?
Giovanni Quindi è un paese agricolo.
Enrico Mmm, sì, però più che agricoltura è l'allevamento.
Giovanni Bestiame?
Enrico Sì, bestiame, o . . . ovini, suini . . .
Giovanni Mmmm, mmmm.
Enrico Bo . . . bovini.
Giovanni Quanti abitanti fa Palombaro più o meno?
Enrico Molto pochi. Siamo in tut . . . in tutto milletrecento abitanti.
Giovanni Allora in confronto a Palombaro Suzzara è una città.
Cesarina Eh, Suzzara non è una città molto grande. È una cittadina dove sono sorte ultimamente alcune industrie. Comunque prevale l'attività agricola.

paese (m.) village, small town; **paesino** small village
collina hill, hillside
catena mountain range (*also* chain)
Appennini Apennines
Maiella a mountain in the Apennines
quindi therefore
agricoltura farming, agriculture (*adj.* **agricolo**)
allevamento animal breeding (**allevare** = to bring up)
in confronto a compared with
sorto past part. of **sorgere** to arise
ultimamente lately
comunque anyhow, anyway, however
prevalere to prevail

5

- **che posto è?** what (sort of) place is it? Other phrases with **posto**: **che bel posto** what a beautiful place; **un posto di montagna** a mountain resort; **tutto è a posto** everything's OK, all is settled; **mettere a posto** to tidy up, to put (things, persons) in their place.

  bestiame (m. sing.), from **bestia** beast, is a general word for cattle and farm animals (excluding poultry which is called **pollame**). It is subdivided into **gli ovini**, which include sheep and goats; **i suini**, pigs; and **i bovini** cows, oxen, and bulls. The names of the various farm animals are listed in *Key words and phrases* opposite.

- **quanti abitanti fa?** how many inhabitants does it have (lit. make)? Enrico might have replied: **fa in tutto 1300 abitanti** it has a total of 1300 inhabitants, but he preferred to include himself among them, saying: 'we are 1300 in all'.

  città town; **cittadina** small town. Note the use of the diminutive also in **paese, paesino**.

- **alcune industrie** a few industries. You could also say **qualche industria**, see note on dialogue 1, p. 177.

Key words and phrases

Expressions of time

due giorni fa	two days ago
una settimana fa	a week ago
l'anno scorso	last year
il mese prossimo	next month
qualche volta/alcune volte	sometimes, a few times

Asking information *(about a visit, home town etc.)*

da quanto tempo è in Inghilterra?	how long have you been in England? *(and are still there)*
(per) quanto tempo è stato in America?	how long were you in America? *(and are no longer there)*
le è piaciuto? **ti è piaciuto?**	did you like it?
si trova bene? **ti trovi bene?**	do you like it? are you comfortable?
che posto è?	what sort of place is it?
quanti abitanti fa?	how many inhabitants does it have?

Giving information

sono in Italia da (due anni)	I've been in Italy (two years) *(and I'm still there)*
sono stato/a in Italia per (due anni)	I was in Italy for (two years) *(and have left)*
sono andato/a per conto mio	I went by myself
la mia città/il mio paese è . . .	my town/my village is . . .
bella/bello	beautiful
grande	big
piccola/piccolo	small
ha qualche industria	it has some industries
fa (1300) abitanti	it has (1300) inhabitants

Farm animals

la pecora	sheep
la capra	goat
il maiale	pig
il bue (pl. **i buoi**)	ox
la mucca	cow
il toro	bull
il cavallo	horse
l'asino	donkey
il mulo	mule
la gallina	hen

Practise what you have learnt

1 Listen to Dino talking about his early life, and see how much you can understand of what he is saying, by answering the following questions. (Answers p. 188.)

a. What is the name of the village where Dino was born?
- ☐ Friuli
- ☐ Tolmezzo

b. How many years did he live there before moving to Bolzano?
- ☐ seven
- ☐ ten

c. Where did he complete his schooling?
- ☐ Bolzano
- ☐ Tolmezzo

d. Did he go to university in Bolzano?
- ☐ yes
- ☐ no

2 Now, using Dino's conversation from Exercise 1, and the following questions as a guide, make up some sentences about your own life and town. Obviously the exact answers can't be given, but on p. 188 you will find some sample sentences you may have used.

Dove sei nato/a?

....

Hai passato l'infanzia lì?

....

Dove hai fatto la scuola?

....

Dove abiti adesso?

....

Che posto è?

....

Quanti abitanti fa?

....

Ti trovi bene lì?

....

3 Listen to the dialogue on tape in which a man is asked about the languages he knows, then answer the following questions. (Answers p. 188.)

a. Which foreign language did he study at school?

☐ French

☐ English

☐ Spanish

b. How good is his spoken English?

☐ he is quite fluent because he practises regularly

☐ he can say short sentences but cannot engage in lengthy conversation

c. How well does he know French?

☐ he learnt French grammar, not how to speak French

☐ he can speak French quite well, with a good pronunciation

4 Imagine that today is Monday 15th March, **lunedì quindici marzo** (for dates you use ordinary numerals in Italian). Write in the spaces below the dates corresponding to the following expressions. You won't need your tape recorder. (Answers p. 188.)

a. tre giorni fa ....

b. la settimana scorsa ....

c. esattamente due mesi fa ....

d. dopodomani ....

e. lunedì prossimo ....

f. la settimana prossima ....

5 Fill in the gaps in the sentences below with one of the following forms of **essere**: **sono, sono stato** (or **sono stata**) **sarò**. You won't need your tape recorder. (Answers p. 188.)

a. ....a Londra un anno fa.

b. ....a Roma la settimana prossima.

c. ....in Italia da due settimane.

d. ....in Inghilterra per due anni.

e. ....a casa dopodomani.

f. ....a Plymouth l'estate scorsa.

Grammar

The imperfect

The imperfect tense can be easily formed by replacing the **-re** of the infinitive with the endings shown below, which are the same for all types of verb.

lavorare to work	**avere** to have	**servire** to serve
lavoravo	**avevo**	**servivo**
lavoravi	**avevi**	**servivi**
lavorava	**aveva**	**serviva**
lavoravamo	**avevamo**	**servivamo**
lavoravate	**avevate**	**servivate**
lavoravano	**avevano**	**servivano**

The only exception is **essere**:
ero, eri, era, eravamo, eravate, erano

It could be misleading to give a 'translation' of the forms above because there is no tense in English exactly corresponding to the Italian imperfect. You should try to understand its use by noticing how it differs from the perfect in the dialogues and in the examples below.

The perfect is used to talk about things which occurred at a definite time or period in the past, and are seen as completed or finished:
Sono stato a Londra la prima volta nel 1968, e ci sono rimasto due anni. I was in London the first time in 1968, and stayed there two years.

The imperfect, on the other hand, leaves things 'unfinished', and is therefore used to talk about situations and states lasting or recurring over an unspecified length of time in the past. It can often be translated into English as 'was -ing' or 'used to . . .'
Quando ero a Londra andavo spesso a teatro. Allora costava poco. When I was in London I used to go often to the theatre. Then it was cheap.

The two tenses may be contrasted in the same sentence:
Lavoravo in un grande albergo, e così ho studiato l'inglese.
I used to work in a luxury hotel, that's why I studied English.

Exercise Complete the following sentences with the verbal forms in the box below. (Answers p. 188.)

a. Quando .... a Londra da studente .... molto andare a teatro.

b. .... a Londra solo due volte e .... molto.

c. Per cinque anni .... come cameriere in un ristorante poi .... un ristorante mio.

ho lavorato	stavo	sono stato/stata
ho avuto	mi piaceva	mi è piaciuta

Did you know?

Population of Italy

In 1861, according to a census organized by the first united Italian government, the population of Italy was about 26 million people. Today it exceeds 56 million: more than twice as many as there were when national unity was achieved. The largest towns are Roma, the capital, with just under 3 million inhabitants; Milano, approaching 2 million; Torino (Turin) and Napoli (Naples) with just under one and a half million people. Genova has just under one million inhabitants, and Firenze (Florence) about half a million. There are furthermore about 40 towns with over 100,000 inhabitants, and 75 with over 50,000 inhabitants. If you remember that Italy was divided for most of its history into several independent states and principalities, and therefore nearly every Italian town of some importance was at some time or other a state or regional capital, you can understand this abundance of large population centres. Probably because of it, Italians tend to underestimate the importance of provincial towns which never reached the status of capital city: in dialogue 3 of the next unit you will hear a student describe his home town, Gambettola, with up to 50,000 people living in it, as **un paesino** (a small village). Thriving provincial centres with more than 100,000 inhabitants are often described as **cittadine** (small towns).

Local government

Italy is divided into 20 **regioni** to which the central government delegates a wide range of administrative powers. Regions are divided into a variable number of **provincie**, each of which contains several **comuni.** The **comune**, of which there are 8050 in the whole country, headed by an elected **sindaco** (mayor), is the smallest local government unit. While the central government has so far remained firmly in the hands of centre and right-wing political parties, large areas of Italy, and some of the most important towns (e.g. Torino, Milano, Napoli, even the capital itself) have come to be administered by the left, including the Communist party. Bologna, often called **Bologna la rossa** not only because of the reddish bricks with which many of its medieval buildings were built, but also because of its long-standing revolutionary traditions, has long been one of the showpieces of Communist local government. Local government powers were enhanced by legislation passed in the late 'sixties, and have resulted in notable administrative improvements and in an increased number of interesting cultural initiatives on a regional level (art exhibitions, concerts, theatrical events, restoration and preservation of ancient monuments etc.).

Read and understand

Read the notes (opposite) on four well-known Roman monuments, such as you may find in a tourist guide. You do not need to understand every word in order to answer the following questions. (Answers p. 188.)

a. Which is the most ancient of the four monuments mentioned?

....

b. Which one is the most recent?

....

c. Where was King Victor Emmanuel II buried?

....

d. How long did it take to build the Trevi fountain?

....

e. For how many centuries did the Terme di Caracalla perform their intended function of public baths?

....

f. Two architects are mentioned in the notes. Give their names.

....

g. Which of the monuments is now used as a summer theatre?

....

ALCUNI MONUMENTI ROMANI

VITTORIANO Lo ha progettato l'architetto Saccone. Il monumento, in marmo bianco, è stato costruito in memoria di re Vittorio Emanuele II, primo re dell'Italia unita. Incominciato nel 1885, è stato terminato solo nel 1911.

FONTANA DI TREVI È stata costruita dal 1732 al 1762, su progetto di Nicola Salvi, e resa famosa, circa duecento anni dopo, dal film *La dolce vita*.

PANTHEON Questo grandioso santuario pagano, dedicato da Agrippa a tutti gli dei nel 27 dopo Cristo, è poi diventato un santuario cristiano. Ora vi si trovano le tombe di italiani illustri, tra cui il pittore Raffaello e i re d'Italia Vittorio Emanuele II e Umberto I.

TERME DI CARACALLA Cominciate nel terzo secolo dopo Cristo dall'imperatore Settimio Severo, inaugurate dal figlio Caracalla e completate dai suoi successori, erano le più grandi terme romane dell'epoca imperiale. Sono state usate come terme fino al sesto secolo. Oggi vi si svolgono concerti sinfonici e la stagione estiva di opera lirica.

Your turn to speak

1 In this exercise you will answer some questions about your language studies. Before you start, just listen again to the dialogue on tape for Exercise 2 of *Practise what you have learnt* which will remind you of some of the vocabulary you'll need. Remember the two verbs **parlare** (to speak) and **studiare** (to study).

2 This time *you* will be asking the questions. You're asking Giancarlo about his home town. You'll need to use the word **ancora** (still) and you'll also hear these new words: **coltelli** (knives) and **forbici** (scissors).

Answers

Practise what you have learnt p. 182 Exercise **1** (**a**) Tolmezzo (**b**) ten (**c**) Bolzano (**d**) no (he went to Pisa).

p. 182 Exercise **2** Here are some sample sentences:
Sono nato a (Londra)
Sono nata in (Inghilterra)
Sì, ho passato i primi quindici anni lì/No, ho passato la mia infanzia a (Birmingham)
Ho fatto la scuola a (Londra)
Adesso abito a (Newcastle)
È una città grande/È un paese piccolo/Ha molte industrie/È un paese agricolo
Fa (100,000) abitanti/Siamo molto pochi
Sì, mi trovo molto bene/No, non mi piace.

p. 183 Exercise **3** (**a**) French (**b**) he can say short sentences but cannot engage in lengthy conversation (**c**) he learnt French grammar, not how to speak French.

p. 183 Exercise **4** (**a**) venerdì dodici marzo (**b**) dall'otto al quattordici marzo (**c**) il quindici gennaio (**d**) mercoledì diciassette marzo (**e**) il ventidue marzo (**f**) dal ventidue al ventinove marzo. (Normally if you write the date, of course, you don't need to write the numbers out in full – this is just to remind you of the Italian numbers.)

p. 183 Exercise **5** (**a**) sono stato/a (**b**) sarò (**c**) sono (**d**) sono stato/a (**e**) sarò (**f**) sono stato/a.

Grammar p. 184 (**a**) stavo, mi piaceva (**b**) sono stato, mi è piaciuta (**c**) ho lavorato, ho avuto.

Read and understand p. 186 (**a**) Pantheon (**b**) Vittoriano (**c**) in the Pantheon (**d**) 30 years (**e**) 3 centuries (**f**) Saccone and Salvi (**g**) Terme di Caracalla.

14 Si potrebbe andare al cinema

What you will learn

- how to talk about things you would like to do
- how to invite friends and acquaintances to an evening out
- how to explain minor health problems to a chemist or to a doctor

Before you begin

Points to remember from Unit 13:

1 the imperfect – used to talk about unspecified states or situations in the past
essere: **ero, eri, era, eravamo, eravate, erano**
avere (and all other verbs): **avevo, avevi, aveva, avevamo, avevate, avevano**

2 how to express duration in the past
faccio il cameriere da cinque anni
I have been a waiter for five years (and still am one)
ho fatto il cameriere per cinque anni
I was a waiter for five years (and no longer am one)

Study guide

	Dialogues 1, 2: listen straight through without the book
	Dialogues 1, 2: listen, read and study one by one
	Dialogues 3, 4: listen straight through without the book
	Dialogues 3, 4: listen, read and study one by one
	Dialogues 5, 6: listen straight through without the book
	Dialogues 5, 6: listen, read and study one by one
	Study the *Key words and phrases*
	Do the exercises in *Practise what you have learnt*
	Study the *Grammar* section and do the exercise
	Do *Read and understand*
	Read *Did you know?*
	Do the tape exercises in *Your turn to speak*
	Finally, listen to all the dialogues again straight through

Dialogues

1 *Annamaria and Giovanni make plans for the evening*

Annamaria Che cosa ti piacerebbe fare questa sera? Si potrebbe andare al cinema.
Giovanni Ma . . . non c'è niente di bello al cinema, niente che vorrei vedere.
Annamaria Se ti piace la musica popolare potremmo andare a un concerto.
Giovanni Mmm . . . un concerto . . . Che cosa danno?
Annamaria Musica popolare dell'Italia meridionale. Canti e danze della Basilicata.
Giovanni Mmm . . . sì, l'idea mi va. Andiamo a questo concerto.

musica popolare folk music
concerto concert
canti songs
danze dances (*also* **balli**; **ballare** = to dance)
Basilicata a region in Southern Italy

2 *Dino invites Giovanni to go to the opera*

Dino A te piace l'opera?
Giovanni Ma, non eccessivamente, devo dir la verità. Perché?
Dino Siccome stasera danno *La Bohème* al teatro mi piacerebbe molto andarci. E, se t'interessa, possiamo andare insieme.
Giovanni Mmm . . . a che teatro la danno?
Dino Al Goldoni.
Giovanni Eh sì, sarebbe una buona idea. Sai a che ora comincia?
Dino Alle otto e mezzo, e . . . quindi, se noi siamo pronti per le otto, arriviamo senz'altro in tempo.

non eccessivamente not very much
siccome as
➧ **teatro** theatre
Goldoni name of the theatre (and of an Italian 18th-century playwright)
cominciare to begin

1 ▸ **che cosa ti piacerebbe fare?** what would you like to do? For **piacerebbe, potrebbe, potremmo, vorrei** etc., see *Grammar* p. 199.
There are other ways of asking basically the same question: **che cosa facciamo questa sera?; che cosa vogliamo fare questa sera?; che cosa si fa questa sera?**

▸ **si potrebbe andare al cinema** one could go to the cinema. Note that in Italian 'one' is used much more often than in English. He could also have said: **potremmo andare al cinema** we could go to the cinema.

niente di bello nothing good. Note the use of **di** after **niente**: **niente di interessante** nothing interesting; **non c'è niente di male** there's no harm in it. Notice also that 'good' for films, plays etc. is **bello**.

niente che vorrei vedere nothing I'd like to see. **Vorrei** is the same form used before in requests like: **vorrei un francobollo da 300 lire** I'd like a 300 lira stamp (it's from **volere**, to want).

▸ **che cosa danno?** what's on? (lit. what do they give?). You can use **dare** (to give) talking of all sorts of performances and entertainments: **danno *Via col vento* alla televisione** they're showing *Gone with the Wind* on television; **danno un'opera di Verdi** they're performing an opera by Verdi.

▸ **l'idea mi va** I like the idea; **ti va?** do you like it? **non mi va affatto** I don't like it at all. (Note **non . . . affatto**, not at all.)

2 **devo dir(e) la verità** I must tell the truth; **per dir la verità** to tell the truth.

stasera (short for **questa sera**) this evening, tonight. Similarly: **stamattina** this morning, **stanotte** tonight.

▸ **se t'interessa, possiamo andarci insieme** if you're interested (lit. if it interests you) we can go together. Note that **ci** (there) joins on to the infinitive, which loses its final **-e**.

▸ **sarebbe una buona idea** it would be a good idea. Or, more simply: **buona idea! che buona idea.**

▸ **pronti per le otto** ready by eight.

▸ **in tempo** (or **a tempo**) on time. Note also the following expressions: **puntualmente** punctually; **in ritardo** late; **in anticipo** early, in advance.

3 *Gianfranco describes his future work prospects*

Gianfranco Fino ad ora ho studiato, però appena ritorno a casa inizierò a lavorare in una scuola materna, perché sono anche maestro.

Giovanni Ah, sei maestro . . . Una scuola materna: quindi insegnerai a bambini piccoli.

Gianfranco Dai tre ai sei anni.

Giovanni Dove insegnerai?

Gianfranco Insegnerò in un paesino vicino a Cesena, che è la mia città natale. Insegnerò a Gambettola, un paesino di circa cinquantamila abitanti.

però but, however
appena as soon as
ritornare to return, to go back
a casa home
iniziare to begin
scuola materna nursery school
bambino, -a child

4 *Giovanni asks Dino about his holiday plans*

Giovanni Quando pensi di prenderti una vacanza la prossima volta?

Dino Probabilmente nell'autunno prossimo, o in ottobre, o in novembre al più tardi.

Giovanni Hai . . . hai deciso dov'è che andrai?

Dino Sì, probabilmente nell'Italia settentrionale, e centrale, non so, tra Milano e Roma, diciamo. La località precisa ancora non, non la so.

Giovanni E perché hai scelto questa stagione per andare in vacanza? La maggior parte della gente va in vacanza d'estate.

Dino Ma, l'estate è troppo calda.

al più tardi at the latest
decidere (part part. **deciso**) to decide
località place, resort
stagione (f.) season
la maggior parte di . . . most

3 **fino a . . .** until, as far as . . . It can be used when speaking of places, e.g. **fino alla stazione** as far as the station; **fino a qui** all the way to here; and speaking of time, e.g. **fino ad ora** until now, up to now; **fino alle tre** until three o'clock; **fino a domani** until tomorrow.

maestro, -a primary schoolteacher. A more general word for 'teacher' is **insegnante** (from **insegnare**, to teach). Secondary school teachers, and all tertiary lecturers, whatever their grade, are called **professore** (**m.**) or **professoressa** (**f.**). Remember that, like all other titles ending in **-re**, **professore** loses its final **-e** when followed by a name: **ho incontrato il professor Rossi** I met/came across (Professor) Rossi.

natale of birth, from **nascere**, to be born, past participle **nato**. Remember from Unit 13: **dove sei nato?** where were you born? **sono nato a Milano** I was born in Milan. **Natale** is also the Italian for Christmas.

4 **quando pensi di prenderti una vacanza?** when do you think you're going to take a holiday? The **-ti** (lit. yourself) attached to **prendere** is idiomatic and can be ignored.

dov'è che andrai? where is it that you'll be going? This is often used instead of the simpler: **dove andrai?**

la gente people. This word is *singular* and goes with singular adjectives and verbs: **c'era molta gente** there were a lot of people; **la gente bene educata** 'nice', well-bred people; **che cosa dirà la gente?** what will people say?

5 *Giovanni asks a chemist's advice about his headache*

Giovanni Ieri ho mangiato un po' troppo. Mi son svegliato questa mattina col mal di testa. Lei che cosa mi consiglia?
Farmacista Ha anche disturbi di stomaco?
Giovanni Leggeri, sì.
Farmacista Il solito Alka-Selzer allora.
Giovanni Alka-Selzer?
Farmacista Sì, se ha disturbi di stomaco e mal di testa, conseguenza di un'indigestione.
Giovanni Alka-Selzer.
Farmacista Una scatoletta da dodici costa mille quattrocento lire.

farmacista (m./f.) chemist
consigliare to advise
disturbo trouble
leggero light, slight
solito usual
conseguenza di because of
indigestione (f.) indigestion
scatoletta small box

6 *In her surgery, a doctor examines a small patient, accompanied by her father*

Dottoressa Ha anche il raffreddore la bambina?
Papà No.
Dottoressa Soltanto della temperatura. Ed . . . è alta la febbre?
Papà Oh sì, è alta . . .
Dottoressa Mm . . . mm. È alta. Quanti anni ha la bambina?
Papà Ha due anni.
Dottoressa Ecco.
Papà Er, Novalgina?
Dottoressa Novalgina a gocce. Sì. Le dà un cinque gocce . . . e tre o quattro volte al giorno. Questo dovrebbe tenere bassa la temperatura e togliere anche un po' il dolore.

dottoressa woman doctor
raffreddore (m.) cold
temperatura temperature
alto high (**basso** low)
febbre (f.) fever, temperature
Novalgina name of a drug
dà give (from **dare**, to give)
dolore (m.) pain.

5 **mi son(o) svegliato** I woke up. This is from **svegliarsi** to wake up, a reflexive verb (note the infinitive of a reflexive verb has **-si** on the end). You can ask reception at your hotel: **mi svegli alle sette** wake me up at seven. **La sveglia** = alarm clock.

mal(e) di testa headache. The phrases for other complaints can be found in *Key words and phrases* p. 196. Note also: **mi fa male . . .** I have a pain in my . . ., e.g. **mi fa male il ginocchio** I have a pain in my knee; **mi fa male l'orecchio** I have a pain in my ear; **mi fa male qui** I have a pain here; and **ho mal di stomaco** I feel sick.

6 **a gocce** drops, in drop form. Medicines and drugs come also in **compresse** tablets, **pillole** pills, **pastiglie** lozenges, **bustine** sachets, **iniezioni** injections, **supposte** suppositories, **pomate** ointments.

un cinque gocce about five drops; **un sei o sette pastiglie al giorno** about six or seven lozenges a day. Other ways of expressing approximate numbers: **una decina** about ten, **una ventina** about twenty, **una trentina** about thirty etc., replacing **-a** of the tens with **-ina**; **un centinaio** about a hundred, **un migliaio** about a thousand.

tre o quattro volte al giorno three or four times a day. Note the use of **a** in the following phrases: **due volte alla settimana** twice a week; **tre volte all'anno** three times a year; **una volta al mese** once a month.

In an emergency you might need a dentist, **un/una dentista**. A medical doctor is **un medico**, although **dottore** and **dottoressa** are also used.

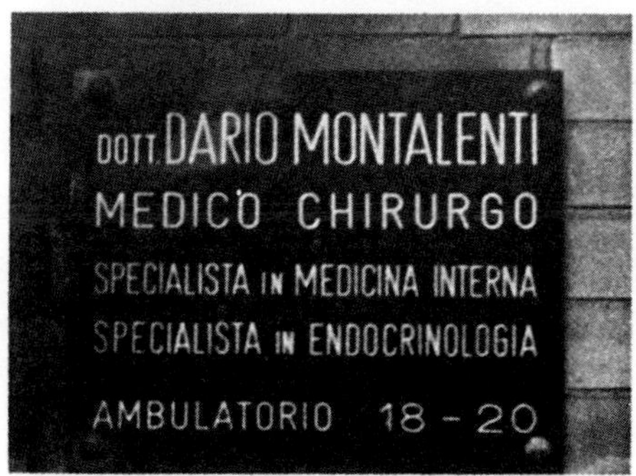

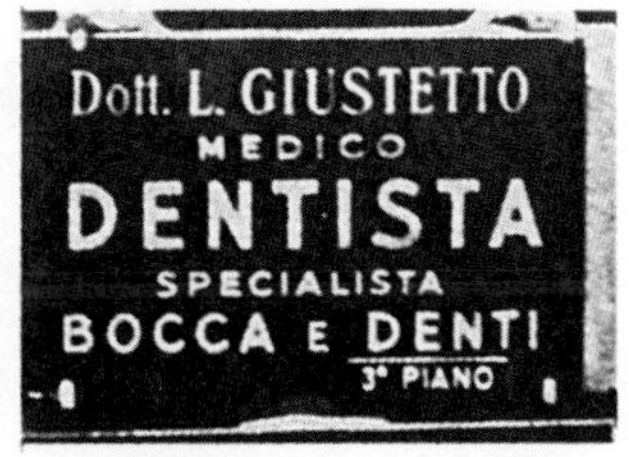

Key words and phrases

Entertainment

che cosa ti piacerebbe fare?	what would you like to do?
che cosa vogliamo fare?	what do we want to do?
che cosa facciamo? **che cosa si fa?**	what shall we do?
se t'interessa. . .	if you are interested . . .
si potrebbe andare . . . **potremmo andare . . .**	we could go . . .
al cinema	to the cinema
al teatro	to the theatre
alla spiaggia	to the beach
che cosa danno?	what's on?
ti va?	do you like the idea?
l'idea mi va	I like the idea
(sarebbe una) buona idea	(it would be a) good idea
fino ad ora	up to now

Health problems

ho mal di. . .	I have a . . . ache
testa	head
denti	tooth
pancia	stomach
schiena	back
mare/aria	I feel sea/air sick
mi fa male . . .	I have a pain in my . . .
il ginocchio	knee
l'orecchio	ear
la gola	I have a sore throat
ho la febbre	I have a temperature

To understand

siamo pronti per le otto	we'll be ready by eight
a tempo, puntualmente	on time, punctually
in ritardo	late
in anticipo	in advance, early

Medicines

gocce	drops
compresse	tablets
pastiglie	lozenges
pillole	pills
iniezioni/punture	injections
supposte	suppositories
pomata	ointment
tre o quattro volte al giorno	three or four times a day

Practise what you have learnt

1 Giancarlo and Gina are discussing their plans for the evening. Listen to the dialogue on tape and answer the following questions. (Answers p. 202.)

a. What do they decide straight away *not* to do?

☐ go to the cinema
☐ stay at home

b. Does Giancarlo like opera?

☐ yes
☐ no

c. Does he want to go to

☐ a play?
☐ a concert?

d. What do they decide to do in the end?

☐ go to a symphony concert next evening
☐ go to a play by Goldoni at the Teatro delle Muse
☐ dine out at a good restaurant

2 Listen to three people introducing themselves on tape and decide which of the entertainments advertised they would each enjoy. (Answers p. 202.)

Carla................................

Luisa................................

Giorgio................................

A

TEATRO DELLE MUSE

Stagione internazionale
presenta
la compagnia del
Birmingham Repertory Theatre in
THE CARETAKER
di Harold Pinter
(in lingua originale)

B

TEATRO LIRICO

Concerto Sinfonico
Orchestra da camera della RAI
diretta dal
Maestro Bruno Nicolai

Musiche di Albinoni, Purcell, Mozart, Bartok.

C

AL CLUB DEL JAZZ
suona il
Quintetto Billy Harper
con
Billy Harper sax tenore
Chris Albert tromba
Armen Donelian piano
Louis Pears contrabbasso
Newman Baker percussione

D

CINEMA ASTORIA
Grande ripresa di
una classica avventura di 007
Il dottor No
con
SEAN CONNERY
URSULA ANDRESS

3 Re-arrange the following dialogue between a patient and her doctor. Then listen to the correct version on tape.

Paziente Sì, credo di aver fatto indigestione.
Dottore Vedrà che domani starà bene.
Paziente Grazie.
Dottore Prenda due di queste compresse adesso, e due dopo cena.
Paziente Da questa mattina.
Dottore Ha anche disturbi di stomaco?
Paziente Ho mal di testa e anche un po' di febbre.
Dottore Da quanto tempo?

Paziente ....

Dottore ....

Paziente ....

Dottore ....

Paziente ....

Dottore ....

Paziente ....

Dottore ....

4 Your friend doesn't know what to do in his free time. Complete the sentences below with the most likely phrases from those in the box beneath. There are a few words you haven't met before but you shouldn't have any trouble in guessing what they mean. You won't need your tape recorder. (Answers p. 202.)

a. Usciamo insieme questa sera? ....

all'Odeon. Ti piacerebbe vederlo?

b. Sei stanco? Allora potremmo stare a casa a ....

c. Oppure andiamo a .... So che Anna e

Flavia saranno al Bar Motta alle otto.

d. Domani, se fa bello, andiamo .... Il mare

è caldo in questa stagione.

e. Se vuoi un po' di cultura, potremmo................................, è

aperto domani.

alla spiaggia	prendere una birra	
visitare il museo	danno un film	guardare la televisione

Grammar

The conditional

The 'conditional' simply means the 'would/should' tense: I would like, they would be able to etc. To form this tense, take away the final **-e** of the infinitive (changing the **-ar-** of **-are** verbs to **-er-**), exactly as in the future, and add the endings shown below:

lavorare to work	**togliere** to take away	**preferire** to prefer
lavorerei	**toglierei**	**preferirei**
lavoreresti	**toglieresti**	**preferiresti**
lavorerebbe	**toglierebbe**	**preferirebbe**
lavoreremmo	**toglieremmo**	**preferiremmo**
lavorereste	**togliereste**	**preferireste**
lavorerebbero	**toglierebbero**	**preferirebbero**

The same verbs that shorten their 'stem' in the future (see Unit 12) do so in the conditional; the endings, however, are the same as above:

andare to go **andrei**
avere to have **avrei**
dovere must **dovrei**
essere to be **sarei**
potere to be able, can **potrei**
rimanere to remain **rimarrei**
vedere to see **vedrei**
volere to want **vorrei**
venire to come **verrei**

This tense is used:
- in making polite requests and expressing wishes
- in expressing opinions, possibilities and expectations

vorrei un caffé I'd like a coffee
le piacerebbe di venire al cinema con me? would you like to come to the cinema with me?
preferiremmo due camere separate we'd rather have two separate rooms
sarebbe difficile it would be difficult
questo dovrebbe togliere il dolore this ought to take away the pain
andrei a teatro, ma ho il raffreddore I'd go to the theatre, but I've got a cold.

Exercise Fill in the gaps in the sentences below with one of the conditionals from the box in the margin. (Answers p. 202.)

dovrebbe
preferirei
potremmo
vorrei
piacerebbe
verremmo
andrebbe
consiglierei

a. Domani sera.. andare a teatro. Mi .... molto, ma non posso.

b. Questa medicina .... tenere bassa la febbre, ma se la febbre non passa, le .... di andare da un medico.

c. Dino .... in vacanza d'estate, ma fa troppo caldo.

d. .... una camera singola con bagno, ma la .... sul cortile.

e. Se siete a casa, ... a visitarvi questa sera.

Read and understand

Here are the programmes shown by a number of film societies in Rome. Read them carefully and answer the following questions. (Answers p. 202.)

CINECLUB

ARCHIMEDE 71, Via Archimede (Parioli). Tel. 875.567. L. 1.500
Non pervenuto

AUSONIA
92 Via Padova (Nomentano-Italia). Tel. 426.160. Feriali-festivi L. 1.500. ridotti L. 800

3: **Il prigioniero di Zenda** di W. Mirisch, con Peter Sellers – 4: **Animal House**, di J. Landis – 5: **The Blues Brothers**, di J. Landis 6: **1941: Allarme a Hollywood,** di Steven Spielberg – 7–8: **The Blues Brothers**, replica.

LA GARBO PARLA! Rassegna di film interpretati da Greta Garbo, in lingua originale con sottotitoli italiani 9–10: **Mata Hari**, di G. Fitz – Maurice.

BOITO
12, Via A. Boito (Vescovio). Tel. 831.01.98 – Feriali e festivi L. 1.500.

Chiuso per restauro

CENTRE CULTUREL FRANÇAIS
3, Piazza Campitelli. Tel. 679.42.87

3. **Touchez Pas Au Grisbi**, di Jacques Becker – 6: **Vivre sa vie**, di Jean Luc Godard – 7: **Arsene Lupin**, di J. Pierre Dercourt.

FARNESE
56, Piazza Campo de' Fiori (Regolo) – Tel. 656.43.95 – Feriali e festivi L. 1.500; ridotti L. 1.000.

RASSEGNA DI FILM INTERPRETATI DA GRETA GARBO, in lingua originale con sottotitoli in italiano – 3: **La Regina Cristina**, di R. Mamoulian – 4: **Anna Karenina**, di C. Brown – 5: **Maria Walewska**, di C. Brown – 6: **Piccoli omicidi**, di Alan Arkin – 8–9: **Stardust Memories**, di Woody Allen.

FILMSTUDIO
1-C, Via Orti d'Alibert (Trastevere) – Tel. 65.73.78 – Tessera Lire 1.500, 4 mesi; ingresso L. 1.500 –

Studio Uno – RASSEGNA DEDICATA A MARLON BRANDO – 3–4–5: **La Caccia**, di A. Penn – 6: riposo – 7–8: **Queimada,** di Gillo Pontecorvo – 9: **Gli ammutinati del Bounty,** di L. Milestone.

a. Where would you go if you wanted to see films with Greta Garbo?

....

b. Which cinema shows the Italian version of *Mutiny on the Bounty*?

....

c. Where can you see French films in the original language?

....

d. How much does an ordinary ticket cost in most of these cinemas?

....

e. Which cinema is closed? ....

f. Does any of these film societies show films produced in Italy with Italian actors? ....

Did you know?

Health problems

In 1980 the Italian government re-structured various forms of state-assisted health insurance into a **Servizio Sanitario Nazionale**. European Community (including UK) nationals going to Italy are entitled to free hospital, medical and dental care, and to prescribed medicines at a reduced charge. If you are a UK national, you should apply before going to Italy to your local National Health and Social Security Office for Form E 111. When in Italy you should show this form to the **Unità Sanitaria Locale** (Local Health Unit), or **USL** for short; or, should there be no **USL**, to another authority known as **SAUB** (**Struttura Amministrativa Unificata di Base**, i.e. Basic Unified Administrative Structure). You will then be issued with a Certificate of Entitlement which you can take to one of the doctors or dentists on the **USL** or **SAUB** panel. Without this certificate you may have to pay for your treatment, and have difficulty in being reimbursed afterwards. Other non-EEC nationals, or people preferring private treatment should, of course, take out a private medical insurance policy before leaving.

For minor ailments most Italians prefer to go to a chemist and ask for his/her advice. Chemists are all university graduates, chartered members of a national professional organization, with a long training and considerable experience in dispensing medicines. They are allowed to sell a number of proprietary drugs and preparations without a doctor's prescription, if they think it's safe to do so. In remote places the chemist may also be willing to give first aid in the case of minor accidents involving simple medication.

Entertainments

Before you decide what sort of entertainment or show to go to, make a point of getting hold of the local paper; or, if you're staying at a hotel, of a copy of the local *What's on* (often printed in Italian and English). It's good to know that regional governments, particularly during the tourist season, earmark a certain proportion of their budget for the sponsorship of free shows and concerts: look out, in your programme, for those marked **ingresso gratuito** entry free.

Italians tend to decide what to do in the evening on the spur of the moment. Only a few very special shows (operas with star performers, or pop concerts) may be sold out (**tutto esaurito**) in advance of their performance. It is normally possible to obtain seats for most shows simply by applying on the same day. In some cases advance booking is positively discouraged!

Theatres and cinemas are divided (going from dearer to cheaper seats) into **platea** stalls, **palchi** boxes, **balconata** circle, **galleria** balcony. Stalls and circle may be divided into **prima fila** first row and **altre file** other rows. Opera houses may have a few rows of cheap seats above the top gallery, called **loggione**. Cinemas often make a single charge for all types of seats (**posto unico**). **Prima visione** means the film is being shown for the first time, in which case the seats are more expensive.

Your turn to speak

1 First you will invite a friend to have an evening out with you. Remember the word **il giornale** (newspaper).

2 Now you are in the chemist's and want something for your sore throat. You will need the verb **consigliare** (to advise).

Answers

Practise what you have learnt p. 197 Exercise **1** (**a**) go to the cinema (**b**) no (**c**) a play (**d**) dine out at a good restaurant.

p. 197 Exercise **2** *Carla:* B *Luisa:* A, B and C *Giorgio:* C and D.

p. 198 Exercise **4** (**a**) danno un film (**b**) guardare la televisione (**c**) prendere una birra (**d**) alla spiaggia (**e**) visitare il museo.

Grammar p. 199 (**a**) potremmo, piacerebbe (**b**) dovrebbe, consiglierei (**c**) andrebbe (**d**) vorrei, preferirei (**e**) verremmo.

Read and understand p. 200 (**a**) Ausonia and Farnese (**b**) Filmstudio (**c**) Centre Culturel Français (**d**) 1500 lire (**e**) Boito (**f**) no.

15 *Un piccolo incidente*

What you will learn

- how to cash a cheque in a bank
- how to ask for a refund
- how to discuss what you have done and to relate past events
- how to complain about overcharging

Before you begin

Points to remember from Unit 14:

1 the conditional (a tense used to express wishes, possibilities, expectations and to make polite requests)
essere: sarei, saresti, sarebbe, saremmo, sareste, sarebbero
avere: avrei, avresti, avrebbe, avremmo, avreste, avrebbero
lavorare: lavorerei, lavoreresti, lavorerebbe, lavoreremmo, lavorereste, lavorerebbero

2 how to complain about pains and ailments
ho male di . . .
mi fa male la testa, la gola etc.
ho la febbre
ho il raffreddore
che cosa mi consiglia?

Study guide

	Dialogues 1, 2: listen straight through without the book
	Dialogues 1, 2: listen, read and study one by one
	Dialogue 3: listen straight through without the book
	Dialogue 3: listen, read and study notes
	Dialogues 4, 5: listen straight through without the book
	Dialogues 4, 5: listen, read and study one by one
	Study the *Key words and phrases*
	Do the exercises in *Practise what you have learnt*
	Study the *Grammar* section
	Read *Did you know?* (this time before *Read and understand*)
	Do *Read and understand*
	Do the tape exercises in *Your turn to speak*
	Listen to all the dialogues again straight through
	Finally, do the *Revision* exercises for Units 13–15 on p. 224.

Dialogues

1 *Giovanni cashes a Eurocheque at a bank*

Impiegato Buon giorno.
Giovanni Senta, vorrei – euh – incassare un assegno Eurocheque. Li accettano?
Impiegato Sì.
Giovanni Ecco.
Impiegato Euh – se mi dà i suoi documenti, mi fa vedere l'assegno . . . e la carta.
Giovanni Ecco il passaporto . . . la carta di credito. L'assegno è qui. Quant'è il cambio della sterlina oggi?
Impiegato Mille novecento venti.
Giovanni Ah! È aumentato. Ieri era mille novecento dieci.
Impiegato Sì, effettivamente è aumentato. Va bene?
Giovanni Va bene, grazie.
Impiegato Mi fa una firma, per favore?
Giovanni Sì, ecco.
Impiegato Si accomodi pure alla cassa dodici.

➧ **incassare** to cash
➧ **assegno** cheque
carta (Eurocheque) card
➧ **cambio** change, rate of change
sterlina pound sterling
effettivamente in fact

2 *A woman applies for a refund on her railway ticket, which she did not use because of her children's illness*

Signora Senta, io ho fatto ieri questi biglietti per Civitavecchia, ieri sera verso le sei; ma io non son partita, ho i bimbi malati e volevo il rimborso.
Impiegato Comunque questo vale due giorni, e stamani poteva partire.
Signora E ma io non son partita perché ho i bimbi ammalati.
Impiegato Eh be', con questo comunque il rimborso doveva chiederlo nella giornata di ieri.
Signora Ma siccome erano per stamani . . . Ieri ero nel caos . . .
Impiegato Cioè, può partire . . . poteva partire anche stamani, però il rimborso veniva chiesto ieri, la data di emissione del biglietto.
Signora E allora? Ma il . . . come, se il biglietto è ancora valido, perché non posso usufruire del rimborso? Io non son partita!

Civitavecchia a coastal town north of Rome
bimbi children
malato, ammalato (pl. **malati, ammalati**) ill
vale is valid
siccome since, given that
caos chaos, state of confusion
data di emissione date of issue
usufruire (**-isco**) to benefit, to be entitled to

1 **li accettano?** do you accept them? Just as you use the **Lei** form to mean 'you' in the singular, e.g. **Lei ha freddo?** are you cold?, so you can use the **loro** form to mean 'you' in the plural. If you go to a restaurant with other people, you may find waiters addressing you in this way: **che cosa desiderano?** what would you like?

è aumentato it's gone up. If it had gone down, Giovanni would have said: **è diminuito** (from **diminuire, -isco**, to diminish). Note how a specific event in the past (the fact that the rate of exchange went up) and a straight description in the past (what the rate was like yesterday), is expressed in the use of (contrast between) the perfect (**è aumentato**) and the imperfect (**era**).

➧ **mi fa una firma?** would you sign here? (lit. would you make me a signature?). You may also hear: **vuole firmare qui?**

➧ **si accomodi pure alla cassa** please go to the cash till. You often hear the phrase **si accomodi** – it is a polite way of asking you to go somewhere or do something, e.g. **prego, si accomodi** please come in/do sit down, make yourself comfortable.

2 **volevo il rimborso** lit. I wanted a refund, but in fact she wants it *now*. For this use of the imperfect to soften a request ('I should like a refund'), see ➧ *Grammar*, p. 212. You may want to ask: **vorrei il rimborso** – or **posso avere il rimborso?** – or **può rimborsarmi il biglietto?** (can you refund my ticket?).

➧ **stamani poteva partire** you could have left this morning. **Stamani**, like **stamattina**, is another way of saying **questa mattina**.

il rimborso doveva chiederlo you should have asked for a refund.

il rimborso veniva chiesto ieri the refund should have been asked for yesterday. Alternatively he might have said **il rimborso andava chiesto ieri**. For this use of **venire** and **andare**, see *Grammar*, p. 212.

3 *A writer reminisces about the past*

Giovanni Io ho studiato a Pisa e mi son laureato con Luigi Russo, no?
Scrittore Ah, io lo conoscevo benissimo . . .
Giovanni Abitava, abitava proprio . . .
Scrittore . . . proprio vicino a me, sì, a poche centinaia di metri da casa mia. Era amico di mio padre. Passavano delle . . . dei pomeriggi, veniva sempre a trovare mio padre. Io ero molto giovane, ma comunque sono stato sempre un suo allievo, insomma vero.

scrittore (m.), **scrittrice (f.)** writer
giovane young
comunque anyhow
allievo disciple, pupil

4 *Dino reminisces about his holiday spent last summer in Val Gardena with his family*

Giovanni Quando sei stato l'ultima volta dalle tue parti con la famiglia?
Dino L'estate scorsa. Abbiamo fatto una vacanza – una breve vacanza nelle Dolomiti, che veramente è stata meravigliosa.
Giovanni In che parte delle Dolomiti sei stato?
Dino Siamo stati in Val Gardena, in una località che si chiama Ortisei, proprio una località ideale per noi, perché ci piacciono le montagne, ci piacciono le passeggiate facili, in montagna.

famiglia family
Dolomiti Dolomites (mountains in North East Italy)
meraviglioso marvellous
Val Gardena Gardena Valley (**val** = **valle**)
montagne mountains, *but* **in montagna** in the mountains

3 **mi son(o) laureato con Luigi Russo** I took my degree, with Luigi Russo as my supervisor. Professor Russo was one of the foremost Italian literary critics in the first half of this century.

lo conoscevo benissimo I knew him well. Note that this same phrase in the perfect: **l'ho conosciuto** would be best translated as 'I met him', as it would refer to a specific occasion. **Conoscere** means 'to know' a person rather than a fact.

veniva sempre a trovare mio padre he always came to see my father. **Andare/venire a trovare** is the same as **visitare**: **sono andato a trovarla ieri** I went to visit her yesterday; **vieni a trovarmi qualche volta** come and see me sometimes.

insomma vero two fillers without direct translations.

4 **dalle tue parti** in your part of the country. On the use of **da** to mean 'in', 'to' or 'at' see *Grammar*, p. 212.

abbiamo fatto una breve vacanza we had a short holiday. Besides **fare una vacanza** you may also use the expression **andare** or **essere in vacanza**: **andremo in vacanza in campagna** we'll go on holiday in the country; **sarò in vacanza dal 3 al 25 luglio** I'll be on holiday from the 3rd to the 25th of July.

le passeggiate walks. 'To go for a walk' is **fare una passeggiata**: **ieri abbiamo fatto una passeggiata in montagna** yesterday we went for a walk in the mountains.

The Dolomites

5 *The holiday was wonderful but the hotelier was not. Dino explains why he had to pay more than he'd bargained for*

Dino Il tempo era molto bello, il cibo era molto buono, la gente era molto simpatica. L'unica eccezione è stato il nostro albergatore che ci ha imbrogliati sul conto: un piccolo incidente che non ci ha rovinato la vacanza.

Giovanni E ve ne siete accorti al momento che vi aveva imbrogliato sul conto, o ve ne siete accorti dopo?

Dino No, me ne sono accorto sul momento, però ho deciso di lasciar correre.

Giovanni Vi aveva imbrogliato sul costo della stanza o vi aveva fatto pagare di più di quello che dovevate pagare?

Dino Sì, ci ha aumentato il prezzo di circa il dieci per cento, e io stupidamente non avevo la lettera che comprovava il prezzo, diciamo, originario.

l'unica eccezione the only exception
albergatore (m.) hotelier, owner/manager of hotel
imbrogliare to cheat, to swindle
incidente (m.) accident
rovinare to ruin
stupidamente stupidly
comprovare to prove, to vouch for

5

- **la gente era molto simpatica** people were very nice (but remember that **la gente** is singular!) Like 'nice', **simpatico** is an all-purpose adjective applying to anyone or anything one likes or approves of: **com'è simpatico** how nice he is; **un ristorante molto simpatico** a very nice restaurant.

- **ve ne siete accorti al/sul momento . . . o dopo?** did you realize (it) at the time . . . or later? Note that **realizzare** in Italian does *not* mean 'to realize' but 'to make something come true or real': **ho realizzato il mio desiderio** I made my wish come true. **Accorgersi**, to notice/realize is reflexive (**mi accorgo, me ne sono accorto** etc.). Remember that **mi, ti, ci, vi** and **si**, when followed by **ne** change their **-i** to **-e** (see Unit 7, dialogue 4): **ce ne siamo accorti** we realized it.

- **vi aveva imbrogliato sul conto** he had cheated you on the bill. If you think your bill is incorrect, say: **c'è uno sbaglio/un errore nel conto** there's a mistake in the bill; **è più di quello che devo pagare** it's more than I ought to pay.

- **lasciar(e) correre** to let it go, to ignore. **Lasciamo correre** let's leave it at that, never mind. Also **lasciare perdere**: **lascia perdere** don't take any notice.

Key words and phrases

To learn

vorrei incassare un assegno	I'd like to cash a cheque
quant'è il cambio?	what's the rate of exchange?
vorrei il rimborso	I'd like a refund
può rimborsarmi il biglietto?	can you refund my ticket?
c'è un errore/uno sbaglio nel conto	there's a mistake in my bill
è più di quello che devo pagare	it's more than I owe you
lasciamo correre	never mind, let's leave it at that
accorgersi di . . .	to become aware of . . ., to realize
ve ne siete accorti?	did you realize (it)?
non me ne sono accorto/a	I didn't realize (it)
venire/andare a trovare	to visit
vieni a trovarci questa sera	come and see us tonight
lo conosco bene	I know him well
l'ho conosciuta a Roma	I met her in Rome
abbiamo fatto una vacanza meravigliosa	we had a marvellous holiday
andremo in vacanza dal . . . al . . .	we'll be on holiday from . . . to . . .
abbiamo fatto delle passeggiate	we went for walks
la gente era simpatica	the people were nice
(Alberto) non era simpatico	(Albert) wasn't nice

To understand

stamani	today, this morning
mi fa una firma?	would you sign here?
si accomodi alla cassa	please go to the cash till
si accomodi	please come in, please sit down

Practise what you have learnt

1 Listen to the dialogue on tape where two friends are talking and answer the following questions. (Answers p. 216.)

a. When was the girl expecting her friend?
- [ ] yesterday afternoon
- [ ] yesterday evening

b. Is her friend
- [ ] working?
- [ ] on holiday?

c. Whom did he meet yesterday?
- [ ] a very young man
- [ ] a friend of his father's

d. What happened?
- [ ] they went together for a long walk
- [ ] they had a long conversation together

e. Did he keep his appointment with the girl?
- [ ] yes: he went to see her at about six in the evening
- [ ] no: he was so absorbed in his conversation with the person he had met that he did not realize how late it was

2 Here is a dialogue about a small problem with a bill. Fill in the missing verbs from the box below and then listen to the correct version on tape to check your answer.

Gina Quando .... che c'era uno sbaglio nel conto?

Giancarlo .... solo dopo aver lasciato il ristorante, infatti .... mia moglie.

Gina Che cosa .... allora?

Giancarlo Quando ...., siamo ritornati al ristorante e .... il rimborso di quello che avevamo pagato in più.

Gina E ve lo .... ?

Giancarlo Sì, ci .... senza discussioni.

me ne sono accorto · **avete fatto** · **hanno dato** · **ti sei accorto** · **ce ne siamo accorti** · **hanno rimborsato** · **se n'è accorta** · **abbiamo chiesto**

3 With the help of the captions to the pictures, complete this postcard to an old friend in Rome who couldn't join you on your holiday on the Italian Riviera, by translating the English sentences below. You don't need your tape recorder. (Answers p. 216.)

andare in barca a vela

fare passeggiate in montagna

andare a nuotare

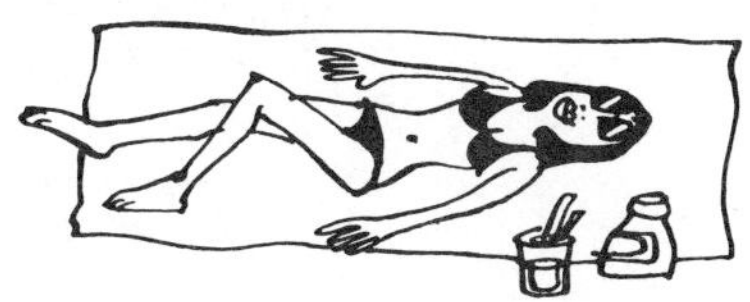

prendere il sole (past part. **preso**)

gente simpatica

andare a ballare

. . . all the people are very nice. Every day we've been swimming and sunbathing. Sometimes we've been sailing and on Sunday we went for a walk in the mountains. Last night we went dancing at the discotheque.

purtroppo unfortunately

Bordighera 1° luglio

Ci è tanto dispiaciuto che non sei potuto venire qui con noi. Siamo qui dal 20 giugno e abbiamo fatto una vacanza meravigliosa. All'albergo . . .

Giorgio Ventura
Via Passetti 12
ROMA
Italia

Oggi purtroppo partiamo!
Cari saluti, Marisa

Grammar

Further uses of the imperfect

The following uses of the imperfect are mostly confined to the spoken language:

- instead of the conditional tense
  stamani poteva partire you could have left this morning
  doveva chiederlo ieri you should have asked for it yesterday
- with **se** (if)
  se chiedeva il rimborso ieri lo aveva subito if you had asked for a refund yesterday you would have got it at once
  se veniva a casa mi trovava if he/she had come to my house he/she would have found me.

Just as the present tense of **essere** and **avere** is used to form the perfect, the imperfect of these verbs, together with the past participle of the verb is used to form another compound tense: the 'pluperfect' which translates as '*had* done something'. You are not going to study this tense but just note two examples of it in dialogue 5:

vi aveva imbrogliato sul conto he had cheated you on the bill
vi aveva fatto pagare di più he had made you pay more.

Venire and andare as auxiliaries

Forms of **venire** may be found before an infinitive instead of **essere**:

questi assegni non vengono accettati (= **non sono accettati**) **dalla banca** these cheques are not accepted by the bank
l'IVA viene aggiunta al totale VAT is added to the total

Forms of **andare** in the same position express a sense of duty or obligation:

questo assegno va presentato a una banca this cheque should be paid into a bank
l'IVA va aggiunta al totale VAT must be added to the total

Use of da

You are already familiar with the use of **da** to mean 'from':

vengo da Roma I come from Rome
dal 3 al 25 luglio from 3rd to 25th July

In some cases **da** can also mean 'in', 'to', or 'at the house of'

posso venire da te questa sera? can I come to your place tonight?
passa dal fornaio e compra mezzo chilo di pane pop in at the baker's and buy half a kilo of bread
abita dalle tue parti he/she lives in your area

Did you know?

The media

As you may remember from a comprehension exercise in Unit 7, there are in Italy a few national newspapers, and several fairly important regional or local papers. The distinction is mostly one of prestige and circulation, rather than coverage, since good 'local' dailies, like *La Nazione* (Florence) or *Il Mattino* (Naples) will give nearly as much space to national and international news as the best known 'nationals' like *Il Corriere della sera* (Milan) or *La Repubblica* (Rome). (The latter was founded only a few years ago but is slowly replacing *Il Corriere della sera* as the establishment paper.) Prestige dailies, on the other hand, will also carry crime stories and other items of local interest. In spite of the fact that many dailies call themselves **quotidiano indipendente**, they are far from being independent of powerful commercial and political interests. In this respect they are not much different from such party dailies as *L'Unità* (Communist) or *Il Popolo* (Christian Democrat), which at least do not make a mystery of their allegiance. All Italian morning dailies have a consistently 'highbrow' tone and layout. It is possible to see some difference between 'quality' and 'popular' press only at the level of the weeklies, but even the most popular magazines, like *Oggi*, *Gente*, or *La Domenica del Corriere* consciously aspire to a quality image. There are no Sunday papers in the British and American sense, only Sunday issues of the everyday papers.

Radio and television are in the hands of a state-controlled organization, **RAI-TV**, with three national radio programmes and three colour television channels, and of a surprising number of private stations, of which there may be more than a dozen in every major town. Some radio stations are sponsored by political parties, like **Radio Radicale**, of the Radical party, which has an embryo national network and possibly the best news service outside **RAI-TV**. The majority are commercial stations, surviving on locally sponsored advertisements, and broadcasting a continuous stream of rock and disco music, interspersed with badly presented and incoherently structured phone-ins. Private TV stations vary considerably. The least bad programmes are shown by stations which have managed to get together into some sort of regional or national network. The rest churn out an astonishing number of cartoons, B-films and (late at night) soft porn, occasionally in the form of live strip shows. The mushrooming growth of all these private and commercial stations has certainly been one of the most interesting social phenomena of the seventies.

Read and understand

Here is a selection of warning notices (excluding road traffic signs) which you can find in Italy. By a judicious process of guesswork, translation and elimination you should be able to match all of them with their English equivalents. (Answers p. 216.)

1 ....

....

2 ....

....

3 ....

....

4 ....

....

5 ....

....

....

....

6 ....

....

Translation of the notices

Danger of fire	Forbidden to cross the rails
Fishing forbidden	Death to whoever touches
Do not lean out	Forbidden to go down
Emergency brake	No through road

Entry forbidden for unauthorized vehicles
It is forbidden to use the alarm signal except in case of danger
Entry forbidden to beggars and travelling salesmen: shut the door
Forbidden to children under 18

7 ....

....

8 ....

....

9 ....

....

....

10 ....

....

11 ....

....

12 ....

....

Your turn to speak

1 First you'll practise changing travellers' cheques at a bank. Before you start, just look at p. 230 and revise the numbers. Remember that 'pounds sterling' in Italian are **sterline**.

2 Now you will complain about a mistake in your hotel bill. Again you will need to know the numbers and it may be a good idea to jot notes on a piece of paper to help you remember the figures as you do the exercise.

Revision

Finish the course by doing the revision section for the last three units you have studied – Units 13–15 – on p. 224. The tape exercise is the last recording on your cassette.

You should now have a good basic knowledge of Italian and an ability to cope in the most common situations – an ability which will improve with practice, and especially if you are able to have a trip to Italy . . . enjoy yourself! **divertiti!**

Answers

Practise what you have learnt p. 210 Exercise **1** (**a**) yesterday afternoon (**b**) on holiday (**c**) a friend of his father's (**d**) they had a long conversation together (**e**) no: he was so absorbed in his conversation.

p. 211 Exercise **3** . . . tutta la gente è molto simpatica. Ogni giorno siamo andati a nuotare e abbiamo preso il sole. Qualche volta siamo andati in barca a vela e domenica abbiamo fatto una passeggiata in montagna. Ieri sera siamo andati a ballare alla discoteca.

Read and understand p. 214 (**1**) Emergency break (**2**) Forbidden to go down (**3**) Forbidden to children under 18 (**4**) Danger of fire (**5**) Entry forbidden to beggars and travelling salesmen: shut the door (**6**) Fishing forbidden (**7**) Death to whoever touches (**8**) Do not lean out (**9**) It is forbidden to use the alarm signal except in case of danger (**10**) Entry forbidden for unauthorized vehicles (**11**) No through road (**12**) Forbidden to cross the rails

Revision Units 1–3

This is a short revision section. Use it to test yourself and see how much you've actually learned (you may surprise yourself!) You'll do better, of course, if you go over the contents of the previous three units once more before you start. Answers to all revision sections can be found on p. 226.

1 Listen to a man and a woman introducing themselves on tape (straight after Unit 3). Then answer the following questions by ticking the correct boxes.

a. The man is called ☐ Giorgio
☐ Franco
☐ Carlo

b. He is from ☐ Varese
☐ Arese
☐ Verona

c. He lives in ☐ Milano
☐ Roma
☐ Como

d. He is a ☐ shopkeeper
☐ English teacher
☐ factory worker

e. The woman is called ☐ Marisa
☐ Luisa
☐ Franca

f. She is from Bologna, but lives in Milan: ☐ true ☐ false

g. She is ☐ a shop assistant
☐ a switchboard operator

h. She works in ☐ the telephone office
☐ a department store

2 Trains in Italy are often identified by numbers. Listen to the station announcements on tape, and write down which train is standing or arriving at which platform. The trains will be of the following four types: **Locale, Diretto, Rapido, Espresso**. They will bear one of the following numbers: 210, 671, 865, 957.

Binario	Treno	Numero
2		
5		
8		
11		

(*Continued on p. 218.*)

3 In this exercise you will ask various questions of two imaginary travelling companions. The instructions are on tape.

4 Finally complete the following sentences.

a. Questo student. . . è ingles. . . e vien. . . da Londra.

b. Il professore d'italiano si chiam. . . Carlo Bianchi.

c. Marcella e la mamma abit. . . a Lurago.

d. Io vad. . . a Roma. E Lei dove v. . .?

e. Questa ser. . . non ci sono vol. . . per Londra.

Revision Units 4–6

In this second revision section you are asked to remember and practise some of the points studied, and skills acquired, in Units 4 to 6. (Answers p. 226.)

1 Form at least ten correct and meaningful sentences using the 'building blocks' below and write them in the spaces provided. Take one 'block' at a time from each column moving from left to right. (You don't have to use a block from every column.) In the answer section (on p. 226) a number of possible sentences will be given, but obviously not a complete list. Most sentences can be preceded by one or more blocks from the pile below. Sentences beginning in the second column must end with a question mark.

mi dica	come	posso	telefonare	colazione	per il centro
non so	dove	devo	fare	il treno	per Roma
	a che ora	voglio	pagare	l'autobus	da Milano
	quando	ferma	prendere	l'aereo	delle 11,45
	quanto	parte	andare	il biglietto	in Inghilterra
	qual'è	arriva	partire	una birra	al mercato
	da dove	costa		un aperitivo	

scusi	per favore	per piacere	senta	allora	dunque

....

....

....

....

....

....

....

....

....

....

2 Listen to the dialogue on tape (straight after Unit 6) between a customer and a bank teller and answer the questions below:

a. How much does the customer want to change into lire?
- ☐ £20
- ☐ £30

b. What sort of document does she show the teller?
- ☐ ID card
- ☐ passport
- ☐ driving licence

c. What rate of exchange for the pound does the teller quote?
- ☐ Lire 2305
- ☐ Lire 2225

d. What is the name of the hotel where the customer is staying?
- ☐ Albergo Risiede
- ☐ Hotel Reale Vittoria

e. From whom does the customer receive her lira?
- ☐ from the cashier
- ☐ from the teller himself

3 This exercise is on tape and follows the usual pattern of *Your turn to speak*. In it you will be prompted to ask for various street directions and other information. The checks are on tape.

Revision Units 7–9

Before you start this revision, look back over Units 7–9, especially the *Key words and phrases* and the *Grammar* sections.

1 Using the 'building blocks' below, construct as many *true* sentences as possible to describe the pictures. Some sample sentences will be given in the answers section on p. 226. Write your answers on a separate sheet of paper.

La bottiglia di	Barolo	è	più	grande	della	bottiglia di	Barolo
	Valpolicella		meno	cara	come la		Valpolicella
	Merlot		così	economica			Merlot
	Chianti						Chianti

2 Listen to your tape (straight after Unit 9). Shop assistants, hotel receptionists, waiters etc. will be offering you various things. You like all of them and decide to have them. Answer as appropriate:
Sì, mi piace, lo/la prendo or
Sì, mi piacciono, li/le prendo

3 Complete the following sentences by writing in the appropriate colour words. (Answers p. 226.)

a. Non mi piace il caffè col latte: lo preferisco ....

b. Quando la luce del semaforo è .... bisogna fermarsi.

c. Quando la luce del semaforo è .... si può passare.

d. Ci sono due tipi di film: a colori e in .... e ....

e. Il colore più comune dei jeans è il ....

f. Le castagne si chiamano anche .... perché sono ....

Revision Units 10–12

1 Fill in the gaps in the following sentences with the appropriate Italian phrase for 'I like' or 'I don't like' indicated by the symbol in the margin. (Answers p. 226.)

a. .... gli antipasti sottoaceto.

b. .... molto lo sport.

c. ....il sole caldo d'estate.

d. ....la neve e la pioggia in inverno.

e. ....mangiare al ristorante.

f. ....viaggiare sull'autostrada in vacanza.

g. ....le lasagne al forno.

2 Complete the following sentences using the appropriate article (**il, lo, la** etc.) and possessive (**mio, mia** etc.) suggested by the English forms in brackets.

a. È (yours, polite) .... questo passaporto? Sì, è (mine) ....

b. (Our) .... camere sono tutte al terzo piano, (theirs) .... sono al secondo.

c. (My) .... automobile ha un motore da 1500 cc.

d. Il cameriere ha portato (our) .... maccheroni ai turisti americani del tavolo a fianco, e (their) .... lasagne a noi!

e. Questi sono (your, plural) .... biglietti di andata e ritorno per Roma.

3 Revise the following passage (based on Unit 6, dialogue 8) changing the present to the future tense in the spaces provided. Cross out the verbs in the present. (Answers p. 226.)

Sabato parto .... per fare una settimana di vacanza. Vado .... in macchina. Viene .... con me Floriana e un'altra coppia di amici. La sera partiamo .... da Milano, poi ci fermiamo .... a Venezia e dormiamo .... la notte lì. Il mattino dopo arriviamo .... a Vienna e, dopo due o tre giorni, ci rechiamo .... a Budapest dove siamo .... tre giorni. Poi da Budapest ritorniamo .... direttamente a Venezia.

4 Listen to the dialogue on tape (straight after Unit 12) and answer the following questions. (Answers p. 226.)

a. When did the man go on holiday?
- ☐ June
- ☐ July

b. Where did he go?
- ☐ Northern Italy, near Adria
- ☐ Southern Italy, on the Adriatic coast of Apulia

c. Was the weather always sunny?
- ☐ yes
- ☐ no, there were one or two stormy days

d. Where did he stay?
- ☐ in a hotel
- ☐ on a campsite

Revision Units 13–15

1 Listen on tape to what Dino has to say about his state of health and answer the following questions. (Answers p. 226.)

a. Why did Dino sleep badly? ☐ there was a lot of noise
☐ he woke up several times during the night

b. What does he complain about this morning?
☐ headache ☐ backache ☐ toothache ☐ cold ☐ 'flu
☐ stomach upset ☐ fever

c. Is he planning to see a doctor? ☐ yes, at once
☐ yes, but only if he does not feel better
☐ no

2 Fill in the gaps in the sentences below with one of the following forms of **ritornare: ritorneremo, ritorneremmo, sono ritornata, sei ritornato, ritornerò.** (Answers p. 226.)

a. .... a Londra un anno fa, per un mese.

b. .... a Roma la settimana prossima.

c. .... con piacere in Italia per le vacanze, ma non possiamo.

d. Mio marito ed io .... a casa alla fine della settimana.

e. Quando .... in Inghilterra, faceva bel tempo?

3 Read the programme (opposite) of shows, concerts and entertainments in Milan for the week 29th June–15th July, and answer the following questions. (Answers p. 226.)

a. On what day is it possible to see the play *An Italian Straw Hat* at the Salone Pierlombardo? ....

b. If you are interested in Islamic music and ceremonies, where would you go, and on what day(s)? ....

c. Walt Disney, 198X and X-Rated are the names of three pop groups. Give the time and place of their performance ....

d. You are free on Sunday 5th July and are interested in ballet. Is there anything you might wish to see? ....

e. There are two matinée performances of *Peter and the Wolf* by Prokofiev. Where, and on what days? ....

Tutti gli spettacoli Milanesi dal 29 giugno al 5 luglio

Lunedì 29 giugno		
Castello Sforzesco	*ore 21.15*	Il Ballo
Salone Pierlombardo	*ore 21*	Un cappello di paglia d'Italia
Teatro Poliziano	*ore 21*	Le intellettuali
Villa Litta	*ore 21*	Quando i contadini vestivano casual
CTH	*ore 21.15*	Divertiamoci a teatro
Martedì 30 giugno		
Castello Sforzesco	*ore21.15*	Il Ballo
Teatro Poliziano	*ore 21*	Le intellettuali
Villa Litta	*ore 21*	Quando i contadini vestivano casual
Mercoledì 1 luglio		
Castello Sforzesco	*ore21.15*	Il Ballo
Teatro Poliziano	*ore 21*	Sufi: Musiche e cerimonie dell'Islam
Villa Litta	*ore 21*	Quando i contadini vestivano casual
Piazza Duomo	*ore21*	Concerto di autori
T.Q. Piazzale Cuoco	*ore 21*	Balletto Spagnolo Rafael De Cordova
Giovedì 2 luglio		
Castello Sforzesco	*ore 21.15*	Il Ballo
Teatro Poliziano	*ore 21*	Le intellettuali
T.Q. Piazzale Cuoco	*ore 21*	Balletto Spagnolo Rafael De Cordova
Cortile della Rocchetta	*ore 15*	Pierino e il lupo
CTH	*ore 21*	Divertiamoci a teatro
Palazzo del Senato	*ore 18.30*	Musica nei cortili
Venerdì 3 luglio		
Castello Sforzesco	*ore 21.15*	Il Ballo
Teatro Poliziano	*ore 21*	Le intellettuali
T.Q. Piazzale Cuoco	*ore 21*	Balletto Spagnolo Rafael De Cordova
Villa Litta	*ore 21*	Walt Disney - 198X - X Rated
Cortile della Rocchetta	*ore 15*	Pierino e il lupo
Cascina Monluè	*ore 21*	Cuntradansa
Chiesa di Santo Stefano	*ore21*	Orchestra Pomeriggi Musicali
CTH	*ore 21*	Divertiamoci a teatro
Sabato 4 luglio		
Castello Sforzesco	*ore 21*	Civica Banda Musicale
Teatro Poliziano	*ore 21*	Le intellettuali
T.Q. Piazzale Cuoco	*ore 21*	Balletto Spagnolo Rafael De Cordova
Villa Litta	*ore 18.30*	Mads - Stingless
CTH	*ore 21*	Divertiamoci a teatro
Cascina Monlue	*ore 21*	Cuntradansa
Domenica 5 luglio		
T.Q. Piazzale Cuoco	*ore 21*	Balletto Spagnolo Rafael de Cordova
Villa Litta	*ore 18.30*	Beggars Banquet - Sheraton Hotel Randa
CTH	*ore 21*	Divertiamoci a teatro
Cascina Monluè	*ore 21*	Cuntradansa

3

f. How many performances of the play *The Intellectuals* does the programme list? ....

g. Where would you go, and when, to be reasonably sure of listening to an orchestral concert? ....

Answers to revision sections

Units 1–3

Exercise **1** (**a**) Franco (**b**) Varese (**c**) Como (**d**) English teacher (**e**) Luisa (**f**) false (**g**) a switchboard operator (**h**) a department store.

Exercise **2** Binario 2 Locale 210 for Bologna, waiting; Binario 5 Diretto 865 from Milan, arriving; Binario 8 Espresso 671 for Fidenza Livorno, leaving; Binario 11 Rapido 957 for Grosseto, arriving.

Exercise **4** (**a**) studente, inglese, viene (**b**) chiama (**c**) abitano (**d**) vado, va (**e**) sera, voli.

Units 4–6

Exercise **1** Here are 10 possible sentences using the 'blocks' – there are many other possibilities:
(scusi) mi dica come posso telefonare in Inghilterra/(per favore) mi dica dove devo prendere il treno per Roma?/(dunque) non so a che ora arriva il treno da Milano/(per piacere) mi dica da dove parte l'autobus per il centro?/(allora) qual'è il treno per Roma?/voglio prendere un aperitivo/dove posso fare colazione?/(scusi) mi dica come posso andare al mercato?/quando parte l'aereo per Roma?/

Exercise **2** (**a**) £20 (**b**) passport (**c**) Lire 2225 (**d**) Hotel Reale Vittoria (**e**) from the cashier.

Units 7–9

Exercise **1** Here are 7 possible sentences, there are many other possibilities:
La bottiglia di Barolo è più cara della bottiglia di Chianti.
La bottiglia di Valpolicella è meno cara della bottiglia di Merlot.
La bottiglia di Merlot è più cara della bottiglia di Chianti.
La bottiglia di Chianti è così grande come la bottiglia di Barolo.
La bottiglia di Chianti è meno cara della bottiglia di Barolo.
La bottiglia di Merlot è più grande della bottiglia di Valpolicella.
La bottiglia di Barolo è meno economica della bottiglia di Chianti.

Exercise **3** (**a**) nero (**b**) rossa (**c**) verde (**d**) bianco, nero (**e**) blu (**f**) marroni, marrone.

Units 10–12

Exercise **1** (**a**) non mi piacciono (**b**) mi piace (**c**) mi piace (**d**) non mi piacciono (**e**) mi piace (**f**) non mi piace (**g**) mi piacciono.

Exercise **2** (**a**) suo, mio (**b**) le nostre, le loro (**c**) la mia (**d**) i nostri, le loro (**e**) i vostri.

Exercise **3** partirò/Andrò/Verrà/partiremo/ci fermeremo/dormiremo/arriveremo/ci recheremo/staremo/ritorneremo.

Exercise **4** (**a**) July (**b**) Southern Italy, on the Adriatic coast of Apulia (**c**) no, there were one or two stormy days (**d**) on a campsite.

Units 13–15

Exercise **1** (**a**) he woke up several times during the night (**b**) headache, cold, stomach upset (**c**) yes, but only if he doesn't feel better.

Exercise **2** (**a**) sono ritornata (**b**) ritornerò (**c**) ritorneremmo (**d**) ritorneremo (**e**) sei ritornato.

Exercise **3** (**a**) Monday 29th June (**b**) Wednesday 1st July, Teatro Poliziano, 9 p.m. (**c**) Friday 3rd July, Villa Litta, 9 p.m. (**d**) Balletto Spagnolo Rafael de Cordova, at T.Q. (Teatro di Quartiere), Piazzale Cuoco, 9 p.m. (**e**) Thursday 2nd and Friday 3rd July, Cortile della Rocchetta (**f**) five (**g**) Friday 3rd July, Chiesa di S. Stefano, 9 p.m., Orchestra Pomeriggi Musicali.

Grammar summary

This section on Italian grammar contains only a general summary of points covered in the course and a glossary of terms. You should refer to the notes and grammar sections of individual units for specific details.

Nouns

A *noun* is the name of a living being (like **segretario, segretaria** secretary; **studente** student) or of an inanimate or abstract thing (like **treno** train, **stazione** station, **partenza** departure). All Italian nouns are masculine or feminine. Nouns can be preceded by *definite articles* (corresponding to 'the' in English), as in **il segretario, lo studente, la partenza**; or by *indefinite articles* (corresponding to 'a', 'an' in English), as in **un treno, una stazione**. See Units 2 and 3, pages 30 and 45.

Adjectives

Nouns may be accompanied by *adjectives* describing or qualifying them (**il segretario privato, la stazione centrale**). Articles, nouns and adjectives that 'go together' as in the previous examples must 'agree', i.e. they must be of the same *gender* (masculine or feminine) and *number* (singular or plural).

Inflection

There are two basic patterns of *inflection* i.e. changes in endings, for nouns and adjectives, a pattern with four separate endings, one for each combination of gender and number; and a pattern with only two endings, for singular and plural. See for details Units 1 and 3, pages 16 and 45.

A few nouns are invariable i.e. don't change: those ending in a stressed vowel like **università** university, **caffè** coffee or café; nearly all those ending in **-ie** and **-si**, like **serie** series and **crisi** crisis; and words of one syllable like **re**, king. They do not change from singular to plural, but they *do* have nevertheless a specific gender and number, with which any accompanying adjective or article must agree, e.g. **l'università italiana, le università italiane; la crisi economica, le crisi economiche**, etc.

Verbs

In any linguistic act (speaking or writing), you can distinguish, regardless of what is being said or written, between:

- the person performing the linguistic act, who appears in it as 'I' or 'we' (1st person)
- the person(s) who is/are the recipient of the act, and appear(s) in it as 'you' (2nd person)
- the person(s) or thing(s) mentioned in the act as 'he', 'she', 'it' or 'they' (3rd person).

Verbs are words that change according to which 'person' (in the grammatical sense) they refer to.

Subject

The words denoting these 'persons' in a sentence are called the *subject* of the verb (in italics in the following examples):

I am tired   *George and I* are tired
You should have told me   *You and George* should have told me
George is tired   *George and his students* went to Italy last summer

In Italian, verbal forms agree with the subject, expressed or implied, and have its same person and number, occasionally also gender.

Object

Sentences may, of course, contain other words apart from subject and verb. Those more closely connected in meaning with the verb are called *object*. It is useful to distinguish between *indirect object*, preceded by a preposition such as 'to', and *direct object*, not preceded by any preposition:
The teacher gave *a book* (direct object) *to each student* (indirect object)

Tense

Verbs also change according to the time indicated in what is being said or written. These changes result in differences of *tense* (present, past, future etc.).

Infinitive

Italian verbs have distinct forms for every person-tense combination. But they also have a form which does not refer to any specific person or tense, called *infinitive*. This is the form used as a dictionary entry word for the verb, and corresponds to forms preceded by 'to' in English, like 'to be', 'to have', 'to play' etc.

Verb patterns

There are three main groups of Italian verbs:

- those with infinitives ending in **-are**, e.g. **studiare** to study, **parlare** to speak, **mangiare** to eat (see p. 17)
- those with infinitives ending in **-ere** e.g. **mettere** to put (see p. 171)
- those with infinitives ending in **-ire**, e.g. **partire** to leave, **finire** to finish (see pp. 86, 115).

Changes in verb form follow mostly regular and easily predictable patterns called *conjugation*. As in all languages, however, the most commonly used verbs are irregular and you need to learn them individually whenever they appear in your grammar notes, e.g. **essere** (p. 17), **fare** (p. 45), **avere** (p. 17).

Pronouns

Pronouns are words that have not only a gender and number like nouns and adjectives, but also a person like verbs. In fact they are often found in conjunction with verbs, particularly *personal pronouns* like 'I', 'you', 'he', 'she' etc., and may function as subject or object.

Personal pronouns are less used in Italian than in English, because they are not needed to distinguish between verbal forms. They are **io** I, **tu** you (informal), **lui** he, **lei** she and you (polite), **noi** we, **voi** you (plural) and **loro** they. These can also function as objects, except **io** and **tu** whose object forms are **me** and **te** respectively, e.g. **con lui** with him; **per me** for me etc.

In most contexts, however, the following object pronouns are used:

mi vedono	they see me
ti vedo	I see you
lo vedo	I see him/it
la vedo	I see her/it
si vede	he/she sees him/herself
ci vedono	they see us
vi vedo	I see you (plural)
li vedo, le vedo	I see them
si vedono	they see themselves

See also Units 3 and 4 pages 45 and 59.

Possessives

Unlike English *possessives* (his, her, mine, yours etc.) which change according to the owner (*his* car, *her* car), Italian possessives behave like adjectives, agreeing with the thing owned (e.g. **la sua automobile** for both his and her car, because **automobile** is feminine singular). See Unit 11, p. 155. Do not expect to find possessives in Italian whenever they are used in English: they are often omitted, e.g. put on your hat **metti il cappello** (NOT **il tuo cappello**).

PREPOSITIONS, ADVERBS and CONJUNCTIONS not only do not change their form, but also do not agree with other words in the sentence.

Prepositions

Prepositions are words indicating relationships between nouns, such as '*in* the room', '*on* the table', '*from* my uncle' etc. In Italian they often combine with definite articles as shown in Units 2 and 4 pp. 30 and 59: **nella stanza, sulla tavola, dallo zio** etc., in which case they change like the definite article. The preposition **del, dello, della** etc. is used as a translation of 'some': **compra dello zucchero** buy some sugar; **c'erano delle nuvole** there were some clouds.

Adverbs

Adverbs are words modifying or qualifying verbs, adjectives or phrases, like 'deeply' in 'thinking deeply', 'deeply resentful' and 'deeply in love'. In Italian they are of two types:

- adverbs formed from the feminine or common singular form of the corresponding adjective, adding the ending **-mente**:
  profondo deep **profondamente** deeply
  veloce quick **velocemente** quickly

  Adjectives having an **-l-** or **-r-** sandwiched between vowels in their ending, drop the final vowel before adding **-mente**: **facile** easy **facilmente** easily; **leggero** light **leggermente** lightly.

- adverbs consisting in invariable forms like **bene** well, **male** badly, **presto** soon; or in 'frozen' masculine singular adjectives not agreeing with the word they qualify, like **molto** much, **poco** little, **troppo** too much etc.

  In this connection it is important to remember that, in Italian as in English, the same word can have different grammatical uses. Think of 'fast' in sentences like 'run fast', 'fast colours do not run', 'monks fast on Friday'. Similarly **troppo** is a noun in the proverb **il troppo stroppia** too much of anything can do you harm; it is an adjective agreeing with **sale** in **c'è troppo sale nella minestra** there's too much salt in the soup; and an adverb in **abbiamo mangiato troppo** we've eaten too much.

Conjunctions

Conjunctions are words like **e** and, **quando** when, **che** that, **perché** because, **mentre** while etc. serving to link together separate parts of the sentence.

Numbers

For numbers beyond 20 follow the pattern of venti: *keep the final vowel except with one and eight.*

0	zero
1	uno
2	due
3	tre
4	quattro
5	cinque
6	sei
7	sette
8	otto
9	nove
10	dieci
11	undici
12	dodici
13	tredici
14	quattordici
15	quindici
16	sedici
17	diciassette
18	diciotto
19	diciannove
20	venti
21	ventuno
22	ventidue
23	ventitré
24	ventiquattro
25	venticinque
26	ventisei
27	ventisette
28	ventotto
29	ventinove
30	trenta
31	trentuno
35	trentacinque
38	trentotto
40	quaranta
41	quarantuno
45	quarantacinque
48	quarantotto
50	cinquanta
55	cinquantacinque
60	sessanta
65	sessantacinque
70	settanta
80	ottanta
90	novanta
100	cento
101	centouno
102	centodue
125	centoventicinque
150	centocinquanta
175	centosettantacinque
200	duecento
300	trecento
400	quattrocento
500	cinquecento
1000	mille
1500	millecinquecento
2000	duemila
5000	cinquemila
10,000	diecimila
100,000	centomila
1,000,000	un milione

Ordinal numbers

1st	primo (1°)
2nd	secondo (2°)
3rd	terzo (3°)
4th	quarto (4°)
5th	quinto (5°)
6th	sesto (6°)
7th	settimo (7°)
8th	ottavo (8°)
9th	nono (9°)
10th	decimo (10°)
11th	undicesimo (11°)
12th	dodicesimo (12°)

Vocabulary

This vocabulary includes only words used in the dialogues and related exercises. It does not include words appearing in the reading sections. When using it please bear in mind the following conventions.

1 Assume that words ending in **-o** (e.g. **albergo**) are masculine nouns, and words ending in **-a** (e.g. **casa**) are feminine nouns. In all other cases the gender will be indicated (e.g. **mano(f)**, **mare(m.)**, **crisi(f.)**, etc.).

2 Words with a double ending (e.g. **studente, -essa**; **italiano, -a**) are nouns or adjectives with separate masculine and feminine endings. Words ending in **-e** (e.g. **sottile**) with no indication of gender are adjectives with a form suitable for both masculine and feminine.

3 Words ending in **-are**, **-ere** and **-ire** are verbs, in the infinitive. They are followed by their main 'irregular' forms, if any (e.g. **prendere, preso**). Words ending in **-rsi** are reflexive verbs (e.g. **vestirsi**).

4 The English translations given refer exclusively to the contexts in which the word appears, and must not be taken as its 'meaning' in all cases. For more complete guidance you should consult a larger bilingual dictionary.

abbastanza rather, enough
abitante inhabitant
abitare to live, to dwell
abito dress
abituarsi to get used
accettare to accept
accomodarsi to make oneself comfortable; **si accomodi** please come in
accorgersi to realize
aceto vinegar
acido,-a acid
acqua water; **acqua minerale** mineral water
acquisto purchase
adatto,-a suitable, suited
adesso now
affatto at all
aggiungere, aggiunto to add
aglio garlic
agosto August
agricolo, -a agricultural
agricoltura farming
agro, -a sour; **agrodolce** sweet and sour
aiutare to help
albergatore(m.), albergatrice(f.) hotelier
albergo hotel
albicocca apricot
alcuni, -e some, a few
alimentare alimentary; **generi alimentari** food
alimentazione(f.) way of eating, food consumption
allevare to breed, to raise
allievo, -a pupil
allora then
altamente highly
alto, -a high
altrimenti otherwise
altro, -a other
amabile (said of wine) medium-sweet
amaro, -a bitter
amico, -a friend
analcoolico, -a without alcohol, alcohol-free
anche also, too
ancora yet, once more
andare, vado, andato to go
angolo corner
anno year
anticipo advance
antigelo antifreeze
antipasto hors-d'oeuvre
anzi on the contrary
ape(f.) bee
aperitivo aperitif
apertura opening
apicultore(m.) bee-keeper
apicultura bee-keeping
appena as soon as, just
appunto precisely
aprile April
aprire, aperto to open
arancia orange
aranciata orangeade
arancione orange (colour)
arrivederci good-bye
arrivo arrival
arrosto roast, roast meat
aspro, -a sour
assegno cheque
assieme together
attendere, atteso to expect
attimo moment
attività activity
atto act; **all 'atto di. . .** at the time of. . .
attraversare to cross
aumentare to increase
autobus(m.) bus
automobile(f.) car
automobilista(m.f.) motorist
autunnale (adjective) autumn, autumnal
autunno autumn
avanti further on
avere, ho, avuto to have

bagno bathroom, bath
ballare to dance
bambino, -a child
banana banana
banca bank
basso, -a low
bastare to be enough; **basta!** that's enough!
bello, -a beautiful
bene well; **benissimo** very well
benzina petrol
bere, bevo, bevuto to drink
besciamella bechamel sauce
bestiame(m.) cattle
bianco, -a white
bietola beet spinach
biglietto ticket
bilancia scales
bimbo, -a child
binario line, platform
birra beer
biscotto biscuit
bisognare to be necessary
bistecca beef steak
blu blue
bollire to boil
borsa travel bag
bottiglia bottle; **bottiglietta** small bottle
botte(f.) cask
bovini cattle, cows, oxen and bulls
bravo, -a good, clever
breve short
brutto, -a bad, ugly
buono, -a good
burro butter
bustina sachet

caffè(m.) coffee, café, coffee bar
caffellatte(m.) milk coffee
caldo, -a hot
cambiare to change; **cambio** change, exchange bureau
camera room, bedroom, hotel room
cameriere, -a waiter, waitress
camicetta blouse
camicia shirt
campo field
candela (motoring) spark plug
candito, -a candied
canto song
caos(m.) chaos
capire, capisco to understand
cappuccino milk coffee made with espresso machine
caraffa carafe, jug
caratteristico, -a typical
carburante(m.) fuel
carciofo artichoke
carne(f.) meat
caro, -a dear
carota carrot
carrello trolley; **carrello portavaligie** luggage trolley
carrozzeria bodywork (car)
carta paper; **carta di credito** credit card
cartella briefcase
cartolina postcard; **cartolina illustrata** picture postcard
casa house
catena (mountain) range, chain
causa cause; **a causa di. . .** because of. . .
cavallo horse
cena dinner, supper
centrale central
centro centre
cercare to try
certo sure, certainly
chi? who?
chiamare to call; **chiamarsi** to be called; **mi chiamo** my name is
chiamata call
chiaramente clearly
chiedere, chiesto to ask for
chilo kilo
chilometro kilometre
chinotto a bitter orange aperitif
chiudere, chiuso to close
chiusura closure
ciao hi, hello
cibo food
ciclamino cyclamen
ciliegia cherry
cinema(m.) cinema
cinque five
cioccolata chocolate
cioè that is
circa about
circolare circular, round
città city, town
classico, -a classic(al)
cliente(m.) customer
clima(m.) climate
coincidenza connection
colazione(f.) breakfast
collina hill
colonia cologne
colorato, -a coloured
colore(m.) colour
come as
cominciare to begin
commerciante(m.) businessman, dealer
commesso, -a shop assistant
comodo comfortable, convenient; **con comodo** at your leisure
completo complete
comprare to buy
compressa tablet
comprovare to prove, to vouch for
comunque anyway, anyhow, at any rate
concerto concert
condire, condisco to season, to dress (salad)
condizione(f.) condition
confezione(f.) packaging
confronto comparison
congresso conference
conoscere, conosciuto to know
conseguenza consequence
consentire to allow
consigliare to advise
conto bill

contorno side dish
contrario, -a contrary
controllare to control
coppia couple
correre, corso to run
cortile(m.) courtyard
corto, -a short
cosa thing; **che cosa** what; **qualche cosa** something
costare to cost; **quanto costa?** how much is it?
costata rib steak
costume da bagno swimsuit
cotoletta cutlet
cravatta tie
crema custard
crisantemo chrysanthemum
crostata short-crust pastry tart
crostino toast (bread)
crudo, -a raw
cucina cooking, kitchen
cuocere, cotto to cook

danza dance
dare to give
data date
dattilografo, -a typist
davanti before
dente (m.) tooth
desiderare to wish
desiderio wish
destra right
di fronte opposite
di nuovo again
dicembre December
dichiarare to declare
dietro behind
differente different
dimenticare, dimenticarsi di. . . to forget
diminuire, diminuisco to diminish, to lessen
dipendere, dipeso to depend
dire, dico, detto to say
direttamente directly, straight
diretto, -a straight
diretto type of train (limited stops)
direzione(f.) direction
discorso speech
dispiacersi to be sorry; **mi dispiace** I'm sorry
distante distant, far
distanza distance
disturbo ailment
ditta firm
diverso, -a different; **diversi, -e** several
doccia shower
documento document
dolce(m.) cake; (adjective) sweet
dolore(m.) pain
domani tomorrow
domenica Sunday
dopo after, afterwards
dopodomani the day after tomorrow
doppio, -a double
dormire to sleep
dottore(m.), dottoressa(f.) doctor
dove where
dovere, devo, dovuto must, ought to
droghiere(m.) grover
due two
dunque well, then
duomo cathedral
durante during
duro, -a hard

eccedenza (luggage) excess weight
eccessivo, -a excessive
eccezione(f.) exception
ecco here it is, here you are, there you are etc.
economico, -a cheap, economical
educato, -a educated; **bene educato** well behaved
elegante elegant
emissione(f.) issue
errore(m.) error
esatto, -a exact
escursione(f.) excursion
esistere, esistito to exist
espresso fast train, express; espresso coffee
essere, sono, stato to be
est east
estate(f.) summer
estero abroad
estivo, -a summer (adjective)
etto a hundred grams

facchino porter
facile easy
facilmente easily
fagiolini(m.pl.) french beans
familiare familiar, family (adjective)
fare, fatto to do, to make
farina flour
favore(m.) favour; **per favore** please
febbraio february
febbre(f.) fever
fegato liver
felice happy
fermare, fermarsi to stop; **fermata** stop
ferrovia railway
fico fig
fiducia trust; **di fiducia** trustworthy
filetto fillet steak
filtro filter
finale final
fine(f.) end
finire, finisco to finish, to end
finocchio fennel
firma signature
fiume(m.) river
fondo bottom; **in fondo** at the bottom
formaggio cheese
fornaio, -a baker
forno oven
forse perhaps
forte strong
francobollo postage stamp
frase(f.) phrase, sentence
freddo, -a cold

freno brake
frequente frequent; **frequenza** frequency
friggere, fritto to fry
frittatina omelet
frizzante fizzy, sparkling
frutta fruit
fungo mushroom
funzionamento working
fuori outside

galleria arcade
garagista(m.) garage attendant
garofano carnation
gasato, -a gassy, fizzy
generalmente generally
genere(m.) kind, gender
gennaio January
gente(f.sing) people
gesto gesture, sign
gettone(m.) token (for telephone)
giacinto hyacinth
giallo, -a yellow
giardino garden
giglio lily
ginocchio knee
giornale(m.) newspaper
giornata day
giorno day; **giorno festivo** holiday; **giorno feriale** weekday, working day
giovane young
giovedì Thursday
giugno June
giusto, -a right, medium (of steak)
goccia drop
gola throat
golf(m.) sweater
gomma tyre, rubber
gonna skirt
gradazione(f.) grade
grammo gram
grana(m.) parmesan cheese
grande big, large
grattugiare to grate
grazie thanks, thank you
grosso, -a big, thick
guardare to look
guardia di finanza customs officer
guidare to lead, to guide
gusto taste

idea idea
ideale ideal
identità identity
ieri yesterday
illustrare to illustrate; **cartolina illustrata** picture postcard
imbarco boarding
imbevere, imbevuto to soak
imbrogliare to deceive
immediato, -a immediate
imparare to learn
impiegato, -a employee
incassare to cash
incidente(m.) accident
includere, incluso to include
incontrare to meet
indigestione(f.) indigestion
indirizzo address
industria industry
inglese English, the English language
iniezione(f.) injection
iniziare to begin
insalata salad
insegnante(m.) teacher; **insegnare** to teach
insieme together
insomma on the whole
integrale integral, wholemeal (of bread)
intenzione(f.) intention
interessante interesting
internazionale international
intero, -a whole
invece on the other hand
inverno winter; **invernale** wintry
isola island
italiano, -a Italian

laggiù down there
lago lake
lampadina electric bulb
lasciare to leave, to let; **lasciar(e) correre** to drop it
latte(m.) milk
lattina tin
laurearsi to take a degree
lavanda lavender water
lavorare to work
leggero, -a light
lessare to cook by boiling
lettera letter
letto bed; **letto matrimoniale** double bed
libero, -a free
lieve slight
limonata lemonade; **limone(m.)** lemon
liquore(m.) liqueur
lira lira
locale local
località locality, place
lontano, -a far
lubrificante(m.) lubricating oil
luglio July
lunedì Monday

macchina machine, car
macinare to grind
magari perhaps, maybe
magazzino department store
maggio May
maglia jersey, sweater
maglietta jumper, T-shirt
magro, -a lean
mai never
maiale(m.) pig, pork
male badly
mamma mother, mummy
mandare to send
mangiare to eat
marca brand, trademark
marciapiede(m.) pavement
mare(m.) sea

margherita daisy
marito husband
marmellata jam; **marmellata d'arancio** marmalade
marrone brown
marrone(m.) chestnut, (colour) brown
martedì Tuesday
marzo March
massimo, -a greatest; **al massimo** at the most
matrimoniale double (said of bed)
mattino, mattina morning
matto, -a crazy
medico doctor
meglio better
mela apple
melone(m.) melon
meno less; **meno male** thank goodness
mensile monthly
mentre while, whilst, in the meantime
meraviglioso, -a marvellous
mercato market
mercoledì Wednesday
meridionale southern
messa a punto overhaul, general check
meteorologico, -a weather (adjective)
metro metre
metropolitana, metrò underground railway
mezzo, -a half; **in mezzo a** in the middle of
mezzo means; **mezzo di superficie** surface transport
mezzogiorno midday, the south of Italy
migliore better
mille one thousand
minestrone(m.) thick vegetable soup
minuto minute
mio, -a mine
misto mixture
modello model
molto, -a much, many
momento moment
montagna mountain
motore(m.) motor, engine
museo museum
musica music
mutande(f. pl.) pants

nascere, nasco, nato to be born
natale of birth
naturale natural
necessario, -a necessary
negoziante(m.,f.) shopkeeper
negozio shop
nemmeno not even
neppure (not) even
nero, -a black
niente nothing
noce(f.) walnut
noioso, -a annoying, dull, boring
noleggiare to book, to hire
nord North
normale normal
nostro, -a our(s)
notte(f.) night, evening
nove nine
novembre November
numero number
nuotare to swim
nuvola cloud; **nuvoloso** cloudy

occidentale western
officina workshop
offrire, offerto to offer
oggi to-day
ogni every
olio oil
omelette(f.) omelet
opera opera
operaio, -a factory worker
oppure or, on the other hand
ora hour
orario time-table
ordinare to order
ordinario, -a ordinary
orecchio ear
organizzare to organize
orientale oriental, eastern
originario, -a original, initial
oro gold
orologio clock
orribile horrible
ospedale(m.) hospital
otto eight
ottobre October
ovest west
ovini sheep and goats

pacchetto packet
paese village, country
pagamento payment
pagare to pay; **paga** pay
pancia belly, tummy
pane(m.) bread; **panino** roll
pantaloni(m. pl.) trousers
parabrezza (m.) windscreen
parlare to speak
parola word
parte(f.) side, area, part
partire to leave, to depart; **partenza** departure
passaporto passport
passare to pass
passeggiata walk
pasta pasta
pastiglia lozenge
patata potato
pelare to peel
penisola peninsula
pensare to think
pensione(f.) retirement; **in pensione** retired
pepe(m.) pepper
peperoncino chilli
per favore please
per piacere please
pera pear
perchè why, because
perfetto, -a perfect
permanenza sojourn, stay
però but, however

persistente persistent, long lasting
persona person
personale(m.) staff
personalmente personally
pesare to weigh
pesca peach
pesce(m.) fish
peso weight
pezzo piece
piacere, piaccio, piaciuto to please; **mi piace** I like
piatto plate, dish; **piatto, -a** flat
piazza square
piccante hot, spicy
piccolo, -a small
piede(m.) foot; **a piedi** on foot
pieno, -a full; **fare il pieno** to fill up
pillola pill
pioggia rain
piovere to rain
piuttosto rather
pneumatico tyre
poco, -a little, few; **un po'** a little
poi then, afterwards
pomata ointment
pomeriggio afternoon
pomodoro tomato
popolare popular
portabiti(m.) wardrobe-suitcase
portare to wear, to bring
portiere(m.) hotel receptionist
possibile possible; **possibilmente** possibly
posta post office
posto place, seat
potere, posso, potuto can, to be able to
pranzo lunch
precipitazione(f.) rainfall
preciso, -a precise
preferire, preferisco to prefer
prego please
prendere, preso to take
prenotare to book
prenotazione(f.) booking
preparare to prepare
presentare to present, to introduce
presso near; **nei pressi di. . .** near
prevalere to prevail
prevedere, previsto to forecast, to foresee
prezzemolo parsley
prezzo price, cost
primavera spring
primaverile spring (adjective)
primo, -a first; **prima base** first thing, in the first instance
primula primrose
problema(m.) problem
professore(m.) professor; **professoressa** female teacher, female professor
profumo perfume; **profumazione(f.)** type of scent
pronto, -a ready; hallo (on the telephone)
pronunciare to pronounce
prosciutto ham
prossimo, -a next
provare to try (on)
proveniente coming from
provincia province, district
prugna plum
pubblico, -a public
pulizia cleaning; **far le pulizie** to clean
pullman(m.) coach, bus
puntuale punctual, on time
pure also
purtroppo unfortunately

qualche a few
qualcosa something
quale which, which one
qualità quality
qualsiasi any
quando when
quanto, -a how much, how many
quarto quarter, fourth
quattro four
quello, -a that
questo this, this one
qui here
quindi then, therefore
quotidiano daily

raffreddore(m.) cold
ragazzo, -a boy, girl
ragione(f.) reason
rapido fast, express train
rapini(m. pl.) turnip tops
realtà reality; **in realtà** in fact
recarsi to go
reggiseno bra
regione(f.) region
regolare regular
resto change
riduzione(f.) discount, reduced price
rientrare to return, to go back
riguardare to look over
rimanere, rimango, rimarrò, rimasto to remain
rimborso refund
riordinare to put things straight
riparare to repair
ripartire to start again, to leave again
riposo rest, closure
riprendere, riprendo, ripreso to take again
riso rice
ristorante(m.) restaurant
ritardo delay
rivista magazine
rosa rose, pink
rossa, -a red
rovinare to ruin
rumore(m.) noise
rumoroso, -a noisy

sabato Saturday
sacrificarsi to sacrifice oneself
salame(m.) salami
salato, -a salty, salted
salsa sauce

salsiccia sausage
saltare to jump, to skip
salumi(m. pl.) preserved meats, salami in general
salumiere, -a grocer, pork butcher
salutare to greet
salvaguardare to safeguard
sandali sandals
sangue(m.) blood; **al sangue** rare (of meat)
sapere, so, saputo to know
sapore(m.) flavour
saporito, -a tasty, flavoursome
sardina sardine
sbaglio mistake
scarpa shoe
scatola box; **scatoletta** small box
scegliere, scelgo, scelto to choose
scelta choice
scendere, sceso to come down, to get out (of a vehicle)
schiena back
sconto discount
scoprire, scoperto to discover
scorso, -a past, last; **la settimana scorsa** last week
scozzese Scottish
scrittore(m.), scrittrice(f.) writer
scrivere, scritto to write
scuola school; **scuola materna** nursery school
scusarsi to excuse oneself; **scusi** excuse me
secco, -a dry
segnare to note down
segretario, -a secretary
seguente following
sei six
semaforo traffic lights
semplice simple
sempre always
senso sense
sentire to listen, to feel
senza without; **senz'altro!** of course, no doubt, without fail
separare to separate
sera evening
serio, -a serious; **sul serio** seriously
servire to serve
servizio service, service charge
seta silk
sette seven
settembre September
settentrionale northern
settimana week; **settimanale** weekly
settore(m.) sector, area
sfuso, -a not packaged, from the cask
sgabello stool
siccome since, given that
sigaretta cigarette
signora Mrs, lady
signore(m.) Mr, sir, gentleman
signorina Miss, young lady
simpatico, -a nice, pleasant
singolo, -a single
sinistral left
sistemare to accommodate
soddisfare, soddisfo, soddisfatto to satisfy
soggiornare to stay, to sojourn
sole(m.) sun
solito, -a usual
solo only
soltanto only
sopra above, on top
sorgere, sorto to arise
sostituire, sostituisco to replace
sostituzione(f.) replacement
sottaceto pickle, pickled
sottile thin
sotto underneath, below
sotto under
sottolio preserved in oil
sottovuoto vacuum packed
spago string
speciale special; **specialità** speciality
specializzarsi to specialize
spiaggia beach
spinaci(m. pl.) spinach
spuntino snack
stagione(f.) season
stamani this morning, to-day
stampa press
stanza room
stare to stay; **mi sta bene** it fits me
stasera to-night
stazione(f.) station
sterlina pound sterling
sterzo steering
stesso,-a same; **lo stesso** all the same
stomaco stomach
strada street
straniero, -a foreign
strato layer
studente(m.) male student; **studentessa** female student
studiare to study
stupidamente stupidly
subito at once
successivo, -a next
succo juice
sud south
sugo sauce, juice
suini pigs
superalcoolico, -a strongly alcoholic, spirit
superiore superior
supermercato supermarket
supplemento supplementary charge
supposta suppository
svegliarsi to wake up

tabaccaio-a, tobacconist
tabacco tobacco
taglia size
tagliare to cut
tanto, -a so much, such
tappa stop, stage in a journey
tardi late
tassa tax
tassì(m.) taxi
té(m.) tea

teatro theatre
telefonico, -a telephone (adjective)
telefonista(m. f.) switchboard operator
telefono telephone
televisione(f.) television
temperatura temperature
tempo time, weather
temporale(m.) storm; **temporalesco** stormy
tenere, tengo, tenuto to keep
tergicristallo windscreen wiper
terminare to end
tessuto cloth
testa head
timbrare to stamp
tinta hue, colour
tipo type
tirare to pull; **tira vento** it's windy
titoli di credito bonds, securities
togliere, tolgo, tolto take away
tonno tuna fish
tornare to return, to go back
torre(f.) tower
torta tart, cake
tram(m.) tram
tranquillo, -a quiet
trasferire, trasferisco to transfer, to move
trattenersi, trattengo, trattenuto to remain
tre three
treno train
troppo, -a too much, (**pl.**) too many
trota trout; **trotella** small trout
trovare to find
turista(m. f.) tourist
tutto all, everything

ufficio office
ultimamente lately
unico, -a only
università university
uno, -a one
uovo,(pl.) uova egg
usare to use
uscire, esco, uscito to go out; **uscita** exit (airport) channel
usufruire, usufruisco to benefit, to be entitled to
uva grapes

vacanza holiday
valere, valgo, valso to be worth
valido, -a valid, worth
valigia suitcase
valuta currency
vapore(m.) steam; **al vapore** steamed
variabile variable
variazone(f.) variation
vasetto jar
vecchio, -a old, elderly
vedere, visto to see
vendere, venduto to sell; **venditore(m.)** seller
venerdì Friday
venire, vengo, venuto to come
vento wind; **ventoso** windy
veramente truly, really
verde green; **verdura** green vegetables
verità truth
vero, -a true
versante(m.) slope
verso about
vestito dress, suit
via street
viaggiare to travel; **viaggiatore(m.)** male traveller; **viaggiatrice(f.)** female traveller
vicinanza neighbourhood
vicino, -a near, nearby
vino wine
viola, violetta violet
visibile visible
visita visit; **visitare** to visit
vitello veal, calf
vivere to live
volante(m.) steering wheel
volentieri willingly
volere, voglio, voluto to want
volo flight
volta time (of a series of times), e.g. **prima volta** first time
vuota, -a empty

zero zero, nought
zucchero sugar
zucchini(m. pl.) courgettes, baby marrows
zuppa soup; **zuppa inglese** trifle

Index

Grammar in the course